Does Business Learn?

Does Business Learn?

Tax Breaks, Uncertainty, and
Political Strategies

Sandra L. Suárez

Ann Arbor

THE UNIVERSITY OF MICHIGAN PRESS

Copyright © by the University of Michigan 2000
All rights reserved
Published in the United States of America by
The University of Michigan Press
Manufactured in the United States of America
♾ Printed on acid-free paper

2003   2002   2001   2000   4   3   2   1

*A CIP catalog record for this book is available
from the British Library.*

Library of Congress Cataloging-in-Publication Data

Suárez, Sandra L.
    Does business learn? : tax breaks, uncertainty, and political
strategies / Sandra L. Suárez.
        p.   cm.
    Based on the author's dissertation (Yale).
    Includes bibliographical references and index.
    ISBN 0-472-11119-1 (acid-free paper)
    1. Corporations—Taxation—United States—Longitudinal
studies.   2. Corporations—Taxation—Law and legislation—
United States—Longitudinal studies.   3. Corporations—
Taxation—Puerto Rico—Longitudinal studies.   4. Business and
politics—United States—Longitudinal studies.   5. Corporations—
United States—Political activity.   I. Title.

HJ4653.C7 S83   2000
336.24'316'0973—dc21   99-051002

To Mauro and
our daughter, Daniela Emma

Contents

Tables

Preface and Acknowledgments

This book offers one of the first longitudinal case studies of the political behavior of the same group of firms throughout the creation, maintenance, and destruction of a policy subsystem. It presents a novel conceptual approach based on organizational-learning theory that allows one to take into account past experience as well as government structures and dominant issues as key factors in the formulation of business political strategies.

By examining how a group of pharmaceutical and electronics companies have attempted to prevent the repeal of an important tax break from the 1970s to the 1990s, I shed light on several major issues. Business firms are the best represented group in our nation's capital and operate more political action committees than any other group in society, and their lobbyists are among the most experienced political operatives. Yet firms are generally unsure about their political power and, consequently, about which political strategies to pursue when their public policy interests are at risk. Firms' decisions about which strategy to pursue among the possible alternatives are always made under conditions of uncertainty about the process, outcome, and effectiveness of their actions. This uncertainty drives firms to use past experiences to guide their behavior. They repeat or change their strategies in light of past political success or failure and independently of the political environment at the time. Hence, only a historical perspective that takes the past as well as the present into account can provide a thorough understanding of business political strategies.

This book has benefited from many people and institutions. My Yale dissertation advisers, David Mayhew and Sylvia Maxfield, have given me excellent suggestions and unwavering support over the past few years. Valuable commentary for improving earlier papers and/or the final manuscript were provided by Professors William Browne of Central Michigan University, James March of Stanford University, Cathie Jo Martin of Boston University, William Ocasio of Northwestern University, Robert Salisbury of Washington University, David Vogel of the University of California at Berkeley, and Graham K. Wilson of the University of Wisconsin at Madison. I am also grateful to David Cameron of Yale University, who has offered his encouragement over the years. Cynthia Enloe of Clark University has been a constant source of support and guidance. I also acknowledge generous financial support from the Ford Foundation,

MIT's political science department, the Institute for the Study of World Politics, Temple University, and Yale University. I am also grateful to the reference librarians at FOMENTO, Yale University, MIT, and Temple University for their assistance.

I am indebted to the many corporate and tax lawyers, lobbyists, government officials and staffers, and journalists who gave so generously of their time to share information and interpretation with me and yet preferred to remain anonymous. Peter Holmes of the Puerto Rico–USA Foundation and Ralph Sierra Jr. of Sierra and Serapión deserve special mention. While they may disagree with my conclusions, I appreciate their willingness to answer my questions about the political activities of the firms and the intricacies of the federal tax break. Salomé Galib-Bras was the Washington correspondent for *El Nuevo Día* when I began to conduct interviews; she was always willing to share information as well as her rolodex with me. I am also grateful to Jeffrey Birnbaum of the *Wall Street Journal* for some extremely valuable contacts. My colleagues at Temple have provided the kind of teaching and research environment that allowed me to complete this book while learning the ropes as an assistant professor: Richard Deeg, Rosario Espinal, Barbara Ferman, Melissa Gilbert, Robin Kolodny, Bernard Mennis, Lynn Miller, Gary Mucciaroni, and Joseph Schwartz.

Parts of this book have been presented at meetings of the American Political Science Association and Midwest Political Science Association, at the MIT and Wellesley College political science departments, the McDonough School of Business at Georgetown University, and the Wharton School of the University of Pennsylvania. Table 1 originally appeared in "Lessons Learned: Explaining the Political Behavior of Business" (*Polity* 31 [fall 1998]: 161–86). I thank my editor at the University of Michigan Press, Charles Myers, for his enthusiasm and advice and the three anonymous referees for their thoughtful commentary.

My greatest debt of gratitude I owe to my husband, Mauro Guillén; my parents, "Mamita y Daddy"; and my sisters, Marin and Dianne Suárez.

Chronology

1921: The Possessions Corporations System of Taxation is enacted as Section 262 (later 931) of the Revenue Act of 1921. It exempted from U.S. taxation all possession-source income of individuals and corporations.

1948: The Puerto Rican Industrial Tax Exemption Act is enacted to match Section 931 of the Internal Revenue Service (IRS) Code.

1950s: The IRS begins to investigate the intercompany transactions of U.S. firms with manufacturing operations in Puerto Rico.

1960s: U.S. pharmaceutical and electronics companies become the biggest beneficiaries of Section 931.

1973: *February:* The House Ways and Means Committee begins hearings and panel discussions on tax reform. The committee also examines the possessions corporations system of taxation.

May: Based on recommendations by the U.S. Treasury Department, the committee adopts provisional changes to the possessions corporations system of taxation that eliminate the main incentive for investing under the rules of Section 931.

June: U.S. firms rely on the implicit threat of an investment strike in Puerto Rico to protect their public-policy interests.

A Puerto Rican delegation goes to Washington to argue that the proposed changes to the possessions tax system would cause U.S. firms to stop investing in Puerto Rico.

Committee Chair Wilbur Mills reverses his committee's decision and instructs his staff to draft a new tax provision that would continue to encourage U.S. investment in Puerto Rico.

1974: *November:* The Tax Reform Act of 1974 containing the new Section 936 dies in committee.

December: Mills resigns.

1975: *December:* The new Ways and Means Committee chair, Al Ullman, reports the Tax Reform Act of 1975, containing many of the tax provision drafted under Mills, including the new Section 936.

1976: *August:* The Senate passes its version of tax reform, which also includes Section 936 as enacted in the House.

October: President Gerald Ford signs the Tax Reform Act of 1976 into law.

1978: *June:* The U.S. Treasury issues its first annual report on Section 936, criticizing the tax law.

1979: *June:* The U.S. Treasury issues its second annual report on Section 936. Like the first report, this one is very critical of the operation and effect of the tax law.

1980: *June:* The U.S. Treasury issues its third annual report on Section 936, continuing its criticism of the tax law.

August: The Internal Revenue Service issues Tax Advice Memorandum 8040019. In response, U.S. firms put on hold their applications for investment grants in Puerto Rico.

1981: *August:* Congress passes President Ronald Reagan's program of tax reductions known as the Economic Recovery Tax Act.

September: The U.S. Treasury briefs Puerto Rican officials on plans to replace Section 936 with a new Section 937.

October: U.S. pharmaceutical and electronics companies begin meeting with Puerto Rican officials to come up with regulatory solutions.

1982: *March:* The "Gang of Seventeen" begins secret meetings. Section 936 becomes part of the budget process.

May: Senator Robert Dole begins working with Senate Finance Committee Republicans on his own revenue-raising package.

June: A Budget resolution calls for $98.3 billion in new taxes.

2 July: The Tax Equity and Fiscal Responsibility Act (TEFRA) is reported out of Senate Finance Committee. After relying on the threat of an investment strike in Puerto Rico, U.S. firms finally decide to mobilize for the protection of their benefits.

23 July: The Senate passes TEFRA with drastic changes to Section 936 included. U.S. firms begin to advocate more aggressively their own particular bills.

August: TEFRA is reported out of conference. Section 936 is not eliminated, but some of its benefits are reduced considerably.

1983: Learning from their political defeat during TEFRA, U.S. firms decide to organize for collective action. The Puerto Rico–USA Foundation (PRUSA) is organized to protect Section 936 from political attacks.

1984: *January:* President Reagan announces that he will ask the Treasury Department to engage in a comprehensive revision of the tax code.

Treasury I is unveiled, containing a proposal to repeal Section 936 and replace it with a temporary wage credit.

PRUSA directs its lobbying effort at the U.S. Congress. The government of Puerto Rico believes that it can get the Reagan administration to eliminate the proposal before sending the tax-reform project to Congress.

1985: *May:* President Reagan and the chairman of the Ways and Means Committee, Dan Rostenkowski, appear on television to promote tax reform.

Treasury II is unveiled, still containing a proposal to eliminate Section 936. By this time PRUSA claims that it has the votes to protect Section 936 in Congress. U.S. firms continue to pursue a cohesive lobbying campaign.

December: After the House Ways and Means Committee approves its version of tax reform, the House passes the Tax Reform Act. The companies never break ranks to advocate their own deals. The government of Puerto Rico is satisfied and ends its own lobbying effort.

1986: *May:* PRUSA and U.S. firms continue to lobby the Senate to get it to eliminate some minor changes to Section 936.

June: The Senate passes tax reform.

October: President Reagan signs the Tax Reform Act into law. U.S. firms are satisfied with the outcome.

1987–91: Section 936 is not a political issue. U.S. Treasury Department staff members are demoralized after their failure to eliminate Section 936 in 1986.

While Congress drafts status legislation for Puerto Rico, Section 936 is safe from political attacks for fear that changes to the tax law could influence Puerto Ricans' preference for statehood, commonwealth, or independence.

1992: *March:* Senator David Pryor's Prescription Drug Containment Act proposes to repeal Section 936 benefits for pharmaceutical companies that raise their prescription drug prices higher than the rate of inflation. The proposal is defeated, but Section 936's visibility is magnified. Pryor vows to continue his campaign to eliminate the tax benefits of Section 936.

July: A class-action suit brought against American Home Products charging that Section 936 results in the loss of jobs in the U.S. mainland is settled. U.S. labor vows to continue its attacks on Section 936.

September: Presidential candidate Bill Clinton endorses Pryor's effort to end tax breaks for pharmaceutical companies during a campaign speech at the headquarters of Merck Pharmaceutical.

November: Pharmaceutical companies are labeled villains by the incoming administration, which campaigned on the promise of health-care reform.

1993: *January:* U.S. Treasury Department staff members begin to target corporate tax expenditures in an effort to come up with the revenues needed for President Clinton's first budget proposal to Congress. Section 936 is targeted, especially pharmaceuticals.

Based on their experiences in 1986, PRUSA companies maintain their unity and refuse to negotiate with Treasury.

February: President Clinton's deficit-reduction budget proposal to Congress includes the elimination of the Section 936 income credit and its replacement with a 60 percent federal tax credit for wages paid.

April: After a meeting with the CEOs of U.S. firms, the governor of Puerto Rico makes his first public statement denouncing Clinton's proposed changes to Section 936.

May: Allergan breaks ranks with PRUSA days before the Ways and Means Committee votes to adopt the president's plan unchanged. Other companies soon follow and begin to advocate their own particular deals.

June: Senator Pryor (under pressure by the White House) and Senator Bradley (responding to the demands of pharmaceutical companies in his state) are forced to compromise on the issue. The Senate votes to keep a significantly reduced tax break.

July: The CEOs of Abbott Laboratories, Johnson and Johnson, G. D. Searle, Motorola, Sara Lee, and Warner-Lambert come to Washington and lobby for their own particular deals before the conference committee votes on the plan. The conference committee votes to adopt the Senate's version of the tax law.

August: Pharmaceutical stock prices fall as a result of the changes made to Section 936. The tax law now has two parts: a reduced income credit and a new wage credit. Companies' preferences change accordingly.

1995: Section 936 becomes a prime example of corporate welfare.

1996: The tax break is eliminated as part of the Small Business Job Protection Act.

CHAPTER 1

Political Uncertainty
and Business Strategy

For interest groups, the law of resources is that *on any given day, any given
group will have more relevant issues before it than it can possibly handle.*
—Jeffrey M. Berry (1997, 90)

The history of the political behavior of American business in the past forty years
is varied. Bauer, Pool, and Dexter's influential account of business political action suggested that in the late 1950s and early 1960s, business was not really
interested in influencing the political process. Then Lindblom explained that
business's political behavior had less to do with its apparent indifference to
Washington than with its privileged position in society. Why would firms need
to be politically active if public policy was designed to favor business? During
the 1970s and early 1980s business attitudes changed as the role of the government in the economy grew. Most accounts agreed at the time that a major
political mobilization by American business occurred in response to new political threats to its interests.[1] All of these studies explain business behavior as a
response to the political environment at the time. Yet it is also clear from the
patterns of firm behavior that even when firms have clear political preferences
which remain constant over time, their political strategies may be inconsistent
with current events.

This book follows over time the political behavior of the same group of
firms concerning a political issue of great importance to them. I reconstruct the
political battles surrounding one of the longest-lasting and most complicated
corporate tax breaks in the Internal Revenue Code: the U.S. government tax
credit applicable to U.S. firms doing business in Puerto Rico, also known as the
possessions tax break. A twenty-year longitudinal analysis suggests that the behavior of firms attempting to protect their political interests is determined not
only by the condition of the political environment but also by the lessons
learned from prior political experiences. Uncertainty about political outcomes
persuades firms to be attentive to politics. But because they are operating in a
fluid and complex political environment with a myriad of interests to pursue,
firms also face uncertainty about the optimum political strategy. Hence, I argue
that to understand why at any given point in time firms may decide to rely on

their structural power, mobilize to lobby in competition with other firms, or engage in collective action, we should consider the consequences of their ability to acquire and preserve knowledge from past political experiences and bring it to bear on current political behavior.

Research has shown that compared to other groups, such as labor, which are concerned with a broad range of social issues, firms concentrate on issues of importance to their business operations.[2] The political behavior of firms is generally geared to profit maximization. It does not follow, however, that firms' political preferences are always clearly identified. Firms may not be aware of the impact of particular or broad policy decisions on corporate profits.[3] And even when the impact of policy decisions is evident, firms may not know how to translate their interests into specific policy preferences.[4] In this book I go a step further. I argue that even when profits are clearly at stake and firms are aware of their interests, their political strategies are not readily formulated.

How do firms develop the strategies they believe will maximize their political influence? An explanation of the political behavior of business must address both external and internal factors.[5] External factors constitute the current political environment, while internal ones are firms' preexisting behavioral tendencies. These internal tendencies embody the lessons firms have learned from prior political experiences and determine the manner in which they will interpret and adapt to a fluid and ambiguous political environment. When their political interests are at risk, firms respond in the same way individuals do when faced with an uncertain environment: they rely on instinct. Firms' political instinct is based on lessons learned from past successes and failures, and it results in a tendency to fight the last war whenever their political interests are threatened. The aim of this book is to specify the process by which firms learn and adapt their strategies to a changing political environment.

Firms' formulation of their political strategies is presented as a two-step process. In the first phase, when firms first realize that the political process threatens their interests, their political behavior will be based on what they have learned from their prior successes and failures. In the second phase of their response, firms may change their behavior as they try to adapt to the political environment at the time. Salient political issues and government structures comprise the political environment to which business attempts to respond as the political process progresses.

Learning, as the term is used here, means acquiring knowledge from experience. Firms get information about the consequences of their political behavior from prior experiences. This experiential learning guides firms' unreflective, automatic responses, serving as a prism through which they assess immediate political threats to their interests and the potential effectiveness of different political strategies. The end result is a political strategy that initially reflects the lessons learned from prior political battles and then slowly adapts to the current political situation. The experiences of firms at this time, in turn, will guide their political responses in the future.

Illustrating the significance of learning by business necessarily requires the study of an issue that has been of importance to the same group of firms for a considerable period of time. For this reason, political battles surrounding the possessions tax break provide an ideal empirical setting. A majority of the firms covered in this study have been investing under the rules of the possessions tax credit for more than thirty years, and since the early 1970s the law was a recurrent element of the public-policy agenda in Washington. Equally important, the costs of the elimination of the tax break were evident to the firms.[6]

For most people not familiar with the intricacies of the U.S. tax code, the possessions tax break remained, until its partial repeal in 1996, an obscure federal provision. But for most U.S. pharmaceutical firms and many electronics companies, the possessions tax credit has been more important in reducing their federal tax bills than have foreign tax credits, tax deferrals, capital gains tax breaks, or investment-tax credits. The conventional wisdom is that before its repeal in 1986, the investment-tax credit was the most attractive tax break for capital-intensive firms. But that was not the case for the group of Fortune 500 companies with operations in Puerto Rico. In fact, "for pharmaceutical companies there was no comparison."[7] For example, in 1973 Eli Lilly used the investment-tax credit to reduce its federal tax liability by $1.1 million but used the possessions tax credit to reduce it by $13.2 million; in 1976 Motorola used the investment-tax credit to reduce its federal tax liability by $2 million and the possessions tax credit to reduce it by $6 million; and in 1984 Merck reduced its federal tax liability by $2.9 million through the investment-tax credit and by a staggering $70.7 million through the possessions tax credit. These examples are typical among the largest pharmaceutical and electronics companies.[8]

The possessions tax credit alone enabled some of these firms to reduce their federal taxes by more than 50 percent. One notorious example was the case of G. D. Searle. In 1975 the federal corporate tax rate was 48 percent, yet the company used the possessions tax break to reduce its liability by 33 percentage points, which translated into a 70 percent reduction in the company's federal taxes owed. Searle's case was not an exception. In 1993 the federal corporate tax rate was 35 percent, and Upjohn used the possessions tax credit to cut its liability by 22.5 percentage points, a 64 percent reduction in the company's federal taxes. And between 1989 and 1994 Johnson and Johnson used the possessions tax credit to reduce its federal tax liability by $1.1 billion.[9] So important was this provision to pharmaceutical companies that the *Wall Street Journal* reported in August 1993 that drug stocks had taken a hit after financial analysts reduced their earning forecasts the moment it became evident that President Clinton would sign into law a significant reduction in the tax credit.[10] Over the years the Internal Revenue Service (IRS) has taken to tax court Eli Lilly (1985), G. D. Searle

(1987), PepsiCo. (1995), the Coca-Cola Company (1996) and others in an effort to recapture some of the federal tax revenue forgone as these companies sought to make the most of the possessions tax credit. The IRS did not always win because the tax court found that companies had followed the law.[11]

This study is also relevant to our broad understanding of the dynamics of business-government relations. Compared to other countries, the American tax system is characterized by an abundance of tax breaks.[12] Political battles involving corporate tax breaks involve government decisions about how to fund public spending and firms' decisions about how to prevent changes to the tax system that could negatively affect their balance sheets. And while the possessions tax credit is one of the oldest U.S. corporate tax provisions, its history is not as exceptional as it might seem. Rather, as Heinz and his colleagues point out, "the business of policy making involves working and reworking issues with a long history. Not many new items get on the agenda, and few matters are disposed of quickly."[13] In this sense, the political battles surrounding the possessions tax break are representative of most political issues and exemplify how well-endowed interests adapt to changing situations and political circumstances.

The narrative reconstructs the political response of U.S. pharmaceutical and electronics firms to U.S. government efforts to repeal the possessions tax credit at four critical junctures: during the processes leading to the Tax Reform Act of 1976, the Tax Equity and Fiscal Responsibility Act of 1982, the Tax Reform Act of 1986, and the Omnibus Budget Reconciliation Act of 1993. The experiences of the firms involved in these battles are not meant to be taken as representative of the experiences of American businesses regarding all issues at each time. Rather, one of the premises of this study is that the political fortunes of business as well as its political strategies vary across issues.[14] Firms pursue different political interests simultaneously. And, in the same way that different issues have different policy-making structures, firms are likely to have different learning scenarios depending on the issue.

The learning model I propose also does not explain the behavior of all individual firms. And while the behavior of U.S. firms with operations in Puerto Rico provides empirical evidence to support the learning view, not all companies behaved in the way the learning model predicts, for two reasons. First, the learning model is based on the general behavior of a critical mass of firms. Accordingly, the model highlights the tendency of individual firms to behave in a certain way when confronted with different political environments. Second, an attempt is made to account for the most important factors that could have an impact on the conduct of firms. But other factors, such as the personal characteristics of the different Washington representatives, for example, may also affect firms' political strategies. The history of the possessions tax credit, however, enables us to test the validity of the learning model to explain the likelihood of firms' decisions to rely on their structural power, engage in fragmented lobbying, or employ a collective-action strategy to protect their public-policy interests at different points in time and in different political contexts.

For example, in the mid-1970s, pharmaceutical and electronics firms doing business in Puerto Rico did not mobilize for political action when Congress proposed eliminating their federal tax break on Puerto Rico–based profits. The companies behaved this way because they had no memory of ever having to mobilize for political action to protect their tax break. Notwithstanding the political behavior of the companies, the tax law was retained and improved as part of the Tax Act of 1976. In 1982 Congress again threatened to eliminate the tax break. Based on their experiences in 1976, the companies initially did not mobilize for political action in spite of the fact that they were operating in a new political environment. The companies eventually adapted and engaged in fragmented lobbying. The failure of the companies to mobilize in time and collectively allowed the political process to continue uninterrupted, in their own view resulting in serious limitations to the tax break.

Based on their 1982 experiences, the companies decided to organize for political action. A lobbying group was formally created in 1983 under the name Puerto Rico–USA Foundation (PRUSA). By the time the Treasury first unveiled President Reagan's tax-reform project containing a proposal to repeal the tax break in late 1984, the companies had been ready for a year. Remarkably, the tax break survived the Tax Reform of 1986, and the companies attributed their success to the strength and unity of their coalition. Finally, President Clinton, who during his campaign blamed pharmaceutical companies, along with the medical community, for the high costs of health care, proposed eliminating the tax break as part of his first budget proposal to Congress in 1993. The companies' automatic response was to rely on the coalition strategy that had worked so well in 1986. Only when the companies adapted to the new political environment did the coalition break down.

The behavior of pharmaceutical and electronic firms in 1976, 1982, 1986, and 1993 suggests that their political strategies were a response to the preceding period as much as they were a response to current dominant political issues and government structures. These four political processes, comprising six different instances of business political response to threats to their interests, support the claim that business learning determines to a great extent firms' ability to adapt in real time to a shifting political environment.

Conventional Views

How do we account for the political behavior of business in the contemporary period? The theoretical literature on business and government does not provide

convincing answers to this question. At any given point firms may choose to respond to threats to their interests by: (a) relying on their structural power, (b)
mobilizing to lobby on behalf of their particular interests, or (c) joining other
firms to lobby for their common good. These three strategic options are mentioned in the literature, but there has been no systematic attempt to explain what
accounts for the variation in the political behavior of firms over time and across
issues.

The structuralist approach, associated with the work of Charles Lindblom,
argues that business enjoys a privileged position in society. Because business
decisions affect unemployment, policymakers will be sensitive to the interests
of business rather than risk an investment strike and the subsequent wrath of
the electorate. Thus, Lindblom argues, the implicit threat of unemployment is
generally enough to "repress" policy decisions, thereby making "government
accommodation of business demands often routine and familiar." There is no
need for "explicit exchange with businessmen" because there is a "tacit understanding . . . with respect to the conditions under which enterprises can or cannot profitably operate."[15]

On many occasions, however, the implicit threat of unemployment alone
does not suffice to protect the interests of business. It cannot be presumed, as
Lindblom does, that policymakers, when presented with a policy issue, immediately consider its impact on business. It also cannot be presumed that policymakers have the time necessary to study issues in depth—that is, they cannot
be expected to always be aware of exactly how a piece of legislation affects
their constituents or exactly how many jobs in their district may be affected.[16]
It is at this time that business may decide to mobilize for political action individually or collectively to persuade policymakers of the connection between a
particular issue and the incentives necessary to continue investing.

An alternative to Lindblom's approach is the interest-group model, associated with the work of David Truman. Truman argues that interests organize
rapidly and easily for political action to protect themselves against threats to
their benefits. In turn, policymakers specifically rely "on interest groups for advice and assistance."[17] Researchers disagree, however, about the likelihood and
easiness of mobilization. Olson provides the dominant critique of the interest-
group approach, arguing that interests behaving as rational actors have an incentive to free ride because they know that either way, they will enjoy the benefits of those that did mobilize for political action. However, Olson agrees that
collective action is possible when a few of the larger units are willing to shoulder the cost of the organization because they have a bigger stake in the outcome
of policy. Accordingly, Moe explains that when compared to other economic
interests, such as farm groups and labor unions, evidence suggests that U.S.
firms are more likely to form or join groups when they share political interests.[18]

The collective action "problem" is not only a question of free riding, however.[19] For firms that have overcome their tendency to free ride, the structure of the state poses another obstacle to collective action. Firms compete in the political arena in the same way they compete in the marketplace. And a federal system of divided government with administrative bureaucracies and specialized committees not only encourages businesses to mobilize politically but also invites them to pursue their own narrow interests. The structure of the state in the United States continues to preclude the development of a single business peak organization such as the Federation of German Industries or the Swedish Employers' Confederation.[20] Furthermore, U.S. firms have become political actors in their own right and have set up offices in Washington to promote their particular interests.[21]

Yet U.S. firms continue to support their trade and industry groups, such as the Pharmaceutical Research and Manufacturers of America and the American Bankers Association; to organize on the basis of size, as members of the Business Roundtable and the National Federation of Independent Business; and to join other firms to form single-issue groups such as the Coalition of Research and Technology to lobby for the R&D tax credit and the Coalition against Regressive Taxation to lobby against excise taxes. Hence, to assume business fragmentation across the board when there is considerable empirical evidence to suggest that firms successfully engage in collective action is as problematic as to assume that business automatically responds to political threats to its interests by organizing into groups or by relying solely on its implicit power to cause unemployment.

A Microhistorical Approach to Business Political Behavior

The historical perspective adopted in this book combines elements drawn from all three explanations of business political behavior. I argue that business strategies vary not only over time and across issues but throughout the political process as well.[22] In the initial phase of the political process, firms' political behavior is automatic and based on knowledge acquired from past successes and failures. After the initial response, their behavior becomes more deliberate, as firms adapt to current political issues and new government structures. To understand why firms may decide to rely on their structural power rather than mobilize to lobby or may be divided instead of united in their political efforts we must understand the relative impact of learning from prior political successes and failures, new dominant political issues, and shifting government structures. This section discusses these three variables in detail.

Experiential Learning

A basic definition of learning is "to acquire knowledge of or skill in by study, instruction, practice, or experience."[23] More than thirty years ago Cyert and March explained that organizations acquire knowledge from experience and record it in their memory. This learning accounts for much of the behavior of organizations, and it is reflected in standard operating procedures that simplify experience and minimize uncertainty.[24] The study of learning is relevant to our understanding of the political behavior of firms in particular because, as Walker explains, "unless liquidation or merger destroys its identity," the corporation, like other institutions such as state and local governments, "has a continuing existence." Corporations "can afford to wait longer than most individuals for the political results they need."[25] As a result, firms accumulate political experiences that are likely to bias their behavior in the future. It should also be noted that learning by an organization occurs primarily at the level of the individual or individuals within the firm. These individuals, however, share their experiences with their colleagues, help set up rules, and write records and reports that facilitate the preservation of "knowledge of the past even when key organizational members leave."[26]

Evidence of experiential learning has been found in a number of empirical studies of business political behavior. For example, Martin has emphasized the importance of social learning and policy legacies to challenge the notion that firms' political preferences are easily explained by their "material circumstance." Specifically, she argues that corporate political preferences with respect to health-care-reform policy in the early 1990s were shaped by firms' membership in regional and national associations: "Companies plugged into national networks learned from their groups and peers, and collectively moved toward a political position." But Martin argues that these firms had become "disillusioned" with prior strategies of health-care cost containment. In other words, past experiences in the form of policy legacies made these firms more open to new policy alternatives.[27]

In his study of U.S. economic policy after World War II, Collins argues that important segments of the business community kept their political influence because, after their experience with the New Deal, they learned that they had to be more flexible in their response to fiscal policy proposals. In his study of the politicization of business in the 1970s and 1980s, Vogel argues that firms mobilized in response to prior political defeats and learned their political strategies from the environmental and consumer groups that fueled those defeats. In another study Martin suggests that the origins of business mobilization can be traced to the efforts of Presidents Kennedy and Johnson to build support for their legislative agendas. She argues that CEO's experiences in the 1960s were instrumental to the organization of the Business Roundtable in the 1970s. And in his survey of Fortune 500 corporations, G. K. Wilson found that the most important predictor of business political activity was not the firms' perceived costs of regulation but the size of their federal contracts. His findings indicate that in spite of the unprecedented degree of environmental and consumer regulation enacted, companies that received government contracts had been better educated as to the "practical importance of government in every-day commercial life."[28] These studies suggest that the time and money firms spend pursuing political goals, their policy positions, and the character of their political mobilization depend to some extent on past experiences. But with the exception of Martin, none of these studies was especially concerned with the impact of experiential learning as a factor in the process by which firms conceive their political strategies. I take the concept of experiential learning a step further by examining its usefulness in explaining firms' political strategies at four critical junctures over a period of twenty years.

Learning affects both perception and action.[29] True or not, firms are likely to believe that their behavior has influenced the outcome of policy in the past. Scott explains this view: "We act and, at least sometimes, elicit a response from the environment, but whether the response is to our actions or completely independent of them is often difficult to determine. Thus, our 'learning' is often superstitious." Because firms believe that earlier political outcomes result from their political strategies, they will instinctively evaluate new political threats through the prism of past experiences.[30]

Experiential learning can affect firms in one of three ways. First, firms repeat past behavior when they acquire knowledge from past successes. As long as the political environment remains stable, firms' political behavior, based on what they have learned from past successes, is likely to be effective. But second, what has been learned from past successes may also blind firms and prevent them from adapting to a new political environment.[31] For example, when issues of importance to firms become politically salient, they may fail to grasp the political consequences of increased public scrutiny. Also, shifting government structures alter the balance of power within the government, but it takes time for firms to realize that they need to change their strategies and seek new allies. On such occasions firms are said to be taken by surprise. They initially fail to recognize new threats because their understanding of reality is clouded by past successes. Hence, to assume that firms learn the right lessons from past experiences is a mistake. When firms win in the political arena, what they learn is a process or standard operating procedure that may or may not be the most appropriate to repeat in the future. As the political process progresses, firms recognize that the old strategy, based on an earlier success, is not working. They will then change their political strategy as they try adapt to the new salient political issues and shifting government structures. Third, learning also occurs after failures—that is, failures decrease the chance that businesses will repeat the same behavior and increase the chance that they will change their strategy.[32]

This view of the process by which firms formulate their political strategies is consistent with the current view of lobbying. As J. Q. Wilson points out in the new introduction to his book, *Political Organization,* today "much of what is called lobbying involves . . . simply gathering information on what an immensely complex, and cross-pressured government is doing or may do in the future."[33] But Feldman and March caution that we should distinguish between two types of information gathering. They argue that while it might be appealing to assume that "information gathered for use in a decision will be used in making that decision," the fact is that "individuals and organizations . . . gather information and do not use it, . . . ask for reports and do not read them [, and] act first and receive requested information later." Hence, while there is a great deal of information gathering by organizations, most of it occurs in a "surveillance mode" rather than in a "decision mode."[34] This finding implies that we should distinguish between well-endowed firms' effectiveness in keeping track of information pertinent to their interests and their propensity to take the time to reevaluate their past strategies in light of new political events, especially if they perceive their past behavior to have succeeded.

It is clear that all issues do not receive the same level of attention simultaneously.[35] The key is to understand why firms may have an incentive to review their political strategies for some issues and not others. March and Simon explain that it is typical for "individuals and organizations [to] give preferred treatment to alternatives that represent continuation of present programs over those that represent change." This preference for repeating successful past behavior is not the result of an ongoing evaluation of alternative strategies; the "persistence comes about primarily because the individual or organization does not search for or consider alternatives to the present course of action unless that present course is in some sense 'unsatisfactory.'"[36] Firms have other things to do, including worrying about other important political issues, besides reconsidering behavior that is believed to be satisfactory. During the debate around the 1986 tax act, for example, a pharmaceutical lobbyist expressed frustration at having to deal with "somewhere around twelve tax issues at a time." Only when they lose in the political arena on an issue that continues to be of importance to them will firms have an incentive to take time away from other activities and critically evaluate their past behavior.[37]

But the primary reason why firms rely on past experiences to guide their behavior is that the political system is marred by uncertainty. Firms are uncertain about outcome and about the means to achieve their interests.[38] So, while in the 1980s and 1990s firms recognized the importance of political issues to the profitability of their operations, it does not follow that they knew how best to advance their interests. As the authors of the most comprehensive study of contemporary Washington representatives point out, Washington lobbyists are not naïve; rather, they are seasoned participants in policy wars.[39] But while they know that they have to be alert to changes in the political arena that could hurt their clients' economic viability, firm representatives are still operating in a fluid and ambiguous environment in which political outcomes are difficult to predict. Firms struggle to cope with a changing political environment, and their political behavior sometimes seems erratic because under conditions of uncertainty they do not always know how to advance their interests and find themselves instinctively relying on past experiences to guide them. Emerging political issues and shifting government structures are exogenous factors that may disturb established relationships between business and government and thereby contribute to the uncertainty of the political environment to which firms have to adapt.[40]

Salient Political Issues

Whatever their past experiences, firms pursue the strategies they believe will maximize their political influence. At a minimum, firms' behavior must respond to newly emerging issues to be effective, because as new issues become part of the political agenda, their political structure shifts, and firms may see themselves losing influence unless they change their established political practices.

Lowi launched the idea that "the relationship among the interests and between them and government vary" depending on the issue. Distributive issues can be dealt with in relative obscurity. For regulatory and redistributive issues, however, choices must be made about winners and losers among economic sectors or social classes, respectively. What is important about Lowi's analysis is not his categories per se but the idea that different issues are characterized by distinct policy-making structures. Over time, issues may undergo transformations and redefinitions, resulting in a corresponding shift in the structure of policy-making.[41] Hence, the importance of the transformation of an issue lies not only in its redefinition but also in the corresponding change of its structural environment.

Alternatively, one might think of the transformation of an issue from distributive to regulatory or redistributive in nature as the process by which a policy subsystem is destroyed. Subsystems are not found in all policy areas, but when they exist they limit the influence of broader political forces. Outsiders will generally defer (or be indifferent) to the preferences of the perceived experts.[42] Policy subsystems may take many forms. For example, "iron triangles" or "subgovernments" generally include bureaucrats, members of Congress (generally senior members of relevant committees or subcommittees), and private groups and/or organizations. By contrast, "issue niches" are characterized by single-purpose organizations that avoid coalitions as a way to maintaining their influence within a particular policy community.[43]

While the traditional image of subsystems is that they are long-lasting, Heclo has called our attention to the shift from iron triangles to "issue networks." The latter he defines as broader aggregation of interests that are likely to disagree. However, the collapse of iron triangles into issue networks can be perceived as part of the process of creation and destruction of subsystems in American politics.[44] Hence, once we acknowledge that modern subsystems are inherently unstable, whether we are referring to the transformation of an issue from distributive to regulatory or redistributive in nature or to the collapse of an iron triangle, what matters is that in both cases the saliency of the particular issue increases, its perceived impact broadens, and its political structure shifts as it becomes an element of the public agenda.

One example of particular relevance to this study is the transformation of the budget in the 1980s from distributive to redistributive in nature. At the time, the increase in defense spending, combined with low economic growth and a decrease in tax revenues, resulted in a federal deficit whose costs were perceived to be widely shared. Overnight, budget policy-making was moved "out of the congressional committees and bureaucratic units, where interest groups wielded power over relatively narrow politics, and onto the floor of Congress, where battles are waged publicly between broad partisan and ideological coalitions."[45]

Members of Congress have played an important role in the maintenance of subsystems.[46] For example, regarding the possessions tax credit, an influential member of the House Ways and Means Committee was, for many years, an instrumental ally of the companies. Specifically, while the redefinition of the budget in 1982 resulted in new legislative threats to the possessions tax break, it also gave jurisdiction over the issue to one sympathetic politician, Representative Charles Rangel (D-N.Y.). The congressman's support for the corporate tax break effectively contributed to the creation and maintenance of a subsystem. Rangel lobbied his colleagues on behalf of the corporations, and when the tax break was again threatened during the 1986 tax-reform process, he shielded the credit from criticism and helped secure its maintenance. Alternatively, political parties, the president, and the mass media are all involved in the creation and/or destruction of subsystems, but they are less involved in the maintenance of subsystems. And while interest groups are an integral part of subsystems, their destruction may also be initiated by opposition from private interests.[47] During the possessions tax battles in 1976 and 1993 in particular, labor unions opposed the tax break, and their activities contributed to issue's increased salience.

Firms are uncertain about how to adapt to the transformation of an issue because they have to respond to a new policy-making structure when the definition of an issue is in flux (i.e., during the creation and/or destruction of a sub-system) as well as to the structural legacies of the redefinition of an issue (i.e., the new policy structure). There are no guarantees regarding their strategies' effectiveness or the outcome of the process. Firms' behavior is guided only by their inferences about its past effectiveness.

Government Structures

In addition to the transformation of an issue, business strategies also respond to government structures. It is common knowledge that private interests take advantage of the multiple points of access characteristic of the U.S. government system. The system, however, is dynamic. State structures fluctuate between centralization and decentralization.[48] And, like the transformation of an issue, changes in government's fundamental structure and rules bring about a shift in the policy-making structure and require business to adapt its political strategies and reassess its political alliances.[49] Because "institutions, procedures, and rules play a key role in determining outcomes, since they inevitably favor some groups more than others, . . . change . . . may come about slowly or during periods of crisis."[50] Accordingly, changes in the structure of government are long-lasting and simultaneously affect the policy-making structure of a broad range of issues.

Congressional reforms have at different times both facilitated and hindered the influence of U.S. firms doing business in Puerto Rico and have led to significant changes in their political behavior. In 1911 reformers wanting to reduce the power of political elites institutionalized the process of seniority selection for committee chairmanships in Congress.[51] More than sixty years later, during the process leading to the Tax Reform Act of 1976, the power of the most senior member of the House Ways and Means Committee, Chairman Wilbur Mills (D-Ark.), facilitated the protection of the possessions tax break without the firms needing to lobby. By contrast, in the 1980s, the increased decentralization of the postreform Congress meant that firms doing business in Puerto Rico could no longer rely on a sympathetic committee chair alone to protect their interests. The companies found themselves in a disadvantageous position when they realized that they needed to secure the votes of all members of the committees with jurisdiction over tax law as well as to gain the sympathies of the increased number of committee staffers, who ultimately are entrusted with writing legislation.

In an effort to deal with exploding budget deficits, Congress changed procedural rules. The new rules also contributed to the saliency of the possessions tax credit. The pay-as-you-go (PAYGO) requirements were enacted as part of the Budget Act of 1990 and require members of Congress who propose tax reductions or spending increases to offset them with spending cuts or tax increases. If new proposals are not deficit neutral, "sequestration," or spending cuts, kicks in automatically. To help members of Congress, the Congressional Budget Office and the Joint Committee on Taxation put together lists of tax expenditures and other revenue-saving ideas. A tax counsel for the Senate Finance Committee explained that the possessions tax credit was invariably on these lists, making any member of Congress looking for revenues to meet the PAYGO requirements aware of the tax revenues foregone with it. In these examples, as in others, new institutional structures and changes in the rules of the game can contribute to the weakening of a policy subsystem, making its borders more porous and open to criticism.

Yet business's political adaptation to the transformation of an issue and new government structures does not always occur when its interests are initially threatened. Rather, the impact of prior experiences determines the way in which business will interpret the implications of a new political environment.

Learning, Issues, and Structures

Table 1 illustrates the relative impact of learning, salient issues, and government structures on firms' political behavior. To analyze this behavior throughout the political process, it is necessary to distinguish between an initial phase, a, and an adaptive phase, b. For example, firms' response to new political threats to their interests during phase a of the political process at time t is a function of their experiences at $t - 1$. If their prior experience was a political success, they are likely to repeat their past behavior unreflectively and automatically. If the political environment (i.e., salient issues and government structures) at t is the same as the political environment at $t - 1$, then firms will have no reason to change their strategy and will continue to behave in the same way during phase b of the political process; therefore, learning will be rein-

TABLE 1. The Political Process and Business Behavior

Political Outcome at $t - 1$	Phase a Initial Response	Political Environment	Phase b Adaptive Response
Success	Automatic Response	$PE_t = PE_{t-1}$	Old Learning Reinforced
		$PE_t \neq PE_{t-1}$	Default Strategy
Failure	Experimental Response	$PE_t = PE_{t-1}$	Experimental New Learning
		$PE_t \neq PE_{t-1}$	Default Strategy

forced. If the political environment at time t differs from $t - 1$, firms will recognize during phase b that their strategy is not working as effectively as before and that their behavior needs to change. At this point, firms employ what I refer to as a default strategy, which generally means that they will fragment and pursue divided lobbying. Alternatively, if firms' prior experience was perceived as a failure, they will not repeat their behavior at time t but will experiment with a new political strategy in an effort to adapt to the political environment they had perceived at time $t - 1$, assuming it remains relevant. If the political environment at t is the same as the political environment at $t - 1$, then firms will continue to pursue the experimental strategy. New learning occurs if firms discover that the new strategy is effective. If the political environment at time t differs from $t - 1$, firms will find that their experimental strategy is not working and will once again adopt their default strategy.

A key aspect of the model outlined in table 1 is that it allows one to predict that the behavior of firms in the first phase of the political process at time t will be either a repetition or a rejection of their political strategy at time $t - 1$, depending on whether their past experience was a success or a failure. Moreover, the model suggests that when the political environment at t differs from the political environment at $t - 1$, firms will employ their default strategy, divided lobbying. When firms realize that their political benefits are likely to be curtailed, they will adopt the same competitive strategy that they employ in the market place. Each firm will try to take advantage of the fragmentation of the U.S. government in an effort to get the best possible deal. As we shall see, the political battles fought by the firms in this study illustrate the two scenarios in phase a and three out of the four scenarios in phase b.

Four Political Battles

Dozens of Fortune 500 corporations, including most of the largest U.S. pharmaceutical and electronics companies, make up Puerto Rico's industrial landscape. Many of these firms have several facilities and manufacture their most profitable products on this Caribbean island. Notable examples include Johnson and Johnson, Baxter International, General Electric, and Westinghouse, each of which operates ten or more plants on the island. Moreover, about 45 percent of all pharmaceutical drugs sold on the U.S. market are manufactured in Puerto Rico. These firms were attracted to Puerto Rico by the possessions tax break.[52] The original provision granted a federal tax exemption to the repatriated profits and interest income of U.S. firms operating on the island. This tax break made Puerto Rico the only offshore location where U.S. firms could enjoy permanent forgiveness (as opposed to a deferral) of their federal tax liabilities.

The possessions tax break was originally enacted in 1921 at the behest of U.S. businessmen operating in the Philippines. In 1946 the Puerto Rican legislature, in an effort to lure U.S. capital to the island, matched the 100 percent federal tax exemption with a 100 percent local exemption. U.S. firms rapidly responded to the combination of tax incentives. By 1972 U.S. pharmaceuticals and electronics had become the first (23.1 percent) and third (10.3 percent) biggest contributors to manufacturing output on the island, respectively.

By the same token, the Puerto Rican subsidiaries of these companies have been very profitable. To take advantage of the tax credit, U.S. firms placed their manufacturing operations on the island and transferred ownership of their products to these subsidiaries. In this way, the companies maximized their Puerto Rican tax-free profits and minimized their federal tax bill by repatriating those profits tax-free. In many cases, this tax break has been the most important individual tax provision (more important than investment-tax credits, foreign tax credits, tax deferrals, capital-gains-tax breaks, and so forth), accounting for a significant reduction in the federal tax liability of most U.S. pharmaceutical and many U.S. electronics companies, and has helped mask slippages in their worldwide profits.

U.S. firms see their Puerto Rican profits as perfectly reasonable. By contrast, the U.S. Treasury has always believed that firms abuse the tax break. Pharmaceuticals, which deduct their R&D costs from their taxable income and then claim a tax credit on the product manufactured in Puerto Rico, have always been considered the biggest offenders. In the 1960s Treasury first tried to control the companies' activities through regulation, but, frustrated over the failure to reduce the "abuses," the department began to advocate the outright elimination of the tax break. Over the years, the tax break also became the subject of increased scrutiny from members of Congress responding to exploding budget deficits, resulting in more calls for repeal. In turn, U.S. pharmaceuticals and electronics employed a variety of strategies in response to the recurring legislative threats to their interests.

The book is divided into seven chapters. Chapter 2 discusses in detail the reasons why U.S. firms have had an interest in preserving the federal tax break. The chapter begins, however, with a necessary historical and factual background, including a brief description of Puerto Rico's industrial-incentive program. Puerto Rican officials traditionally maintained that the tax break was integral to the island's economic survival. And, at times, the islanders proved to be valuable allies of U.S. firms during their efforts to protect the tax law from political attacks.

Chapter 2 continues with an explanation of why for most pharmaceuticals and many electronics firms, taxes are one of the most important considerations when deciding where to locate manufacturing operations. The analysis shows how these firms structured their worldwide operations to take advantage of the possessions tax break. Some firms went as far as attributing more than half of their worldwide consolidated after-tax profits to their Puerto Rican operations. The discussion also shows that the firms in this study were aware of the costs and benefits of the possessions tax break, which is why its history provides an excellent case to test the learning view.

To highlight the way in which business learning, dominant issues, and government structures shape the political strategies of business, the case study chapters follow a chronological logic. Chapters 3 through 6 examine the U.S. companies' political strategy for the protection of their tax benefits during the processes leading to the Tax Reform Act of 1976, the Tax Equity and Fiscal Responsibility Act of 1982, the Tax Reform Act of 1986, and the Omnibus Budget Reconciliation Act of 1993, respectively. I examine in detail the companies' relationship to both the executive and the legislative branches of government and their component parts, and I highlight the major debates and key arguments espoused by the different interested parties. Domestic politics in Puerto Rico are discussed insofar as they are relevant to the political process in Washington.

By employing both a historical and a comparative case-study approach (i.e., the behavior of a relatively stable group of firms is studied at different points in time), it can be shown that business strategies vary a great deal depending on the relative impact of learning, issues, and government structures. It is important to note that while the history of the tax break is divided into four major political events, the total number of observations that I seek to explain is six: the varied political responses of firms to political threats to their interests.[53] To protect the federal tax break, U.S. pharmaceutical and electronics companies relied on the implicit threat to cause unemployment in 1976 and won; initially relied on their implicit threat to cause unemployment and subsequently engaged in fragmented lobbying in 1982, losing a substantial portion of their benefits; organized for collective action in 1986 and won; and initially engaged in collective action but subsequently fragmented in 1993 and lost. All along, firms' understanding of new political realities was shaped by their political experiences in the preceding period, and their political behavior was guided initially by what they had learned from prior successes and failures. Chapter 7 assesses the contributions of a learning approach to our understanding of the political influence of U.S. firms over time and across issues. Finally, in the long run, this is a story of a business loss. In August 1996 the U.S. Congress repealed Section 936 of the Internal Revenue Code as part of its Small Business Job Protection Act. Firms with existing operations in Puerto Rico can continue to benefit from Section 936 until 2006, but new firms are not eligible for the tax break. The events leading to the elimination of the tax break seventy-five years after it was originally enacted are discussed briefly in the epilogue.

This book is based on a variety of empirical materials. Public sources include congressional hearings, company annual and 10-K reports, political action committee contributions, and other documentary material. The bulk of the research, however, consisted of more than seventy semistructured interviews. Interviewees included lobbyists for ten pharmaceutical companies, one biotechnology firm, one beverage concern, and four electronics companies; twelve private consultants and tax lawyers, all of whom had lobbied on behalf of various companies;[54] fifteen present and former staff members of the Joint Committee on Taxation, Senate Finance Committee, and Ways and Means Committee; five lobbyists for PRUSA and for the Pharmaceutical Manufacturers Association (now Pharmaceutical Research and Manufacturers of America); eight White House and Treasury Department officials; ten Puerto Rican officials; and six Washington-based journalists who covered the possessions-tax-credit debates. In-depth interviews provided insights into the motivations guiding the political activities of firms that could not be obtained through documentary material. These interviews took place over a number of years, and whenever possible, meetings with representatives from the companies were repeated and/or their political activity was followed via telephone. The goal was to capture as closely as possible a picture of each firm's views about its political behavior—that is, its cognition of how its behavior may have contributed to its successes and failures and its rationale for employing different political strategies. Complementing these interviews were extremely valuable private reports and correspondence obtained from the interviewees. It should be noted that company representatives and public officials were not always comfortable providing information that they viewed as sensitive. Unless otherwise noted, these interviews were granted on the condition that they would not be attributed to their sources.

CHAPTER 2

Corporate Interests
and Government Policy

Ireland, Hong Kong, Singapore—all of the tax havens combined did not
come close to what Section 936 represented to these companies.
—U.S. Corporate Tax Lawyer

The possessions-corporation system of taxation became enormously significant
to U.S. firms more than thirty years after it was first enacted in 1921. In the late
1940s, many U.S. companies began to aggressively tailor their investment
strategies to take advantage of the possessions tax break. The federal tax provision enabled them to maximize their Puerto Rican tax-free profits via intercompany transactions and minimize their federal tax bill. By the 1970s, the tax
break was the most important factor for reducing the federal tax liability of most
pharmaceutical and many electronics firms. Given the degree to which these
two industry groups benefited from their investments in Puerto Rico, they had
a political interest in the preservation of the federal tax provision when the U.S.
government targeted it for elimination in 1976, 1982, 1986, and 1993. The companies have, at times, found Puerto Rican administrators to be important allies
because they had an interest in using the federal tax break in combination with
a local tax exemption to attract U.S. manufacturing investment to the island.

This chapter covers the history of the possessions-corporations system of
taxation from 1921 to 1975 to lay the ground for chapter 3, which deals with
the response of U.S. firms to congressional efforts to eliminate the federal tax
exemption as part of the Tax Reform Act of 1976. It is important to clarify how
the possessions-corporation system of taxation differed from the basic taxation
of foreign operations of U.S. corporations. Therefore, this chapter begins with
a review of the three basic Internal Revenue Code provisions applicable to foreign income. The bulk of the discussion is about Section 931, the predecessor
of Section 936.

I.   U.S. Tax Treatment of Foreign-Source Income

Foreign direct investment (FDI) occurs when a parent company makes an investment in plant, equipment, or other assets of affiliated foreign companies.

FDI implies that the U.S. company has sufficient voting stock to have control of the foreign company. The U.S. government defines control as ownership of 10 percent or more of a foreign corporation. U.S. taxation of FDI generally has two main features: a foreign tax credit and a tax deferral. But until its partial elimination in 1996, a third provision, the possessions-corporation system of taxation also applied to U.S. investments in the possessions.

The United States imposes taxes on U.S. corporations on a worldwide basis—that is, all income is included in the tax base regardless of its geographic origin. The U.S. government then allows a tax credit for taxes paid to foreign governments. This is the federal tax treatment accorded to foreign branch operations of U.S. corporations. Before the tax credit was enacted, foreign taxes were simply deducted from the taxable income of the foreign affiliate. In 1918 a witness appeared before the House Ways and Means Committee and complained that this practice amounted to double taxation and made the tax burden of U.S. investors higher than the tax burden of their competitors.[1] Thus, the tax credit was amended to allow the affiliate to credit its foreign taxes against the U.S. tax liability.

Foreign corporations are subject to tax only on income from U.S. sources. Since the foreign subsidiaries of U.S. corporations are organized under the laws of a foreign country, their profits are not subject to U.S. taxation. The U.S. parent corporation is taxed only on any dividends received from its foreign subsidiary. Thus, the subsidiary can reinvest its earnings abroad without being subject to any immediate U.S. tax liability, a process known generally as tax deferral. The tax deferral has been in place since the corporate income tax was established in 1913 and followed the established practice of taxing individuals' dividend income rather than their share of a corporation's retained earnings. In addition to the tax deferral, taxes paid by the U.S. subsidiary to a foreign government when dividends are repatriated can also be taken as credits against the U.S. tax liability. U.S. multinationals usually can choose whether to organize as a branch or a subsidiary operation. Organizing as a subsidiary offers U.S. firms a deferral. Conversely, organizing as a branch enables the U.S. investor to deduct foreign losses from any tax liability.

Even though Puerto Rico is a U.S. possession, for the purposes of the Internal Revenue Code (IRC), U.S. firms doing business on the island are foreign corporations. They are organized under the laws of the Commonwealth of Puerto Rico. Under Section 936 of the IRC, a U.S. company organized as a 936 subsidiary in Puerto Rico or any other U.S. possession enjoyed a tax credit that effectively eliminated its federal tax liability from activities in the possessions.[2] The subsidiary, also known as a 936 company or possessions corporation, was granted a federal tax credit even if, as it was the case in Puerto Rico, it was subject to little or no taxation in the possession.

Section 936 was preceded by Section 931. The latter was enacted as Section 262 of the Revenue Act of 1921. Section 262, as originally proposed, would have exempted foreign-source income from U.S. taxation regardless of the country of origin.[3] Pressure for this provision came from businessmen in the Philippines, who complained that the United States taxed their foreign income as it was earned, while Britain deferred taxation on foreign-source income until it was repatriated. Since the government of the Philippines also taxed all persons within its jurisdiction, U.S. businesses argued that they were being subjected to double taxation.[4] Thus, proponents of the bill argued that U.S. investors were at a competitive disadvantage relative to their British counterparts. The House Ways and Means Committee version of the bill would have resolved this problem by exempting from U.S. taxation the unrepatriated foreign-source income of "foreign traders" and "foreign trade corporations." The latter were defined as U.S. citizens and domestic corporations 80 percent or more of whose gross income was derived from foreign sources.[5]

As explained earlier, foreign subsidiaries of U.S. corporations could defer the taxation of foreign-source income until profits were repatriated to the U.S. However, at the time, U.S. companies generally preferred to conduct their foreign operations through a U.S. branch or a U.S. chartered subsidiary.[6] Consequently, these companies were subject to U.S. as well as Philippine taxes on their current income.

During the debate on the House floor, it was suggested that the entire proposal be struck from the revenue bill. In an effort to make the provision more attractive to members of Congress, Representative Nicholas Longworth (D-Ohio) proposed that benefits of the proposed exemption be restricted to individuals and corporations that, in addition to deriving 80 percent or more of their income from abroad, "derived 50 percent or more of their income from the active conduct (as opposed to interest income) of a trade or business without the United States." This amendment was meant to limit the benefits of the provision to businesses by making it difficult for "some very rich man [to] transfer all of his investments abroad and be exempt from taxation on 80 percent of them."[7]

When the 1921 revenue bill was introduced in the Senate, the most ardent opponent of the provision was Senator Robert LaFollette (R-Wis.). He argued that at a time when Congress was "exhausting [its] ingenuity to wring from the small taxpayer the last penny possible to meet government expenses," it would be inconceivable to support a proposal "to exempt great aggregations of wealth from taxes altogether." Furthermore, he wondered why, if capital was needed here in the United States, Congress should support a proposal that promoted U.S. foreign investment. Finally, a number of senators argued that the provision would encourage citizens and domestic corporations doing a large volume of business abroad to organize in such a way that 80 percent of their income was derived from foreign sources with the sole purpose of avoiding taxation. In the end, the provision was eliminated from the revenue bill.[8]

The Senate Finance Committee reintroduced the exemption to cover only individuals and corporations deriving 80 percent or more of their gross income from a U.S. possession.[9] As finally enacted in the Revenue Act of 1921, the possessions-corporation system of taxation exempted from U.S. taxation all foreign-source income of individuals and corporations that met the 80-50 income test in any U.S. possession except the Virgin Islands. However, a possession corporation was treated as a foreign company, and thus it had to pay taxes on any dividends paid to a U.S. shareholder. In essence, under this provision, "a possessions corporation was taxed . . . as if it were a foreign corporation and received the same benefits of tax deferral as enjoyed under British law by its British rivals in the Philippines and elsewhere."[10]

According to the U.S. Treasury, "little attention was paid to the effect of this law on the Philippine economy; Puerto Rico was virtually ignored in the public debate."[11] The Puerto Rican economy, however, would reap the greatest benefits from the tax law in the long run. In 1947, in an effort to attract U.S. investment, the island government decided to match the federal tax exemption with a Puerto Rican exemption. The following section examines how the possessions-corporation system of taxation contributed to the transformation of the island from the "poorhouse of the Caribbean" into a developing economy. The importance of this federal tax law to the island's economy explains why the government of Puerto Rico has traditionally had an interest in its preservation.

II. "The Economic Miracle"

Puerto Rico has been the richest country in Latin America on a per capita income basis since 1958. Economic success derived not only from the island's industrial-incentive program, known as Operation Bootstrap, but also from the federal tax exemption for the attraction of U.S. investment, a fact that would help the firms justify the tax break on the basis of its contributions to Puerto Rico's development and Caribbean stability. Thus, reviewing Puerto Rico's economic and political history since its separation from Spain is key to understanding the evolution of the tax break over time and the companies' political strategies. It is analytically helpful to differentiate among three periods: the Puerto Rican economy before Operation Bootstrap (1898–1940); the first phase of the government's development program (1940–48); and the second phase of the program (1948–70).

1898–1940

In one of the most comprehensive studies of U.S.–Puerto Rican relations, Gordon K. Lewis noted that at the end of the Spanish-American War in 1898,

"Americans looked at the new territory, characteristically, in terms of its business opportunities." Scarcely two weeks after U.S. occupation of Puerto Rico began, "the first advance guard of business representatives arrived."[12] The new acquisition opened big investment opportunities for U.S. private interests, and they wasted no time in taking advantage of the situation. By the early 1900s, the island had become a monocrop economy based on sugar, with absentee U.S. investors reaping the profits.

Prior to 1898, coffee production had been protected by a Spanish tariff. After the war, Americans decided to invest in sugar given that the American consumer was used to non–Puerto Rican coffees. Accordingly, sugar production soared. However, although the economy appeared to be productive statistically, virtually all sugar profits were being repatriated to the mainland, with little benefit to the island's economy.[13]

In time, as more and more large tracts of land were devoted to sugar production, small planters sold their land and became day laborers. Another consequence of the increase in sugar production was a steady decline in the production of food crops, which forced island consumers to import high-priced foods from the United States or from other markets with tariffs imposed on them.[14] To make things worse, in addition to the negative effects of the great economic depression of the 1930s, a devastating hurricane hit Puerto Rico in 1928. Before the island could recover, a second one struck in 1932.

In the mid-1930s, the New Deal programs were expanded to Puerto Rico. But, as Raymond Carr explains, "a policy conceived to deal with the domestic economic problems of America—a highly industrialized continental state plagued by depression—could not cure a feeble island economy confronting the problems of a banana republic." Puerto Rico needed a comprehensive development program.[15] In the 1940s, sugar production—and, to a lesser extent, coffee and tobacco production—remained the island's main economic activities. Agriculture dominated both national income (31.1 percent) and employment (42.7 percent). In second place came the much smaller manufacturing sector, 25 percent of which was in tobacco and sugar processing.[16]

1940–48

Under these economic circumstances, the Popular Democratic Party, led by Luis Muñoz Marín, won control of the Puerto Rican legislature in 1940. This election was the first time in forty-two years of U.S. rule that Puerto Rican political elites had shifted the political discourse from a concern with the political status of the island to the economic well-being of its inhabitants.[17] The Populares, as they were called, found support for their economic development efforts in the last appointed governor of Puerto Rico, Rexford G. Tugwell. An economist by training, Tugwell was a New Dealer who believed in "public corporations and state financed industry; [and] autonomous planning boards, under democratic control" as a middle ground between "the straitjacket of 'doctrinaire socialism'" and laissez-faire capitalism.[18]

The first phase of Operation Bootstrap focused on agriculture. Tugwell's Puerto Rican appointees tried to settle farmers on their own plots; some sugar plantations were bought in an attempt to establish a profit-sharing operation with workers; and a rural housing program was organized. With the exception of the housing program, these efforts failed; there were "too many farmers and too little land, high costs, insufficient water, etc."[19]

Among the public corporations set up as part of this first development effort were the Water Resources Authority, the Aqueduct and Sewer Authority, the Communications Authority, the Development Bank, and the Puerto Rico Industrial Development Company (PRIDCO).[20] PRIDCO began operations by investing in government-run cement, glass, paper, pottery, and shoe factories.[21] But like the agricultural program, government-owned enterprises fell short of expectations. Most operated at a loss and created only a small number of jobs.

1948–70

By the mid-1940s, Puerto Rican administrators recognized that agriculture and government-owned enterprises could not lead the economy to full employment and economic growth. As a result, the government dramatically reversed its economic policies. It was decided that Puerto Rico had "to industrialize, and industrialize rapidly." And because the government lacked the financial resources to undertake an industrialization program on its own, Puerto Rican officials looked outside for investment capital. As Carr explains,

> the investment needed for such a crash program could only come from *private* American investors. . . . Private "absentee" capital, which the earlier "socialist" program had sought to drive out, was now to be attracted by the building and leasing of factories on favorable terms to businesses that were prepared to come to Puerto Rico. But the measure that would revolutionize the Puerto Rican economy came in 1947: the [Puerto Rican] Industrial Incentives Act.[22]

Indeed, the Puerto Rican government targeted American investors. But the feasibility of this courtship depended on Washington-made policies, not just Puerto Rican measures. Thus, the Puerto Rican government devised its industrial-incentives program to match Section 931 of the Internal Revenue Code, which, up until that time, had been largely ignored by prior island administrators.

The Puerto Rican legislature enacted the Industrial Tax Exemption Act in

1948.[23] It provided qualified firms with exemptions from operating-income, property, and municipal taxes. To qualify for the exemptions, a manufacturing firm had to produce either an item that was not already produced on a commercial scale or certain specified items, such as wearing apparel or processed food items. In addition to tax breaks, the Economic Development Administration (FOMENTO) advertised the island's surplus of low-wage labor and offered factory buildings and low-interest loans through the Government Development Bank. Moreover, protection under the U.S. tariff schedule helped to make Puerto Rico a competitive location for U.S. firms.

U.S. investors rapidly took notice of Puerto Rico. A mainland newspaper described the benefits of investing in the island during the 1950s in a vivid, yet accurate, way:

> Investors dreaming of paradise might visualize a place where a factory owner doesn't have to pay any taxes or rent. If their imagination were working overtime they might daydream of workers happy to toil for as little as 17½ cents an hour. Actually there is no reason for such dreaming according to Charles E. Boyd, secretary of the Detroit Board of Commerce's retail and wholesale division. For such a place—Puerto Rico— exists in reality.[24]

Responding to these incentives, the island's apparel, textile, shoe, leather, mechanical, electrical, and electronics industries grew rapidly in the period after the enactment of the Industrial Incentives Act. As a result, the manufacturing sector's contribution to the GDP grew from 16.4 percent in 1948 to 20.2 percent in 1954.

Initially, the period of total exemption was designed to end in 1959. The amount of exempted income would be 75 percent in 1959, 50 percent in 1960, and 25 percent in 1961. All income would be taxable by 1962. But, by 1954 it became clear to Puerto Rican government officials that the phaseout was reducing the incentive for new manufacturing companies to start operations in Puerto Rico. Thus, in 1954 the Industrial Tax Exemption Act was amended to provide that certain businesses would be exempt from taxes on income for a period of ten years.[25] A third version of the act, passed by the Puerto Rican legislature in 1963, continued the exemption program for firms establishing manufacturing operations in Puerto Rico. However, instead of general exemptions related to specific types of industry, the 1963 Act provided several lengths of exemptions (from ten to thirty years), depending on the location of the new business. For example, firms establishing business in underdeveloped zones could receive exemptions for up to thirty years.[26]

Finally, as part of Puerto Rico's Overall Economic Plan of 1966, FOMENTO directed its promotional efforts toward "larger, well-known main-

land companies." While FOMENTO had succeeded in attracting U.S. manufacturing firms to the island, the economy had proved vulnerable to cyclical
variation in the mainland economy and increasing labor costs. FOMENTO then
began to focus "on types of industry thought to be less subject to cyclical
changes, less vulnerable to increasing wage costs, and capable of providing
linkages which would result in a more integrated sector structure."[27] New emphasis would be placed on capital-intensive industries such as pharmaceuticals
and petrochemicals.

Puerto Rico's economic growth in the two decades after 1948 has often
been called an economic miracle. Some vital statistics give an idea of the ex-
traordinary transformation of the island's economy. Real gross national product (GNP) increased at an average annual rate of 5.3 percent in the 1950s and
7.0 percent in the 1960s. Real per capita GNP rose at an average annual rate of
4.7 percent in the 1950s and 5.5 percent in the 1960s, compared to an annual
growth rate of 3.7 percent and 2.2 percent of real GNP and GNP per capita, respectively, in the United States for the same period. By 1958, per capita income
in Puerto Rico was the highest in Latin America. "By any historical or international yardstick, the growth in total and per capita GNP was remarkable." Economic growth was also accompanied by advances in health and education. Between 1940 and 1970, life expectancy rose by thirty years, and enrollment in
secondary schools more than doubled.[28]

In terms of the island's transformation from an agricultural economy to a
"burgeoning neo-industrial society," by 1957, manufacturing had become the
most important economic activity, and, by 1960, more than 660 firms had been
established.[29] From 1950 to 1974 the manufacturing sector produced a net
92,000 additional jobs, an average increase of 3,833 per year. The growth in
manufacturing and construction jobs was not strong enough to offset the decline in agriculture. The overall unemployment rate fell, however, as Puerto Ricans emigrated to the mainland and as new jobs opened up in the Puerto Rican
government, trade, and services sectors. By 1970, unemployment reached its
lowest level in the postwar period, 10.7 percent.[30]

Between 1947 and 1975 a number of changes occurred in the composition
of the manufacturing sector. New industries had been attracted to the island at
the time the U.S. Congress first began to discuss the elimination of the federal
tax incentive. Table 2 shows that in 1947, food, apparel, and, to a lesser extent,
tobacco accounted for 61.1 percent of the manufacturing sector's contribution
to GDP. By 1974 these industries represented only 25.3 percent of the sector's
output, as other industries began to assume increasing importance. Pharmaceuticals had become the single biggest contributor to manufacturing output
(17.2 percent), followed by apparel (10.6 percent), electrical machinery (10.5
percent), and alcoholic beverages (7.1 percent). Industry's contribution to employment also experienced some changes. However, although the relative num-

ber of jobs created by the different industry groups changed, table 3 shows that with the exception of sugar, major contributors to employment remained consistent. For example, in 1949 pharmaceuticals and electrical machinery had no significant impact on employment, and by 1975 they had grown to represent 4.4 and 7.3 percent of manufacturing employment respectively. Apparel and food, however, remained among the most important industries in terms of employment in the period between 1949 and 1975.

In terms of each industry's contribution to labor income, table 4 shows that apparel and food products remained among the biggest contributors, although the growth of other industries had also been remarkable. By 1976, four industries—electrical machinery, petrochemicals, instruments, and pharmaceuticals—were among the top seven industry contributors and represented 26.4 percent of manufacturing labor income.

The data in tables 2, 3, and 4 suggest that during the 1970s, labor-intensive investment on the island had begun to stagnate. There are a number of reasons why Puerto Rico had begun to lose its attractiveness for labor-intensive

TABLE 2. Industry Group Contribution to Puerto Rican GDP (% of total)

	1947	1965	1970	1972	1974	1976
Food[a]	39.9	19.1	11.9	9.9	9.4	9.0
Apparel	15.0	13.4	14.8	11.8	10.6	8.9
Tobacco	6.2	5.8	6.5	5.6	5.3	4.3
Stone, clay, glass	3.0	5.4	4.9	5.1	4.1	2.6
Wood and furniture	2.7	2.4	2.3	2.5	1.4	1.0
Textiles	.6	3.4	3.5	2.8	2.7	1.5
Printing/publishing	2.3	2.2	1.9	1.6	1.6	1.4
Paper	—	1.0	1.1	0.7	0.6	0.6
Leather	—	3.9	3.2	1.9	1.6	1.2
Rubber and plastics	—	—	2.5	1.6	1.5	1.5
Primary metals	—	—	1.0	0.8	1.1	0.6
Fabricated metals	—	—	3.1	3.5	3.2	2.6
Transportation equipment	—	—	0.2	0.2	0.2	0.2
Other chemicals	—	—	0.6	0.6	0.4	0.6
Alcoholic beverages	—	11.8	10.7	10.0	7.1	7.1
Soft drinks	1.1	1.2	2.3	2.3	1.6	1.6
Instruments	—	—	3.2	3.8	3.8	4.6
Pharmaceuticals	—	—	8.0	14.1	17.2	23.1
Petrochemicals	—	—	1.6	3.7	5.0	8.7
Petrorefining	—	—	3.8	2.5	4.7	2.5
Other petroproducts	—	—	2.0	2.2	3.5	1.2
Machinery	—	—	1.2	1.7	2.3	2.9
Electrical machinery	—	—	8.4	9.7	10.5	10.3

Source: U.S. Commerce Department 1979.
[a]Includes, sugar, beer, and other food products.

investment. First, though modified for the island, the U.S. Fair Labor Standards Act establishing a federal minimum wage had been applicable to Puerto Rico since 1938.[31] Second, "to some extent, Puerto Rico was the victim of its own economic success: as per capita incomes rose, so did the wage at which labor would work." Moreover, after the Kennedy round of tariff negotiations reduced tariff rates by 40 to 50 percent, Puerto Rican products were hurt by Japanese and other competitors utilizing low-wage foreign labor. At the same time "U.S. companies lost their inhibitions about manufacturing in low-wage countries and exporting back to the United States." Ultimately, the wage differential between Puerto Rico and these low-wage countries was considerable, and it discouraged labor-intensive investment on the island.[32]

In addition, not all of the capital-intensive industries that had come to the island were profitable. By the mid-1970s, the Puerto Rican petrochemical industry was in dire straits. The petroleum-refining industry began operations in Puerto Rico in the mid-1950s with the establishment of the Caribbean Gulf Refining Company and the Commonwealth Oil Refining Company. By presidential proclamation, the United States granted Puerto Rico quotas for imports of

TABLE 3. Puerto Rican Manufacturing Employment (% of total)

	1949	1967	1970	1972	1975	1976
Sugar	25.8	3.2	2.5	1.4	2.5	2.4
Food	10.5	8.4	8.6	12.3	11.1	11.2
Apparel	19.6	28.5	25.9	26.6	26.4	25.6
Tobacco	12.9	5.6	4.5	3.8	3.6	3.1
Stone, clay, glass	4.6	5.1	5.0	5.1	4.5	—
Wood and furniture	4.0	3.6	3.7	3.4	2.8	2.6
Textiles	2.6	5.4	6.5	5.2	3.6	3.0
Printing/publishing	2.6	1.9	1.9	1.9	1.9	2.0
Paper	0.5	1.0	1.0	0.8	0.9	1.0
Leather	1.7	8.5	6.1	4.1	3.8	3.4
Rubber and plastics	—	2.6	3.0	2.6	2.0	2.4
Primary metals	—	0.7	0.8	0.7	0.7	0.7
Fabricated metals	—	2.9	3.4	4.0	3.4	3.3
Transportation equipment	—	0.5	0.4	0.3	0.3	0.2
Other chemicals	2.3	0.6	1.1	2.0	1.1	1.3
Alcoholic beverages	—	11.8	10.7	10.0	7.1	7.1
Soft drinks	1.6	1.4	1.2	1.2	1.2	1.2
Instruments	—	2.6	3.8	5.2	7.9	7.3
Pharmaceuticals	—	1.1	1.2	2.4	4.4	5.1
Petrochemicals	—	—	1.3	2.0	2.3	2.3
Petroleum	—	1.6	2.1	2.2	1.9	2.0
Machinery	1.1	0.9	1.0	1.0	2.2	3.0
Electric machinery	—	6.9	7.8	8.3	7.3	9.2

Source: U.S. Commerce Department 1979.

foreign oil when the price was below that of domestic oil. Puerto Rican officials "hoped to refine foreign crude and the use the by-products to establish a
petrochemical complex," but "before these linkages could be developed, the
price of foreign crude rocketed."[33] By contrast, tables 2, 3, and 4 suggest that
Puerto Rican administrators had been successful in attracting other capital-intensive industries that would be more resistant to the effect of cyclical economic
changes on the mainland. In the 1970s, manufacturers of pharmaceuticals and
electrical and electronic components were among the island's fastest growing
industries.

In brief, while the U.S. tax break for doing business in the possessions had
existed since 1921, U.S. firms began to notice Puerto Rico only after a local tax
exemption was offered to work in conjunction with the federal tax provision.
Given the success of the combination of federal and local tax incentives in attracting U.S. investment to the island, it is no wonder that the preservation of
the possessions tax provision would become an interest for Puerto Rican government officials. Traditionally, Puerto Rican administrators believed that with-

TABLE 4.   Puerto Rican Labor Income by Industry Group (% of total)

	1947	1967	1970	1972	1974	1976
Food products	9.9	9.7	9.2	10.2	10.6	10.8
Beer	2.6	2.4	2.4	1.8	1.3	1.3
Sugar	26.2	5.5	3.5	2.7	2.6	2.6
Apparel	25.2	21.1	21.9	18.5	18.0	17.6
Tobacco	10.6	4.5	3.5	3.0	2.7	2.8
Stone, clay, glass	2.1	6.9	6.5	6.5	6.4	5.2
Wood and furniture	3.0	3.5	3.5	3.1	2.7	2.1
Textiles	1.1	4.6	4.9	4.0	3.7	2.7
Printing/publishing	4.1	2.8	3.0	2.7	3.2	2.9
Paper	—	1.3	1.3	1.1	1.0	0.9
Leather	—	5.5	4.8	3.3	2.8	2.5
Rubber and plastics	—	2.4	2.4	2.7	2.3	2.4
Primary metals	—	1.5	1.4	1.3	1.3	1.6
Fabricated metals	—	3.3	3.6	4.0	3.9	3.7
Transportation equipment	—	0.4	0.3	0.5	0.4	0.4
Other chemicals	—	0.9	0.7	0.8	1.0	1.6
Alcoholic beverages	4.2	1.9	1.9	2.0	1.7	1.6
Soft drinks	1.6	1.7	1.8	2.2	2.1	2.1
Instruments	—	2.7	3.5	4.5	4.8	6.0
Pharmaceuticals	—	1.2	1.7	3.3	4.7	7.0
Petrochemicals	—	1.6	2.6	4.2	4.8	3.9
Petroleum	—	3.6	4.0	4.0	3.7	4.1
Machinery	—	1.6	1.4	1.8	2.3	3.0
Electrical machinery	—	6.8	7.5	9.3	9.8	9.5

Source: U.S. Commerce Department 1979.

out the possessions tax system they would be unable to attract U.S. investment to the island. As a result, the Puerto Rican government proved to be an important political ally of U.S. pharmaceuticals and electronics firms, for which the federal tax break had also become extremely significant.

III.   U.S. Firms and Tax-Free Profits

While many different kinds of U.S. firms had taken advantage of the combination of federal and Puerto Rican tax exemptions, only specific kinds of manufacturing affiliates could continue to benefit from the possessions tax break in spite of increasing labor and energy costs. Specifically, pharmaceutical and electronics companies benefited by transferring ownership of products developed on the mainland to their island affiliates and then setting intercompany prices in a way that allowed the reduction of U.S. tax liability. In fact, when compared with their rates of return on the mainland, the rates of return for some of these companies in Puerto Rico suggest that they were shifting much of their profits to their island affiliates to take advantage of the tax haven. The U.S.–Puerto Rican tax regime was a gold mine to these U.S. firms because, while other countries also offered tax incentives to attract manufacturing investment, island subsidiaries could repatriate their profits tax-free. Nowhere else in the world were U.S. firms able to invest free of federal and host-country taxation.

As explained earlier, under Section 931 all income from a possessions corporation was excluded from U.S. taxation as long as it met the 80-50 income test—that is, as long as 80 percent or more of its gross income was derived from a U.S. possession and at least 50 percent of its gross income was derived from the active conduct of trade and business within the possession. Technically, the parent corporation had to pay taxes on dividends repatriated to the mainland. However, possessions corporations got around this requirement by using Section 931 in conjunction with the rules of Section 332, which permitted the tax-free liquidation of a domestic subsidiary. This meant that a possessions corporation could defer taxation and then be liquidated free of federal tax. As a result, 931 companies would accumulate earnings derived on the island and reinvest them outside the United States and Puerto Rico until the subsidiaries were liquidated. As long as no more than 20 percent of their repatriated profits were earned outside the United States or a possession, foreign income was also exempted from U.S. taxation. According to the U.S. Treasury,

> companies operating in Puerto Rico frequently placed large investments in the "Eurodollar" market . . . , either directly or through Guamanian banks. (Since Guam is a possession, interest on a bank deposit in Guam was "possession source," and therefore helped the 931 corporation meet

its 80 percent test.) After a number of years, usually at the end of the Puerto Rican tax exemption, the company would be liquidated (tax-free) into its U.S. parent.[34]

With tax planning of this kind, a mainland publication argued, U.S. investors could "augment the accumulated exempt earnings by at least 40 percent over the life of" their Puerto Rican "incentives grant."[35]

But the most important incentive for U.S. companies was their ability to set transfer prices to maximize tax-free profits. As suggested in a tax-planning publication,

> The use of pricing arrangements in transactions between the Puerto Rican enterprise and its United States affiliate to shift income from the United States to Puerto Rico might be advantageous. For example, the Puerto Rican firm might sell to its United States parent at an unusually high price; without reimbursement the parent might incur expenses for products manufactured by its Puerto Rican subsidiary; the Puerto Rican subsidiary might use the parent's patents or industrial property free of royalty.[36]

Suppose that a U.S. multinational owns the patent for a new product, which is manufactured in the Puerto Rican affiliate. The Puerto Rican affiliate then sells the finished product to the parent at an inflated price, and the parent company then sells it to distributors for the same price. This practice allows the parent to shift a substantial portion of its income to the tax-free affiliate in Puerto Rico. At the same time, the parent corporation retains most of the costs of researching and developing this new product, enabling it to offset some of its tax liability in the United States.

Under Section 482 of the IRC (generally applicable to all U.S. multinationals), the Internal Revenue Service (IRS) may reallocate income or expenses between two or more corporations commonly owned to prevent tax evasion resulting from the aforementioned practice. In the 1950s the IRS began to investigate the intercompany pricing activities of 931 corporations. In 1959 the Puerto Rican governor complained to the secretary of the U.S. Treasury that IRS investigations were "hurting Puerto Rico's ability to attract U.S. investment." As a result, pending IRS investigations were suspended until 1963. At that time the IRS issued new rules applicable only to transactions between the Puerto Rican affiliate and its U.S. parent. These new guidelines noted a number of situations in which "improper shifting of profits might occur," making a Section 482 ruling necessary. According to the Treasury, the "most difficult and contentious cases ... typically involve intangible property: patents, trademarks, brand names, access to established marketing and distribution channels, and goodwill with customers."[37]

According to the 1963 regulations, to assess where the profits from the intangible property belonged, the first step was to determine whether the parent or the Puerto Rican affiliate owned the intangible property. Thus, U.S. tax lawyers quickly advised firms to "transfer the industrial property to the Puerto Rican enterprise."[38] After 1963, the establishment of a U.S. subsidiary in Puerto Rico was "accompanied by the execution of legal documents irrevocably assigning exclusive patent and other rights to the newborn company." This procedure made it difficult for the U.S. Treasury to argue that the parent rather than the Puerto Rican affiliate was "entitled to the return of the intangible."[39]

Clearly, there were a number of legal ways in which U.S. firms could minimize their federal tax liability through their investments in Puerto Rico.[40] However, not all U.S. firms benefited equally from tax planning because not all firms benefited equally from the tax exemption.

A tax holiday does not automatically mean higher rates of returns for a manufacturing affiliate. A firm needs to consider additional costs when it decides to invest overseas. Besides taxes, other costs of production include labor, transportation, rent, infrastructure, political stability, and so on. Hence, the relative importance of taxes in explaining location decisions "varies considerably across industries and business activities." For some firms—especially pharmaceuticals—taxes are one of the most important or the most important consideration when deciding where to locate their manufacturing operation. Moreover, even when taxes are the most important consideration for a multinational corporation, flexibility in setting transfer prices might be an equally important consideration.[41] U.S. multinationals benefit from low taxes and flexibility to set transfer prices in a host country as long as the U.S. tax rate exceeds the foreign tax rate.[42] And if there is little or no tax in the host country, as in Puerto Rico, the incentives to locate manufacturing operations there are even greater for this type of firm.

The Pharmaceutical Industry

Success in the pharmaceutical industry "depends on a company's ability to discover effective new drugs, get them through the regulatory approval processes in various countries, and market them quickly to harvest profits before their patents expire."[43] Until 1984, the duration of a U.S. patent was seventeen years. However, the approval process could take between eight and thirteen years, meaning that the effective life of a drug could be as short as five years.[44]

For a drug company, manufacturing and distribution costs are but a small portion of the selling price.[45] Rather the selling price must reflect the costs of research and development of the patented drug as well as research costs of losers. Thus, "regardless of whether current profits represent a low, reasonable, or high return on past R&D, the tax saving of assigning those profits to a tax-exempt subsidiary can be substantial."[46] In his study of location decisions of manufacturing corporations, G. P. Wilson found that tax benefits are the among the principal reasons driving location decisions for pharmaceutical corporations in Puerto Rico. In fact, in the 1970s, "taxes were the primary driver" of foreign location decisions.[47]

Table 5 lists the names and years in which the biggest firms in the pharmaceutical industry first established their operations in Puerto Rico. The first U.S. pharmaceutical company began operation in Puerto Rico in 1960, and by 1974, twenty pharmaceutical companies had operations there. The list is misleading, however, because some of these companies had multiple operations. For example, in 1975, seven U.S. firms alone (Eli Lilly, G. D. Searle, Warner-Lambert, Abbott Laboratories, Bristol-Myers, Pfizer, and Upjohn), had established a total of nineteen plants on the island. According to the U.S. Commerce Department, it was expected that "any suitable exclusive new product successfully introduced on the market by a U.S. pharmaceutical company [would] be taken to Puerto Rico for production."[48]

Table 6 shows the tax savings in the possessions for a sample of Section 931 companies for 1971–75. The U.S. statutory corporate tax rate during this period was 48 percent, but, as the table illustrates, the 931 provision enabled some of the pharmaceutical firms to reduce their U.S. tax burden by between

TABLE 5.   Pharmaceutical Companies: Year of Initial Puerto Rican Operation

Abbott Laboratories	1968
Alcon	1974
Allergan	1971
American Hospital Supply	1971
Baxter Laboratories	1958
Bristol-Myers	1971
Johnson and Johnson	1966
Eli Lilly	1966
Merck	1972
Pfizer	1973
Richardson-Merrell	1974
A. H. Robins	1974
Schering	1972
G. D. Searle	1969
SmithKline	1970
Squibb	1970
Sterling	1950
Technicon	1970
Upjohn	1973
Warner-Lambert	1960

Source: U.S. Commerce Department 1979.

TABLE 6. U.S. Firms Reporting a Tax Savings under Section 931, 1973–76 (in percentage points)

	1973	1974	1975	1976
Pharmaceuticals				
Abbott Laboratories	12.0*	15.4*	12.6*	—
American Hospital Supply	1.6	2.1	3.5	6.7*
Baxter Laboratories	21.9*	23.0*	22.3*	—
Becton Dickinson	—	3.6	5.1	—
Eli Lilly	5.2*	6.2	6.0	4.2
Johnson and Johnson	—	0.5	2.5	3.6
Merck	2.2*	2.7	4.5	—
Pfizer	—	13.5	—	—
Schering-Plough	4.5	8.9	14.0*	—
G. D. Searle	24.3*	28.1*	33.6*	—
SmithKline	17.2*	19.1*	21.7*	—
Squibb	12.0	—	12.7	14.6*
Upjohn	—	—	—	8.0
Electronics				
Digital Equipment	—	—	7.6*	—
Motorola	—	—	8.2	—
Textile and Apparel				
Cluett Peabody	7.0	—	0.2	—
Bluebell	—	—	—	3.4
Hanes	—	11.0*	—	—
Food Processors				
H. J. Heinz	—	—	7.5	—
Esmark	—	—	—	4.9
Beverages				
PepsiCo	—	—	4.1	2.8
Instruments				
Perkin Elmer	—	—	4.5	—
Federal Statutory Tax Rate	48.0	48.0	48.0	48.0

Source: Tax Notes and 10-K reports, 1973, 1974, 1975, 1976.

Note: U.S. firms have to file 10-K reports with the U.S. Securities and Exchange Commission. These 10-K reports require companies to indicate the tax provisions that reduced their U.S. tax liability by more than 2.4 percent. However, not all companies break down their tax savings by country or statute. General Electric, for example, combines its possessions tax break savings with other savings and places them under a "miscellaneous" category.

(—) Information not available or no tax savings reported.

*Indicates that the possessions tax break was the most important factor reducing federal taxes.

0.5 and 33.6 percentage points. For many of these drug companies, Section 931 was the most important factor in reducing their federal tax liability, even exceeding the savings from foreign tax credits, tax deferrals, tax-exempt investment income, and capital-gains exempted income.[49] For example, in 1974 SmithKline owed an estimated $83.6 million (48 percent of its income) in taxes to the U.S. government. The company used Section 931 to reduce its federal tax liability by $33.3 million (19.1 percentage points). By comparison, foreign tax credits, tax deferrals, and other miscellaneous tax provisions combined enabled the company to reduce its federal tax liability by $17 million (11.8 percentage points). The company's statutory corporate tax rate was reduced from 48 percent to 17.1 percent, or $47.8 million.

For the rest of the pharmaceutical companies, foreign tax credits were the most important factor (followed by Section 931) for reducing their federal tax liability. However, contrary to the 100 percent federal tax exemption granted under 931, foreign tax credits represented income taxes paid to foreign governments. For example, in 1975 Eli Lilly's statutory tax liability was an estimated $288.5 million. The company used Section 931 to reduce its federal tax liability by $36.0 million (6.0 percentage points). The company's share to foreign governments enabled it to reduce its U.S. tax liability by $45.0 million (7.5 percentage points).

For many of these companies, their Puerto Rican affiliate was slowly becoming their principal pharmaceutical operation. Table 7 shows the estimated after-tax earnings of U.S. multinationals derived from their Puerto Rican operations. Note that Puerto Rican earnings represented between 1.0 percent and 68.7 percent of pharmaceutical companies' consolidated after-tax earnings. The table suggests that some of these companies were indeed taking their most profitable products to Puerto Rico. The profit margins of the island activities of pharmaceuticals' generally compared favorably with the profit margins of their counterparts on the U.S. mainland. Only twice between 1967 and 1976 did the profit-to-sales ratio of the Puerto Rican affiliates fall below 50 percent (compared with average profit-to-sales ratios of 12 percent on the mainland). The island affiliates' tax-free condition partially explains the higher profit margins. However, there was also "upward bias" in the Puerto Rican rates caused by the tendency of U.S. multinationals to structure their investments in a way that maximized the profits attributed to their island subsidiaries."[50]

Eli Lilly and G. D. Searle are two of the most notorious transfer-prices cases in which the IRS took the companies to tax court to make the parent liable for additional taxes. In both cases the IRS argued that the price that the island affiliate charged the parent company for its products was too high. Table 8 shows the return on assets for both the parent and its island affiliate for the years covered by the cases.

While their Puerto Rican profits seem excessive, U.S. firms were simply responding to tax incentives. Moreover, although the IRS complained that some of the companies' tax-free profits were questionable, government guidelines for intercompany transactions remained unclear.

The Electronics Industry

The case of electronics differs somewhat. The first step in the manufacturing process for this industry is the production of semiconductor integrated circuits and chips. These devices are the basic component parts of a wide range of prod-

TABLE 7.   Tax-Free Puerto Rican Earnings as a Percentage of Consolidated after-Tax Earnings, 1973–76

	1973	1974	1975	1976
Pharmaceuticals				
Abbott Laboratories	25.0	32.0	26.2	—
American Hospital Supply	3.3	4.3	7.2	13.9
Baxter Laboratories	45.6	47.9	46.4	—
Becton Dickinson	—	7.5	10.6	—
Eli Lilly	10.8	12.9	12.5	8.7
Johnson and Johnson	—	1.0	5.2	7.5
Merck	4.5	5.6	9.3	—
Pfizer	—	28.0	—	—
Schering-Plough	9.3	18.5	29.1	—
G. D. Searle	50.6	58.5	68.7	—
SmithKline	35.8	39.7	42.5	—
Squibb	23.9	—	26.4	30.0
Upjohn	—	—	—	16.6
Electronics				
Digital Equipment	—	—	15.8	—
Motorola	—	—	17.0	—
Textile and Apparel				
Cluett Peabody	14.5	—	0.4	—
Bluebell	—	—	—	7.8
Hanes	—	22.9	—	—
Food Processors				
H. J. Heinz	—	—	15.6	—
Esmark	—	—	—	10.2
Beverages				
PepsiCo	—	—	8.5	5.8
Instruments				
Perkin Elmer	—	—	9.3	—

Source: Tax Notes and 10-K reports, 1973, 1974, 1975, 1976.

(—) Information not available or no tax savings reported.

ucts, such as telephones, fax machines, satellites, computers, robotics, auto electronics, videocassette recorders, and a wide range of defense products.[51]

Profit margins in the semiconductor industry are "higher than most industries, but lower than the pharmaceutical industry" because manufacturing costs are higher for semiconductors than for pharmaceuticals, although for both industry groups the "bulk of the expenses are incurred prior to the start of manufacturing" (i.e., during research and development). Product life is short for this industry, but unlike the pharmaceutical industry, such is the case not because of patent expiration but rather because of "product obsolescence."[52]

In his study, G. P. Wilson examined the location decisions of a number of semiconductor companies. He found that location decisions for this industry were "strongly influenced" by "tax considerations," although other factors, such as "labor force, infrastructure, political stability, proximity to markets and financial systems," and so on were also important.[53] By October 1976 of a total of 134 electronic establishments in Puerto Rico, 122 were owned by fifty-eight U.S. firms. General Electric operated twenty-three plants on the island, and Westinghouse operated sixteen facilities. In Puerto Rico, this industry was dominated by the manufacture of products for industrial and communications use, including "computers, testing and measuring instruments, industrial control and processing equipment, television and radio broadcasting equipment, and medical and therapeutic equipment."[54]

The two electronic companies listed in table 6, Motorola and Digital Equipment, used Section 931 to reduce their U.S. tax liability by 8.2 percentage points and 7.6 percentage points, respectively. For Digital, Section 931 was the most important factor reducing its federal tax liability in 1975, and for Motorola it was the second most important factor. The electronics industry's Puerto Rican activities showed higher profits than their mainland counterparts, although not by the margins of the pharmaceutical industry. For example, in 1973 and 1975, two years for which comparable data are available, the Puerto Rican rate of return exceeded the U.S. rate. In 1973 the rate of return on equity for the

TABLE 8.   Return on Average Assets Employed by Two Pharmaceutical Companies (in percentages)

	1971	1972	1973	1974	1975
Eli Lilly					
Parent	20	24	30		
Affiliate	138	143	101		
G. D. Searle					
Parent				31	42
Affiliate				109	119

Source: Scholes and Wolfson 1992.

industry was 13.1 percent in the United States versus 20.7 percent in Puerto Rico. In 1975 the rate was 9.0 percent in the United States versus 20.6 percent in Puerto Rico. Likewise, in 1973 and 1975, the profit-to-sales ratios in the United States were 4.3 percent and 3.2 percent, respectively, versus 25.0 and 26.8 percent in Puerto Rico.[55] That is, the profit-to-sales ratio of the Puerto Rican affiliates was at least five times greater than the return of the mainland firms in 1973 and eight times greater in 1975. As in the case of pharmaceuticals, these margins suggest that electronics firms were taking advantage of their ability to shift income to their Puerto Rican affiliates.

U.S. Treasury data support the conclusion that pharmaceuticals were the biggest beneficiaries of Section 931. Treasury estimates show that between 1973 and 1975, approximately 50 percent of the total federal tax savings associated with 931 were concentrated in the pharmaceutical industry. Pharmaceutical industry benefits were also evident in the Treasury's estimates of tax benefits per employee. For example, in 1975, the tax savings per employee in both pharmaceutical and electronic firms were among the highest of all possessions corporations. However, the tax savings per employee for pharmaceuticals was $34,873, which was more than three times the average employee compensation of $10,032. The tax savings per employee for electronics was $7,423, almost equal to the average employee compensation of $7,412. For every dollar of wages and benefits paid to Puerto Rican workers, the U.S. Treasury lost three dollars in tax revenues for the pharmaceutical industries and one dollar in tax revenues for the electronics industry.[56]

Although pharmaceuticals and electronics were not the only industry groups with operations in Puerto Rico, they clearly benefited the most from the existing tax regime. First, for industry groups such as these, with high gross-profit margins, taxes are an important consideration for manufacturing-location decisions. Second, as their profit figures suggest, these firms benefited from the flexibility in transferring ownership of their products to their island affiliates and in setting intercompany prices. Third, Puerto Rico offered these U.S. firms a unique advantage because it was the only jurisdiction where they could invest and repatriate profits to the U.S. without incurring federal tax liabilities. For example, U.S. pharmaceuticals traditionally viewed Ireland as an attractive alternative to Puerto Rico. Ireland also had an aggressive program to attract foreign investment through local tax breaks, but unlike the case of Puerto Rico, the profits of U.S. firms doing business in Ireland were subject to federal tax upon repatriation.

IV. Conclusion

At the time of its enactment in 1921, the possessions-corporation system of taxation represented a departure from the basic federal tax treatment of U.S. companies doing business abroad. Moreover, while this federal tax exemption was originally enacted with no intention of contributing to the economic development of the possessions, Puerto Rico became one of the provision's biggest beneficiaries. Another important beneficiary of the federal tax break was the U.S. firms that established subsidiary operations on the island. U.S. pharmaceutical and electronics companies took advantage of the combination of federal and Puerto Rican tax exemptions by shifting a great deal of their profits to their island affiliates and then repatriating them tax-free. Given that the federal tax break had been one of the most important factors for reducing the federal tax liability of many of these firms, it is exceedingly likely that they would have an interest in the perpetuation of this tax regime. The next chapter discusses the political reaction of U.S. firms to congressional attempts to eliminate this very lucrative federal tax provision as part of the Tax Reform Act of 1976.

CHAPTER 3

Learning to Rely on Implicit Threats:
The Tax Reform Act of 1976

> I have said on many occasions that sometimes there is a loophole in the
> law that you cannot fully close or eliminate without creating more prob-
> lems in the process of doing so than you have as a result of the loophole.
> —Chairman Wilbur Mills (D-Ark.)

In 1973, as part of its work on tax reform, Congress proposed eliminating the
investment incentives U.S. firms enjoyed with the possessions tax credit. Although it was in their interests to protect their tax-free earnings in Puerto Rico,
the companies made no attempts to become involved in the political process.
They relied on the implicit threat to cause unemployment in Puerto Rico to persuade Congress to retain the federal tax incentives. It is likely that the companies relied on this strategy because they had no memory of ever having to mobilize for political action regarding this issue. Their political strategy worked
because by the time tax reform was drafted, the political pressure to control the
activities of U.S. multinationals through taxation had subsided. Moreover, the
chair of the House Ways and Means Committee believed that U.S. firms needed
incentives to invest. The concentration of committee power in the hands of its
chair would have rendered a lobbying campaign by the companies redundant
because members were expected to follow the lead of their chair. In 1981–82
this scenario would change, but the fact that in the early 1970s the companies
succeeded in protecting their interests by relying solely on their structural
power to cause unemployment would have important consequences for their future political behavior.

I. Section 931 Becomes an Item
on the Public-Policy Agenda

In the early 1960s, there had been a general consensus for a liberal U.S. trade
policy. In 1962 Congress passed the Trade Expansion Act with support from the
AFL-CIO as well as the Chamber of Commerce and paved the way to the
Kennedy round of multilateral trade negotiations. In the area of foreign direct

investment, the U.S. government, though lacking a coherent policy, was perceived as encouraging the expansion of multinational enterprises. As the decade progressed, however, the global dominance the United States had enjoyed during the previous twenty years began to erode. The U.S. government could no longer ignore its balance-of-payments deficits. The outflow of capital was increasing, more and more industries were showing negative trade balances, and unemployment was on the rise.[1] As a result, capital control programs were established, protectionist demands increased, and U.S. multinationals came under attack.

Organized Labor and the Taxation of U.S. Multinationals

The AFL-CIO gradually reversed its traditional free-trade position to one in which it supported import restrictions and changes in the tax laws that would have significantly increased the federal tax liability of U.S. multinationals. Since the early 1960s, "small" unions had complained that increasing imports were threatening their jobs.[2] But the AFL-CIO leadership continued to support free trade. Eventually, however, as the rate of unemployment continued to increase, more unions complained, and labor's official reversal on free trade became inevitable. Labor began to argue that multinationals exported jobs and transferred U.S. technology to low-wage countries, enabling their workers to "produce at almost the same level of productivity as high-waged American workers." In addition, labor argued that U.S. multinationals were nothing more than "a device for escaping the full burden of U.S. corporate taxes."[3]

Mills and Tax Reform

In the meantime, during his brief bid for the Democratic presidential nomination in 1973, the chair of the Ways and Means Committee, Wilbur Mills (D-Ark.) had promised a thorough review of the tax code. He kept his promise and at the start of the 93rd Congress in 1973, Mills announced that general tax reform would be the committee's first order of business. On 5 February, the committee began panel discussions and hearings on the topic of tax reform. Given the controversy concerning the taxation of multinationals, the committee decided to spend considerable time studying the issue, which also included a review of the possessions tax provision. It would be the first time that a congressional committee would examine in such detail the taxation of U.S. multinationals.[4]

During the ensuing panel discussions, the committee's direction on the issue of the possessions tax break was unclear. Panelists explained that the argument had been made that Section 931 "contribute[d] to the exports of jobs from the United States to our possessions, and in particular to Puerto Rico." They also suggested that the committee review the rules of Section 332 of the Internal Revenue Code (IRC), which permitted the tax-free liquidation of a U.S. subsidiary. It was argued that Section 332, in conjunction with Section 931, "obviously provide[d] substantial tax incentives for locating plants in a possession such as Puerto Rico." Panelists were aware that Puerto Rico also exempted U.S. manufacturing subsidiaries from Puerto Rican income tax for a period of years. Finally, it was argued that "the special relationship of the United States to its possessions, including the Commonwealth of Puerto Rico, would suggest that tax changes . . . should not be lightly and precipitously undertaken."[5]

Both the panel discussion and the hearing testimony made it clear that, in the fifty-two years since the enactment of the possessions tax break on behalf of U.S. investors in the Philippines, Congress had never really reviewed the provision. However, the panelists' testimony suggests that they viewed Section 931 not as tax policy for U.S. firms doing business in the possessions but as U.S. tax policy for the possessions in general and for Puerto Rico in particular. For the first time in the history of the provision, it was suggested that a review of the tax law "necessarily [went] far beyond questions of tax policy" and should include consideration of the relationship of the United States with Puerto Rico.[6]

The committee began the markup of tax reform in May 1973, by which time labor had lost its momentum. Dollar devaluations in late 1971 and early 1973 had turned the trade deficit into a $1 billion surplus. As the domestic economic situation began to improve, labor's protectionist arguments were undermined.[7] However, although the political pressure to make the tax rules for doing business abroad more strict had subsided, the tax-reform process kept the issue alive.

Treasury Proposes Changes

During markup, Treasury lobbied to limit the tax benefits for U.S. firms doing business in Puerto Rico. Since it was customary for Mills to have officials and staff of the Treasury Department sit with the committee during meetings at which legislation was being marked up, department officials had an advantage in making this kind of recommendation unopposed. Treasury argued that Section 931 had not been enacted to allow the tax-free repatriation of profits from the possessions. Moreover, as explained in chapter 2, since the late 1950s, the IRS had maintained that U.S. firms had been abusing the tax provision by transferring ownership of their products to Puerto Rico and then inflating the prices at which they sold island products to the mainland headquarters. Such intercompany transactions, the U.S. Treasury argued, enabled U.S. multinationals to increase their federal tax-free Puerto Rican profits.

Based on Treasury recommendations, on 22 May the committee proposed a number of changes to Section 931 and Section 332 of the Internal Revenue

Code. In particular, the committee decided to tax the accumulated profits of U.S. firms doing business in Puerto Rico at the time of liquidation. "The tentative proposal approved by the committee would have imposed a capital gains tax on the transfer of the accumulated profits on liquidation."[8] As a result, income from doing business in Puerto Rico would be exempted from U.S. taxation only as long as the money was not repatriated to the U.S. mainland. As far as U.S. taxes were concerned, investing in Puerto Rico would be no different from establishing a subsidiary operation in a foreign country. For all practical purposes, the proposal eliminated one of the most important incentives for doing business in Puerto Rico under the rules of Section 931.

By the time Congress devised its proposal to eliminate the benefits of the possessions tax credit, U.S. firms had been profiting significantly from their Puerto Rican operations for years. The companies had also tried to deflect Treasury efforts to increase their federal tax liability by taking them to tax court.[9] Hence, it is likely that once the firms learned of congressional attempts to eliminate nearly all of the benefits of investing under the rules of Section 931, they would oppose it. But the companies' political reaction was to rely on the implicit threat of an investment strike in Puerto Rico to protect their interests. Specifically, interviews with company and government officials revealed that U.S. firms' automatic response was to rely on the Puerto Rican government to communicate to Congress that it was in business's interest that the benefits of the possessions tax break be preserved. The companies did not purposely decide to rely on the Puerto Rican government because it would make for a better lobbyist and did not pressure Puerto Rican officials to lobby on their behalf. Rather, the firms' behavior suggests that they expected their structural power would be enough to convince both Puerto Rican and U.S. public officials that Section 931 should not be altered in any way.

Reaction of Puerto Rican Administrators

On learning about the committee's proposal, Puerto Rico's resident commissioner,[10] Jaime Benítez, called a meeting with the governor, Hernández Colón; Puerto Rico's treasury secretary, Salvador Casellas; and the head of Puerto Rico's Economic Development Administration (FOMENTO), Teodoro Moscoso, to get their opinions. The Puerto Rican administration comprised members of the ruling Popular Democratic Party, and they were convinced that without the ability to repatriate their Puerto Rico–based profits free of federal taxation, U.S. firms would stop bringing in new investment to Puerto Rico.

According to Casellas,

> time was of [the] essence. [It was agreed] that one of us should appear before the Ways and Means Committee immediately to inform the members

of how injurious their action could be for Puerto Rico . . . especially since we were in the midst of our worst recession since the 1930s.[11]

Benítez arranged for Casellas to appear before the committee on 30 May. On arriving in the committee room, Casellas was greeted by representatives of the U.S. Treasury and by Lawrence Woodworth, executive director of the Joint Committee on Taxation, who also sat with the committee during markup.[12]

Casellas began his testimony by explaining that Puerto Rico's industrial-incentives program had been devised to work with U.S. tax laws. He argued that "Puerto Rico needed jobs and it had to be provided with the basic tools to create them . . . otherwise Puerto Ricans would depend primarily on welfare for their living." According to Casellas, the reaction of committee members was "most favorable, and Chairman Mills personally opened the door for a reconsideration by the Committee."[13] Mills explained that they did not intend to hurt Puerto Rico and granted Casellas another opportunity on 3 June to appear before the committee with Benítez and Moscoso. Mills also instructed Woodworth to meet with Casellas and work on alternatives. Woodworth had been looking into the concept of tax sparing and suggested it as a possible alternative to Section 931 in Puerto Rico. A tax-sparing agreement allows multinationals to take advantage of a tax holiday in the host country. It provides for a home-country tax credit in the amount of taxes they would have paid to the host country. The U.S. Treasury officially opposes tax sparing, and the U.S. government has never included such provisions in any of its tax treaties.

After Casellas finished his presentation, members of the business community who had been present during his testimony (including lawyers and Washington representatives of possessions corporations) introduced themselves and expressed their support. According to Casellas, although the business community had at no time been directly involved in the issue of the possessions tax credit, the committee was, after all, marking up major tax legislation, and U.S. companies were on the alert.[14]

On 3 June, Benítez, Moscoso, and Casellas appeared before the committee with an extensive memorandum from Governor Hernández Colón. First, they apprised the committee on what Puerto Rico's industrialization program had done to "transform [the island] from a monocrop economy to a developing one, from the poorhouse of the Caribbean to a modern example of industrial development."[15] The Puerto Rican delegation made it clear that U.S. firms would stop investing in Puerto Rico if they could no longer repatriate their earnings free of federal taxes. Puerto Rican officials also sought to make the economy of Puerto Rico a local issue for committee members by arguing that the U.S. economy would also be hurt by the elimination of the federal tax incentives. Thus, Governor Hernández Colón, in his memorandum to the committee, explained,

> I am assured that U.S. manufacturing firms no longer able to enjoy the tax free . . . [liquidation] . . . incentive will not continue to establish factories in Puerto Rico, with the consequent disastrous effect on our industrial development program. This is so in as much as Puerto Rico offers no other major incentive to attract such plants. [As a result], unemployment in Puerto Rico will increase sharply, social unrest will become epidemic and net inward migration from the U.S. will reverse and once again flow heavily towards the mainland, as it did in the past. In addition, welfare expenditures on the continent will increase and there will be great pressure on the Congress to make special appropriations to deal with "the Puerto Rican situation."[16]

The Puerto Rican delegation argued that 90,000 to 100,000 Puerto Ricans would migrate to the United States every year, most of them taking up residence in New York City, Chicago, Philadelphia, and Ohio. Finally, the Puerto Rican representatives argued that Puerto Rico was the sixth-largest customer of U.S. mainland products, thus generating 168,000 jobs in the States. These jobs would be lost if Section 931 and Section 332 were eliminated or modified.[17]

Reacting to the testimony of Benítez, Moscoso, and Casellas, Mills reflected,

> I am sure I express the opinion of the members of the committee when I say we certainly do not want to reverse this progress that you are making. The effects would not only be felt in your country, but of course they would be felt here.
>
> I have said on many occasions that sometimes there is a loophole in the law that you cannot fully close or eliminate without creating more problems in the process of doing so than you have as a result of the loophole. This is, in my opinion, an example of what I have been talking about. As far as I am concerned, I am willing to forget it.

Likewise, Representative Al Ullman (D-Ore.) said, "I join with the Chairman expressing our hope that we might continue programs in effect just as they are." Representative James A. Burke (D-Mass.) concurred: "I think we have a moral responsibility here not to do anything to injure Puerto Rico."[18]

None of the committee members questioned whether the implied threat of unemployment in Puerto Rico was real. As Lindblom would have expected, the presumption was that business needs incentives to invest. Because labor's demands regarding the federal treatment of the foreign profits of U.S. firms had subsided, Mills had the freedom to concentrate on promoting what he thought was good public policy.[19] And, at the time, good policy meant using tax breaks to achieve socioeconomic goals.

Economic Growth and Democracy

Why would Mills think that protecting Puerto Rico's economic growth was good public policy? The final Ways and Means Committee report on the Tax Reform Act provides only a general explanation for the decision to retain the federal tax break. It reads as follows:

> Your committee, after studying the problem, concluded that it is inappropriate to disturb the existing relationship between the possession investment incentives and the U.S. tax laws because of the important role it is believed they play in keeping investment in the possessions competitive with investment in neighboring countries.[20]

The only thing that becomes apparent from reading the report is that the committee did not want to be responsible for eliminating a tax incentive that could affect Puerto Rico's economic growth. The question is, why would the U.S. government feel that it had a stake in protecting Puerto Rico's economic health? The answer is that, in the context of the cold war, democracy and political stability in the Caribbean was an important concern of U.S. policymakers.

In the 1950s and 1960s, American policymakers based foreign-assistance policies on the belief that economic aid contributes to economic development, which, in turn, contributes to the growth and stability of liberal democratic political systems.[21] While there is no direct evidence that this kind of argument was decisive, it is likely Mills believed that economic growth in Puerto Rico would secure a politically stable and democratic island. In turn, Puerto Rico's well-being may have been in the interest of Congress because the U.S. government had used the island as a model of democracy and economic development to be copied by other less-developed countries. It is probable, then, that Mills did not want to be responsible for hurting the economic progress of Puerto Rico, especially when a few years earlier the U.S. government had presented the island as an alternative model to Cuba in the Caribbean and Latin America.[22] Carr explains,

> To many American policymakers, Castro's Cuba was more than a direct political and strategic threat. It was a moral affront; it bred an ideological virus that could not be allowed to spread. The Caribbean became a battlefield between the democratic values of the West and Soviet totalitarianism.
>
> In this battle, Puerto Rico [was] cast to play an important role: it was a "showcase of democracy," a proof that democracy and free enterprise could bring well-being and political stability.[23]

Ultimately, Mills's favorable disposition toward Puerto Rico was everything that Puerto Rican officials and U.S. firms could hope for and more. His

support alone ensured the permanence of the possessions tax break without re-
quiring business to exert any additional effort. In turn, Mills's support was
grounded in the belief that the companies would leave Puerto Rico if the committee followed the suggestions of the Treasury staff.

II. Centralized Committee Structures

Once the chairman of the Ways and Means Committee agreed that the possessions tax break should be preserved, any political mobilization by business
would have been redundant because committee members were expected to follow his lead. Mills's influence resulted from the manner in which he conducted
business within the committee. In 1961 Mills banned the use of subcommittees,
thereby making the committee very centralized. Mills's control was also attributed to the fact that he was "as responsive to the Committee as the Committee [was] to him." The committee's decisions were "shaped and articulated
by Mills, but his word [came] close to being law in the Committee because he
[had] listened to other members." The end product was sound legislation written in a "collegial" and professional manner—even if the final vote was split.
Proof of Mills's and the committee's effectiveness lies in the fact that the House
rejected committee bills on only two occasions between 1961 and 1968. Most
important, however, the reason most often given to explain Mills's influence
within the committee was his expertise. Members less knowledgeable than he
on revenue issues trusted him to make the decisions.[24]

In turn, the Ways and Means Committee has controlled revenue legislation in the House since the committee's inception in 1795. Combined with the
fact that during the Mills era (1958–75), most committee legislation passed the
full House unamended, this control made the committee an inherently important government actor in all revenue legislation. The committee's importance
in the House was also heightened by the fact that it was "the committee on committees"—that is, it was the group in charge of committee assignments for
House Democrats.[25] Because the committee was seen as highly responsive to
the interests of House members, they gave Mills the tools he needed to maintain his exclusive control over revenue legislation, including closed markup
sessions, closed rules prohibiting floor amendments, and "exclusive" use of the
Joint Committee on Taxation.[26]

Mills's formidable influence within the committee, combined with its control over revenue legislation, facilitated the protection of the possessions tax
break in relative obscurity and without the need for U.S. firms to engage in any
kind of explicit political mobilization. Once Mills had decided on the basic sub-
stance of the legislation dealing with U.S. firms doing business in Puerto Rico,

his technical support staff—Woodworth, with representatives from the U.S. Treasury—worked out the details. After several meetings with Casellas and Moscoso, they fashioned Section 936 to replace Section 931 before the end of the 93rd Congress.

New Incentives to Invest

The new Section 936 was designed to harmonize U.S. and Puerto Rican interests. First, there was a consensus among U.S. officials that Puerto Rico needed to be able to offer U.S. firms tax-free investment and current repatriation to the mainland to "create job opportunities on the island." The committee report listed a number of disadvantages of investing in Puerto Rico.

> The U.S. Government imposes upon the possessions various requirements, such as minimum wage requirements and requirements to use U.S. flagships in transporting goods between the United States and various possessions, which substantially increase the labor, transportation and other costs of establishing business operations in Puerto Rico. Thus, without significant local tax incentives that are not nullified by the U.S. taxes, the possessions would find it quite difficult to attract investments by U.S. corporations.[27]

Thus, tax breaks were the only alternative considered by U.S. officials. The only point of contention was whether U.S. firms should get a 100 percent exemption or less. Finally, the committee decided that the U.S. government would give U.S. firms a 100 percent exemption and Puerto Rico would impose a tollgate tax of 15 percent.[28]

At the same time, Treasury officials were concerned that U.S. companies were investing billions in the Eurodollar market and then repatriating the money tax-free via Puerto Rico. Section 936 would make these investments taxable. Hence, one important difference between Section 931 and Section 936 was that, under Section 936, instead of excluding income earned in the possession, a 936 company would enjoy a 100 percent tax credit on income from the "active conduct of a trade or business in the possession" or from qualified possession source investment income, which was defined as "passive investment income" from within the possession. This provision ensured that only income from within the possession would be free of tax. But the most important difference between Section 931 and the new law was that under Section 936, the parent company would pay no taxes on dividends received from a 936 subsidiary.[29] As a result, U.S. firms would not need to liquidate their Puerto Rican operations to repatriate their island profits free of federal tax.

Treasury strongly opposed Section 936, not a surprising position given the IRS's problems in attempting to regulate the intercompany transactions of the companies under Section 931. Moreover, Treasury had never really understood how Section 931 worked. Because under 931 income from the possessions was exempted from U.S. income tax, in spite of the 10-K requirements, Treasury did not really know how much money was being earned in Puerto Rico free of federal tax; the department also had not undertaken a comprehensive study of the tax law. Some Treasury analysts requested that "action on 936 should be delayed pending a study of the existing situation under 931." Treasury's petition "was transformed" by the Ways and Means Committee into a request for the department to examine the effectiveness of the tax law as a mechanism for job creation on the island, to look at the revenue effects to the U.S. Treasury, and to produce an annual report.[30]

When the drafting of Section 936 had been completed at the end of 1973, Puerto Rican officials "started to receive positive feedback from the business community." According to Casellas, the general feeling among the business community was that the proposed Section 936 was an improvement over Section 931. U.S. firms could now invest in the island and enjoy the flexibility to repatriate their profits to the mainland free of both Puerto Rican and federal taxes anytime they wanted. The new provision was much better than anything the companies could have envisioned.

In spite of the more generous tax incentive being discussed and the fact that "there was much uncertainty with respect to its ultimate passage," U.S. firms continued to have a seemingly relaxed attitude and limited their political activity to monitoring the progress of the proposed tax law. By all accounts, possessions corporations felt that if the reform did not pass, the worst that could happen was that Section 931 would remain unaltered. After all, the federal tax break had remained unchanged for more than fifty years, and Puerto Rican and U.S. officials were responding to the companies' implicit threat to leave the island if the tax regime was made less favorable. Accordingly, in 1974 and 1975, U.S. firms continued to establish manufacturing operations on the island. Expansions of existing plants continued uninterrupted. Between July 1974 and June 1975, ninety-six U.S. firms added to their existing operations on the island. "Chief among the expansions were those companies dealing with the manufacture of electrical equipment such as General Electric, Westinghouse, and Digital" as well as pharmaceutical companies.[31]

Some members of the Puerto Rican financial community expressed the fear that if Section 936 were enacted "it might turn out to be too much of a good thing." They were aware of the fact that very few members of Congress really knew how Section 931 worked and that it was possible that "once the Pandora's Box of congressional scrutiny was opened, it might be difficult or impossible to close it again."[32]

The Long Process of Reform

Finally, in November 1974, under pressure to report a reform bill after almost two years of deliberations, the committee reported H.R. 17488. The bill combined sections of an energy bill the committee had tried to pass at the end of 1973 and some tax-reform provisions, including Section 936.[33] However, there was little enthusiasm for tax-reform legislation in the House, and the Rules Committee rejected a request to send the bill to the floor, effectively killing it. Roughly at the same time, Mills was hospitalized after being criticized for "erratic behavior" during a public incident regarding a stripper. He resigned as committee chairman in December 1974.

Mills's resignation was accompanied by a series of reforms directed at the House Ways and Means Committee, which many congressional reformers argued was "unresponsive and obstructionist." These reforms included an enlarged committee membership, the creation of subcommittees, no power over House committee assignments, and increased opportunities for committee bills to be open to amendments on the floor.[34]

These changes lengthened the tax-reform process. However, in terms of the possessions tax break, the changes in both the committee's operation and its membership had little impact on the outcome of legislation. In spite of some earlier legislative setbacks, when the possessions tax break was first being discussed, Mills still remained the undisputed leader of the committee; before his departure, the proposal replacing Section 931 with 936 had already been drafted per his instructions. By 1975 the committee was in a hurry to enact a tax-reform project because, after two years of deliberations, the failure to produce a bill had become an embarrassment. Hence, rather than changing the tax bill as it had been drafted under Mills, the new committee chairman, Ullman, used it as a blueprint for his own tax-reform project. In the end, committee members retained Section 936, along with other tax-reform provisions drafted during Mills's tenure, as part of the 1975 tax act.[35]

On 4 December 1975, the House passed the Ways and Means tax-reform bill together with a tax-cut extension. The bill was sent to the Senate Finance Committee. By all accounts, the committee acted to provide "remedial assistance to clientele groups who appeal to [its members] for redress from House decisions." The committee's chairman, Senator Russell Long (D-La.), who believed that "one person's tax reform is another person's loophole," argued that the House version of the tax-reform bill "went too far." Almost every industry "fared better in the Senate committee than in the House." On 6 August 1976 the Senate passed its version of the bill after twenty-five days of debate, including a discussion over whether it should continue to be labeled "reform."[36]

The Senate Finance Committee paid very little attention to the possessions tax break, except to adopt the House version of the law. On 4 October 1976, almost four years after the legislative process began in the House Ways and Means Committee, the Tax Reform Act was signed into law by President Ford.

III. Banking on Structural Power

It might be argued that U.S. firms chose not to mobilize for political action during the process leading to the Tax Reform Act of 1976 because the protection of the possessions tax break was not really in their interest. Without the federal tax benefits for doing business in Puerto Rico, the companies could always seek alternative low-tax jurisdictions. Multinationals presumably can shift income to continue to minimize their U.S. tax bills. However, it is likely that pharmaceuticals and electronics would oppose such an outcome for four reasons. First, as explained in chapter 2, U.S. firms had been reaping huge profits by investing under the rules of the possessions tax break. It seems improbable, then, that they would feel indifferent toward any changes in the tax law. Second, it could not be argued that the companies were not aware of their preferences. By all accounts, the firms were aware of the importance of Section 936 to the profitability of their operations. Not only did Puerto Rican tax-free profits represent a substantial portion of the companies worldwide earnings, but the companies had been protecting those profits from IRS regulation and the U.S. Tax Court since the 1960s. As a rule, all companies keep up with IRS regulation (they have to comply with it when they file their taxes) and with any tax court proceedings that may affect their operations (the IRS also takes companies to tax court to send a message to other companies).

Third, U.S. firms had structured their worldwide operations to take advantage of the tax benefits. Had Section 931 been eliminated, costs would have been involved in devising alternative ways to minimize taxation.[37] Fourth, there were no real alternatives. While other countries offered tax holidays to attract foreign investment, conditions in Puerto Rico were unique in that on liquidation, U.S. firms could repatriate their earnings free of taxes. Without Section 931, the companies' tax bills would have risen. Consequently, in the mid-1970s, U.S. firms had an interest in the permanence of a unique federal tax law that enabled them to maximize their tax-free Puerto Rican–source profits via intercompany transactions and to minimize their federal tax bills by repatriating those profits tax-free. What explains, then, the companies' seemingly disinterested reaction to congressional threats to their interests?

According to Charles Lindblom, when U.S. businesses see their interests threatened by government action, they know that they do not need to lobby the government to communicate their interests to politicians. Businesses know that they have a privileged position vis-à-vis other groups in society. Because business decisions affect the level of unemployment, politicians will always be sensitive to the interests of business lest they risk layoffs and the subsequent wrath of the electorate. Lindblom explains,

> In the eyes of the government officials . . . businessmen do not appear simply as representatives of a special interests, as representatives of interest groups do, they appear as functionaries performing functions that government officials regard as indispensable. When a government official asks himself whether business needs a tax deduction he knows that he is asking a question about the welfare of the whole society and not simply about a favor to that segment of that population which is what is typically at stake when he asks himself should he respond to an interest group.[38]

This argument implies that business relies on the implicit threat of unemployment because it believes doing so to be an efficient strategy for protecting its political interests. That belief, however, is grounded on past experiences. Regarding the possessions tax break, it is likely that U.S. firms' automatic response was to rely on their structural power because they had no recollection of ever needing to mobilize for the political protection of their tax benefits in Puerto Rico. Indeed, as explained in chapter 2, in a prior incident the government of Puerto Rico complained that IRS investigations were interfering with the island's ability to attract U.S. capital to the island. In response, the U.S. Treasury ceased all investigations for four years. Firms knew that, because the tax break meant so much to its economic development strategy, the island administration could be counted on to defend the tax credit. And the firms' reliance on the Puerto Rican government to lobby on their behalf is consistent with Lindblom's concept of structural power. U.S. pharmaceuticals and electronics did not plan this strategy or mobilize to persuade Puerto Rican officials to go to Washington. The firms' reliance on their power to cause unemployment was their strategy of choice to deal not only with the U.S. Congress but also with the Puerto Rican government.

IV. Conclusion

Past political experiences of U.S. firms doing business in Puerto Rico, combined with current political realities, guided their political behavior throughout the political process leading to the Tax Reform Act of 1976. Labor's demands for a stricter tax treatment of U.S. multinationals initially increased the saliency of the tax provision and moved the issue out of Treasury and into Congress, where it received close scrutiny. In spite of having an interest in the preservation of the benefits of the possessions tax break, U.S. firms did not become openly involved in the political process. They relied on their structural power to protect their interests, probably because they had never needed to formulate a political strategy to explicitly influence policymakers regarding this issue. As the political process progressed, a review of the tax break remained an element of the tax-reform agenda even as labor dropped its demands. U.S. firms had no reason to change their political strategy, however, because a centralized congressional committee structure allowed the polemic over the tax break to be resolved in relative obscurity. Chairman Mills was persuaded that the tax break enticed U.S. firms to perform the service of creating jobs and ensuring Puerto Rico's economic and political stability. In turn, committee members were expected to follow the lead of their chair.

In hindsight it could be argued that firms did not mobilize initially because they shrewdly and correctly interpreted the current political environment as favorable. However, prior to 1973 important segments of corporate America had suffered a number of legislative setbacks that led to an upsurge in many firms' political mobilization.[39] In the early 1970s the broader political environment was anything but certain, and the outcome of the tax-reform process was not guaranteed, yet U.S. firms with operations in Puerto Rico responded in a way that suggests that they were confident that their interests would not be hurt. This confidence was most likely based on the knowledge that they had never had to lobby the U.S. government for the protection of their interests in Puerto Rico. Their behavior also indicates that large corporations are not unitary actors and that the political behavior of individual firms may vary depending on the issue.

In the end, a favorable political environment was conducive to a victory by business regardless of the character of its political strategy. The political success of U.S. companies at this time, however, would have important implications for their political behavior and likelihood of success in the future. What will be the political strategy of the same group of firms when the U.S. government, strapped for money, argues that encouraging U.S. investment in Puerto Rico does not justify the amount of tax revenue foregone by keeping the tax exemption in place? What will U.S. firms do when power in Congress becomes so dispersed that there is no single individual to whom they can appeal for the protection of their political interests? How will the experiences of U.S. firms in 1976 affect their political response to an entirely new political environment?

CHAPTER 4

Failure to Adapt: The Tax Equity and Fiscal Responsibility Act of 1982

> My boss used to say that the hardest thing in lobbying is keeping down-town together—the hardest thing is getting companies to say the same thing when they go to the Hill. Human nature dictates that if I can protect my company's interests, even if it means that I can get a better deal than Merck and Johnson and Johnson, well, so be it.
> —Executive Director of Government Relations, Pfizer

The experiences of pharmaceutical and electronics companies during the process leading to the Tax Equity and Fiscal Responsibility Act (TEFRA) of 1982 are one example of when learning from an earlier success prevents business from reacting effectively to a new political environment. In the 1980s, budget deficits became the most important factor influencing most political decisions, especially tax legislation. Revenue issues were redefined. Tax preferences were no longer perceived solely as a tool for socioeconomic growth but were also seen as the means to control exploding budget deficits.[1] All tax breaks, including Section 936, came under increased scrutiny, as tax policy became a relevant issue for most members of Congress. In addition, Congress's new structure and rules had been in place for a number of years. In a decentralized Congress, U.S. firms could no longer rely on sympathetic committee chairs to protect business interests: they needed to secure the individual members' votes as well.

The redefinition of tax issues combined with new government structures required the 936 companies to update their political strategies. But when the controversy erupted, pharmaceutical and electronics companies, based on what they had learned in 1976, relied on their structural power to cause unemployment. As the policy process progressed, however, firms began to realize that the political environment had changed and that they could not rely on their structural power alone to protect their public policy interests. The companies decided to mobilize and tried to form a coalition, but they quickly succumbed to their default strategy, divided lobbying. Consequently, while the political effort was unprecedented—it included contacting members of Congress and White House officials, hiring political insiders, and bringing CEOs to Washington to lobby for the maintenance of Section 936—the companies' fragmentation only helped to weaken their mobilization's potential effectiveness. Ultimately, the companies were not happy with the outcome of TEFRA, and the failure to protect their interests at this time would guide their political behavior when a new political battle over Section 936 materialized a few years later.

I. The Learned Political Response

Treasury investigations into the practices of the companies in early 1980 resulted in an investment strike in Puerto Rico. According to the companies, they were simply responding to the uncertainty of the situation, but the implicit message was that if Section 936 were to be altered in any way, thousands of jobs would be lost in Puerto Rico because the companies would leave the island in search of more attractive investment sites. Their reliance on an investment-strike strategy followed their privileged structural position. Their political behavior, however, was also a factor of their experiences during the process leading to the Tax Reform Act of 1976. At that time U.S. companies learned that they did not have to mobilize for political action to protect their interests in Puerto Rico. Accordingly, during the initial phase of the process in 1981, no effort was made to devise a political strategy, negotiate deals, or contact members of Congress or the Reagan administration to get them to interfere with Treasury on the firms' behalf.

U.S. Firms and Their Spectacular Profits

In the 1980s, U.S. firms had an interest in the protection of Section 936 because, since the enactment of the new version of the tax break in 1976, they had continued to profit from their tax-free investments in Puerto Rico. In 1981 Congress had enacted President Reagan's program of tax reductions known as the Economic Recovery Tax Act of 1981 (ERTA). But while ERTA made investing on the U.S. mainland more attractive, Puerto Rico remained the only jurisdiction that did not give rise to U.S. taxation after profits were repatriated to the mainland, and within the United States, Puerto Rico remained the only place where company profits were 100 percent free of federal taxes.[2]

As table 9 shows, for many U.S. firms, the possessions tax credit remained the most important individual tax provision, accounting for a material difference between the effective tax rate and the federal statutory rate. Moreover, as table 10 indicates, for some electronics companies, such as Westinghouse (1979, 1980, and 1981) and Medtronic (1980 and 1981), Puerto Rican profits represented between a quarter and a third of their worldwide consolidated after-tax profits. For some large pharmaceutical companies (Abbott, Pfizer,

TABLE 9.   U.S. Firms Reporting a Tax Savings under Section 936, 1977–81 (in percentage points)

	1977	1978	1979	1980	1981
Pharmaceuticals					
Abbott Laboratories	12.2*	10.6*	11.3*	11.8*	—
American Hospital Supply	8.2*	9.6*	11.2*	12.5*	13.0*
Baxter Laboratories	—	—	—	25.7*	—
Becton Dickinson	—	6.1*	6.1	6.7	—
Carter-Wallace	—	—	21.1*	22.5*	16.0*
Eli Lilly	5.2*	5.1	4.5	4.2	3.8*
Johnson and Johnson	5.0	3.9*	3.9*	5.0*	5.7*
Merck	5.1	5.1	4.0	4.4	5.2
Pfizer	—	17.0	15.2	10.3	—
Schering-Plough	19.8*	20.3*	18.7*	19.0*	19.1*
G. D. Searle	19.1	29.7*	24.9*	30.7*	36.2*
SmithKline	14.9	10.5	14.0	17.5*	—
Squibb	18.5*	18.0*	23.4*	22.5*	—
Sterling Drug	—	1.8	2.1	1.9	2.8
Upjohn	14.1*	13.4*	16.9	20.0*	25.9*
Warner-Lambert	7.3	7.7	—	8.2	—
Electronics					
Digital Equipment	7.9	7.9	2.3	—	—
Medtronic	—	—	11.3*	21.7*	18.4*
Motorola	5.0	1.1	—	—	
Westinghouse	—	—	13.3*	14.0*	14.1*
Textile and Apparel					
Hanes Corporation	9.6*	10.6*	—	—	—
Food Processors					
ConAgra	8.2*	7.4*	18.6	—	—
CPC International	1.4	—	1.5	—	—
H. J. Heinz	5.9	—	—	—	—
Esmark	7.5	7.4	4.4	—	—
Beverages					
PepsiCo	—	—	5.3	—	—
Instruments					
Bell and Howell	1.3	—	8.1	—	—
Millipore Corporation	—	—	2.4	8.6*	18.5*
Pall Corporation	—	—	3.6*	5.8*	8.2*
Perkin Elmer	3.2	3.2	3.9	—	—
Federal Statutory Tax Rate	48%	48%	46%	46%	46%

Source: Tax Notes and 10-K reports, 1977, 1978, 1979, 1980, 1981.

(—) Information not available or no tax savings reported.

*Indicates that the possessions tax break was the most important factor reducing federal taxes.

TABLE 10.   Tax-Free Puerto Rican Earnings as a Percentage of Consolidated after-Tax Earnings, 1977–81

	1977	1978	1979	1980	1981
Pharmaceuticals					
Abbott Laboratories	25.4	22.0	24.5	25.6	—
American Hospital Supply	17.0	20.0	24.3	27.1	27.0
Baxter Laboratories	—	—	—	—	27.1
Becton Dickinson	—	12.7	13.1	14.5	—
Carter-Wallace	—	—	44.4	48.9	34.7
Eli Lilly	10.8	10.6	9.7	9.1	8.2
Johnson and Johnson	11.4	8.1	8.4	10.8	12.3
Merck	10.6	10.6	8.6	9.5	11.3
Pfizer	—	35.4	33.0	22.3	—
Schering-Plough	41.4	42.2	38.9	41.0	41.5
G. D. Searle	39.7	60.4	54.1	66.7	78.7
SmithKline	31.0	21.8	30.4	38.0	—
Squibb	38.5	37.5	50.8	48.9	—
Sterling Drug	—	3.7	4.5	4.1	6.0
Upjohn	29.3	27.9	36.7	43.4	56.3
Warner-Lambert	15.2	16.0	—	19.3	—
Electronics					
Digital Equipment	16.4	16.4	5.0	—	—
Medtronic	—	—	24.5	47.7	40.0
Motorola	10.4	8.9	17.8	—	—
Westinghouse	—	—	28.9	30.4	30.6
Textile and Apparel					
Hanes	20.0	22.0	—	—	—
Food Processors					
ConAgra	17.0	15.4	40.4	—	—
CPC International	2.9	—	3.2	—	—
Esmark	15.6	15.4	9.5	—	—
H. J. Heinz	12.2	—	—	—	—
Beverages					
PepsiCo	—	—	11.2	—	—
Instruments					
Bell and Howell	2.8	—	17.6	—	—
Millipore Corporation	—	—	5.2	18.6	40.2
Pall Corporation	—	—	7.8	12.6	17.8
Perkin Elmer	6.9	6.6	8.4	—	—

Source: Tax Notes and 10-K reports, 1977, 1978, 1979, 1980, 1981.

(—) Denotes information not available or no tax savings reported.

Schering-Plough, G. D. Searle, SmithKline, Squibb, and Upjohn), Puerto Rican profits represented between a quarter and a half of their after-tax profits. Searle (1978 and 1981) and Squibb (1979), in particular, stand out because their Puerto Rican profits represented more than half of their after-tax profits.[3]

U.S. pharmaceuticals agreed that "the high profitability of their Puerto Rican operations may look suspicious to the government." However, they argued that their Puerto Rican profits were perfectly reasonable: "the ideal is to go to Puerto Rico with the product that has the highest volume and margin. . . . [E]veryone has their best product there, since they want to maximize their tax-free profits."[4] U.S. firms—particularly pharmaceuticals—clearly had a continued interest in the protection of the possessions tax credit.

Since early 1980, pharmaceutical companies had reason to believe that something was brewing at Treasury.[5] In fact, according to Nelson Famadas, chief economist for the Puerto Rican government, the pharmaceutical companies alerted the Puerto Rican government to check on Treasury to find out what the agency was planning to do about the 936 companies. As U.S. firms had suspected, Puerto Rican officials learned that Treasury was planning a major cutback in the Section 936 benefits.

Treasury Threatens U.S. Firms' Interests

Treasury bureaucrats had opposed the idea of Section 936 before it was enacted in 1976. As chapter 3 revealed, they lost the battle. But, as compensation, Congress gave Treasury the power to report on the federal tax revenue foregone under Section 936 and its effects on Puerto Rico. In those reports, three of which had already been published, Treasury argued five major points:

1. Tax expenditures associated with Section 936 had increased rather than decreased after 1976.[6]
2. Section 936 did not really benefit the economy of Puerto Rico because it continued to be more attractive for capital-intensive businesses rather than labor-intensive industries, thus resulting in relatively few jobs for Puerto Rico.
3. Section 936 did not create new profitable investment opportunities in Puerto Rico but merely made already profitable investments more profitable (thus implying that the same number of jobs could be created in Puerto Rico by U.S. firms without the tax law and the federal tax expenditures).
4. Contrary to what had been expected, possessions corporations chose to retain earnings in Puerto Rico rather than repatriate them to the mainland. (Section 936 was enacted, in part, to encourage the repatriation of U.S. multinationals' earnings to the mainland.)

5. Finally, the reports also listed the firms' "abuses" of Section 936:

> Since the amount of tax savings depends directly on the amount of profits attributed to the possessions corporations, the exemption system creates very strong incentives to shift profits from fully-taxed operations in the United States to the tax exempt operations in Puerto Rico. There are a number of ways such profit shifting can occur. For example, a possessions corporation may overcharge its parent for exports; the parent may undercharge the possessions corporation for raw materials or component parts, or fail to charge it for expenses undertaken in its behalf; or the possessions corporation may benefit from intangibles developed by the parent (e.g., a patent or trademark) without proper accounting for the costs incurred in developing the intangible or the manner in which it is used.[7]

Treasury claimed that although the tax code has a number of antiabuse provisions aimed at "improper income shifting" for possession corporations, the issue remained "complex" and "unresolved." The reports implied that when "improper income shifting" was found, the U.S. firm likely had established its operations in Puerto Rico to take advantage of the flexibility in determining intercompany prices.[8] To make its case, Treasury pointed out that pharmaceuticals and electronics sold only 1.0 and 10.7 percent of their output respectively to the Puerto Rican market. The remainder of sales were mostly exports to the U.S. market.[9]

All in all, opponents of Section 936 at Treasury believed that U.S. companies were primarily attracted to Puerto Rico to take advantage of the flexibility to transfer ownership of their intangible property to their island affiliates and to set intercompany transfer prices. Since pharmaceuticals accounted for most of the tax expenditure associated with Section 936, it followed that this group was thought to be the biggest abuser of the tax exemption.[10] Consequently, the pharmaceutical group had been subject to most of the IRS audits.

In retrospect, it was not surprising that Treasury reported negatively on Section 936. Treasury had never understood how Section 931 had worked, and it had opposed the enactment of 936 in 1976. More important, however, Congress had put an agency responsible for collecting revenue in charge of analyzing a nonrevenue provision. In 1980, however, President Reagan's supply-siders had invaded the Treasury and, in accordance with their belief that little or no taxation was the key to economic growth, wanted the Treasury staff to report more positively on the tax provision. Greg Ballantine, deputy assistant secretary for tax analysis, recalled that the "Treasury Department in '81 was a really odd place. We had the two high priests of supply side-economics, [Paul] Craig Roberts [assistant secretary for economic policy] and Norman Ture [undersecretary for tax policy]." Ture, in particular, was adamant that Section 936 was good policy and that the tone of the reports had to be changed to emphasize the "indirect" effects of the tax law on the Puerto Rican economy. Ballantine recalls that Ture clashed with "the economists in the department who thought 936 was abusive."

Corporate Earnings under IRS Scrutiny

Internal Revenue Service agents were also at odds with supply-siders over the Section 936 issue. The IRS uses a process in which an agent, during an investigation of a corporation, presents the facts and asks the agency for an opinion, known as a technical advice memorandum or private letter ruling. Though these opinions cannot be used as precedent in the courts, they are indicators of IRS policy and may inhibit the foreign-investment plans of multinational corporations.[11] Such an opinion had been requested for a transfer-pricing situation between a U.S. parent and its island affiliate.

Technical advice memorandum 8040019 was issued in July 1980. In the opinion, the IRS argued that "though the parent corporation had taken all steps to legally transfer intangibles to its affiliated possessions corporation, the intangibles would not be treated as 'belonging' to the possessions' affiliate." The agency concluded that the transfer of intangibles had been "motivated solely by tax avoidance and that Section 482 would be applied to reallocate *all of the income* produced by the intangibles to the parent corporation."[12] In other words, the IRS was suggesting that the company operated as a "contract manufacturer," which meant that it was not really manufacturing the product in Puerto Rico but only using the labor. Consequently, the profits did not really belong to the island subsidiary.[13] According to a tax lawyer for 936 companies, the memorandum implied that the IRS would now "tell" the U.S. multinational "how much they made in Puerto Rico."

Ture and Roberts also became involved in revising the IRS regulation. But according to a Treasury official, eventually it became clear that working with Ture would not be easy. Moreover, "it was unusual for policy types and nonpolicy types" to be working together. There was no "acrimony," but the "tension" between Ture and the staff continued even after Treasury Secretary Donald Regan designated his deputy, Tim McNamar, to mediate "this sort of task force on 936." Ballantine explained,

> I remember having many debates with Norm [Ture] that the enormous productivity that he saw in Puerto Rico was fictional, that the patent was just transferred there; but for Norm, Puerto Rico was very productive. Our view was that it was just simply a transfer of technology; that if you wanted real activity you needed a labor rather than an intangible incentive.

In September 1981, Treasury devised a proposal to replace Section 936 with a new Section 937 (that is, it proposed a legislative solution for the abuses). Section 937 would have required that before a U.S. firm established an operation in Puerto Rico, it would enter into an agreement with the IRS whereby the agency would determine the value of its transfers to Puerto Rico. Thus, even before the company started operations in Puerto Rico, it would have an agreement on how much it would have to pay the U.S. Treasury.[14]

Reaction of Puerto Rican Officials and U.S. Firms

As in 1976, Puerto Rican officials continued to have an interest in the protection of Section 936. But they also had an interest in reaching a compromise with Treasury. The Treasury reports were so negative that some Puerto Ricans felt that each report would be the final one. Moreover, the controversy over the U.S. parent's transfer of intangibles to the island affiliate created uncertainty over the future of the tax law. Puerto Rican officials argued that this uncertainty affected Puerto Rico's ability to attract U.S. investment. According to a Puerto Rican official, FOMENTO, the government agency in charge of promoting U.S. investment, "was dead." He explained that, when other 936 companies learned about the IRS ruling, they said "That applies to me," and, as a consequence, they had stopped applying for investment grants in Puerto Rico.

The tax director of a 936 corporation explained,

> In August 1980 people were gathered in Cincinnati and given a draft of a technical advice memorandum. That resulted in a change in the mood of settlements [between IRS and 936 corporations]. Agents were told not to settle on a basis inconsistent with the memorandum.

U.S. firms argued that Treasury was "trying to change the law by audit techniques," thereby affecting the companies' investment decisions. Businesses that might have been considering beginning or expanding their operations in Puerto Rico presumably could not assess adequately the costs and benefits of their investment because they could not ascertain what their ultimate tax bill would be. As the tax representative of a U.S. computer company explained at the time, "We need certainty and we need incentives. Section 936 is an incentive, but because of [the memorandum], the incentive is being repealed."

Although U.S. firms wanted to minimize the uncertainty surrounding Section 936, what they feared most was the possibility that the tax law would become a legislative issue if Treasury decided to push for the enactment of Section 937. The outcome of a legislative battle was presumed to be less secure than merely dealing with the Treasury because the final law might differ substantially from the sponsors' original proposal. Moreover, U.S. firms argued that an administrative (i.e., regulatory) solution is always more easily challenged than a statutory one.

The 936 companies also had specific objections to a new Section 937. They argued that Section 937 would still leave open to contest the issue of determining the fair market value of the intangibles transferred from the parent to the island affiliate. In addition, all companies agreed that they would not take the risk of investing in Puerto Rico if they would be subject to substantial up-front taxes on uncertain long-term profits (resulting from product obsolescence or technological developments). U.S. firms also complained that up-front charges would have a negative effect on companies' current reported earnings and cash flow before any benefits were realized.

Yet in spite of their opposition to the activities of Treasury officials and staff, these companies made no effort to contact members of the Reagan administration or Congress to ask them to intervene. This inaction is consistent with a learning view because the companies were relying on the same strategy that they understood to succeed in the past. U.S. firms are also constituents of the government of Puerto Rico, however, and their investment strike forced island officials to negotiate with the U.S. Treasury on behalf of the corporations. The companies' attitude might seem puzzling because some of this firms had extensive Washington experience—a few of the electronics firms were government contractors and pharmaceuticals were known to urge members of Congress to pressure the Food and Drug Administration to approve new drugs. But the conduct of 936 corporations indicates that, as long as the government of Puerto Rico effectively acted as their representative during its negotiations with Treasury officials, the companies felt no need to change their investment-strike strategy for the protection of Section 936. After all, if the strategy had worked in 1976, why wouldn't it work in 1981?

Pharmaceuticals and Electronics at Odds

In an effort to end the companies' investment strike, Puerto Rican officials started to work with Treasury and the IRS to try to solve the income-shifting problem in a way that would be acceptable to all parties. In addition, in October, Ralph Sierra, a well-known expert on Section 936 who had been brought in as a consultant to the Puerto Rican government, along with Nelson Famadas and Cheo Madera, head of FOMENTO, began a series of meetings with U.S. firms' tax directors. The purpose of the meetings was to draft regulatory guidelines for computing multinationals' profits in Puerto Rico that would be acceptable to all the companies as well as to the U.S. Treasury. These meetings initially were somewhat adversarial.[15] While the firms knew that their interests had previously been tied to those of Puerto Rico, there was uncertainty in the knowledge that Puerto Rican officials were willing to negotiate with the

U.S. Treasury. There was also a rumor that some Puerto Rican officials had favored the enactment of Section 937. Puerto Ricans made it clear that they were not in cahoots with the Treasury and that these meetings sought ideas and feedback.

During the Puerto Rican officials' meeting with the pharmaceutical group, some of the companies reiterated their policy of an investment strike in Puerto Rico until it became clear that the tax law was out of danger. Specifically, representatives from Pfizer, SmithKline, and Johnson and Johnson pointed out that they had, in fact, reversed some of their decisions to take some of their products to the island because of the uncertainty with the law.[16] Moreover, the companies' made it clear that without the flexibility to transfer intangibles to their island affiliates, Section 936 would mean very little. That is, they argued that if, in accordance with the memorandum, "the 'contract manufacturer' concept is used, all of the incentive is gone for pharmaceuticals." After intangibles, company officials argued that flexibility to set transfer prices was the second-most important aspect of the tax law for pharmaceuticals. Given that flexibility to transfer intangibles and set transfer prices were the most controversial aspects of the tax law, it was clear that pharmaceuticals wanted Treasury to leave Section 936 alone. Pharmaceuticals wanted Puerto Rican officials to get Treasury to reverse itself on the memorandum and forget about Section 937. A Puerto Rican official recalled that it became evident these companies would never agree to negotiate with Treasury. They felt confident that whatever regulatory changes Treasury came up with could be challenged in court. Island officials responded, "we can't wait three or four years [after litigation has been concluded]. We need to promote investments [in Puerto Rico]."

By contrast, electronics firms were more willing to compromise with Treasury on the issues of transfer of intangibles and transfer pricing because they were not as important to this industry as to pharmaceuticals. Indeed, the friction between these two industry groups was apparent during the meetings. Specifically, electrical, electronics, and computer companies argued that the uncertainty created by the IRS audits was the result of Treasury's opinion that pharmaceutical companies were abusing the tax law. One after another of the tax representatives of this group expressed the same concern. According to the tax official of one computer company, Treasury believed that pharmaceutical operations on the island involved "putting everything in a box in the United States, shipping it to Puerto Rico and returning it to the United States." In a separate meeting, an electronics company official argued that "pharmaceuticals were taking the fruits of R&D into Puerto Rico and realizing enormous profits. At a Citibank seminar [we were told] that this is the most serious problem. Knowing that a solution is needed, we think that intangibles need to be dealt with." Another official complained that "what concerns many companies now is that someone else is getting a better deal in Puerto Rico." Others argued that if "the Section 937 proposal is passed, we think that 936 should be left intact for companies that have no problem with intangibles."

Electronics did not have the same problems that pharmaceuticals had with intangibles simply because, on average, the profit margins for the electrical and electronic products produced in Puerto Rico were never as stupendous as the profit margins for pharmaceuticals. As one computer company representative explained, "We don't work like pharmaceuticals. A pharmaceutical develops know-how specifically for, say, Darvon. Our know-how builds on each other." In contrast to the manufacturing process of a drug, there are a number of different stages involved in the manufacture of electrical and electronic components, and each of these stages usually takes place in a different country. Hence, the value attributed to the electronics products assembled in Puerto Rico did not compare to the value of a patented drug. Moreover, as explained in chapter 2, the profit margins for electronics are generally lower than for pharmaceuticals because manufacturing costs are lower for the latter. Ultimately, because their tax expenditure per employee was not as excessive as for pharmaceuticals, electronics knew that their activities were not perceived as abusive by the Treasury Department.

Still, the Puerto Rican government continued with its effort to devise regulatory solutions that would please both industry groups before Treasury decided push for a legislative change to the provision. Based on the companies' suggestions, Puerto Rican officials came up with the idea of cost sharing and fifty-fifty profit split as regulatory guidelines for computing the tax-exempt income from intangibles attributable to the possessions corporations.[17] Cost sharing was supposed to be the attractive option for companies with patents (that is, pharmaceuticals); profit split was supposed to be attractive for companies with marketing intangibles (that is, electronics).

In the interim, U.S. firms continued to rely on an investment strike as their only strategy for the protection of Section 936. In spite of the uncertainty surrounding the tax law, U.S. firms felt that they did not have to mobilize politically because Puerto Rican officials had the firms' interests in mind. Puerto Rican officials were negotiating with Treasury to devise a compromise that the companies would accept. The firms did not blindly trust Puerto Rican officials but expected that the process would succeed in 1981 in the same way that it had in 1976. As explained in chapter 1, firms have a tendency to repeat past behavior when it is based on prior success. While they may keep up with events that may affect their operations' profitability, they will be less likely to engage in an evaluation of past strategies if their past behavior was considered satisfactory. Hence, the firms did not feel it necessary to contact members of Congress or the administration, they had become accustomed to relying on the Puerto Rican government for the defense of the tax law. By mid-1982, however, this scenario would change.

Late in 1981 the meetings between the Treasury and Puerto Rican officials came to a standstill. The sides could not come to an agreement. According to Puerto Rican officials, Treasury wanted to make the rules for the allocation of income between the parent and its affiliate too restrictive. In spite of the friction within the department, it was clear that Treasury opponents of Section 936 would not be persuaded by the companies' investment strike to leave the tax law alone. Then, in early 1982, Section 936 became part of the budget process. Suddenly, after years of the IRS investigating and legally challenging the intercompany transactions of possessions corporations, the Treasury staff would finally have the opportunity to suggest legislative changes to Section 936 to a Republican Finance Committee chairman who welcomed such revenue-raising ideas. Their suggestions went beyond what had been negotiated with Puerto Rican officials.[18]

II. Tax Issues Are Redefined

According to White and Wildavsky, the 1980s was "the era of the budget." They explained that the budget "is to our era what civil rights, communism, the depression, industrialization, and slavery were to other times."[19] This trend implied that budget deficits had become the most important factor influencing most political decisions, especially tax legislation. As one Ways and Means Committee member explained,

> Tax bills used to be used to reduce taxes. And those bills could be used by members to achieve social objectives . . . as well as for special interest provisions. The big change of the last couple of years is that because of the deficit and the need to raise revenue it is very difficult to imagine the tax code being used anymore to be an engine for social and economic changes.[20]

Heightened concern for the political and economic impact of budget deficits began shortly after ERTA's enactment.[21]

Even before Reagan won the presidency in the fall of 1980, support for a program of tax reductions to spur economic growth was already apparent. During the campaign Reagan embraced the most important component of his tax program: a three-year, across-the-board reduction in individual income-tax rates. When Reagan won the presidency, Republicans won control of the Senate for the first time in twenty-six years and gained thirty-three House seats; consequently, there seemed to be a "very favorable climate for the enactment of tax policies sought by the new administration."[22]

Supply-side economics, the theory behind the administration's tax-cutting effort, was simple: "tax cut[s] would produce so much economic growth that revenues on the increment of growth would exceed the loss from lower tax rates."[23] Shortly after the inauguration, the administration started to work on its tax proposals. They were embodied in the Conable-Hance bill introduced in the House on 14 June, at the same time that the Senate Finance Committee and the House Ways and Means Committee began markup of their own tax bills. After the Finance Committee approved its bill on 25 June, the administration began a bidding contest with the new Ways and Means chairman, Dan Rostenkowski (D-Ill.), to see which side could come up with more attractive cuts.[24] Ultimately, on 29 July the Republican version of the tax bill passed both the House and the Senate.

But even before the president signed ERTA on 13 August, the administration faced pressure to do something about the looming deficit.[25] On 3 August, the director of the Office of Management and Budget, David Stockman, warned the president and his top economic advisers that if something was not done about the deficit it would "spook the markets." In addition, when the administration sent its tax-cut recommendations to Congress, it was estimated that they would result in deficits for fiscal year (FY) 1982 of $45 billion. However, the large tax reductions, combined with the recession that developed later in the year (which resulted in lower tax revenues and an increase in spending for programs), and higher interest rates (which increased the costs of servicing the national debt) forced those projections upward. As the economy worsened, supply-siders began to lose their influence in the White House; pressure began to grow for increasing revenue through higher taxes rather than through tax cuts.

On 24 September 1981, during a nationally televised address, President Reagan proposed a number of tax increases and spending cuts and promised to balance the budget by 1984. However, even by his own admission, his proposal was not enough to close the deficit gap. In the end, the administration did not send its revenue proposals to Congress, which had little enthusiasm for raising taxes anyway, and rejected most of the proposed spending cuts.[26]

On 5 February 1982, the Congressional Budget Office estimated the deficits would reach $157 billion in FY 1983.[27] But, despite a worsening outlook for the budget, the White House and the Ways and Means Committee refused to take responsibility for raising taxes. Members of Congress in general were not enthusiastic about raising taxes in an election year and did not think it was a good idea during a recession.[28]

In May, the White House and Senate Budget Committee Republicans reached a compromise (approved as a budget resolution on 28 June) that called for the two congressional tax-writing committees to find $98.3 billion in new taxes for FY 1983–85. Again, however, the White House refused to specify how the revenue targets would be met. Ways and Means Committee Democrats also refused to act. First, they wanted to be assured that the president was serious about deficit reduction. Moreover, they believed that the only way to meet the revenue targets was by repealing or delaying the tax cuts enacted under ERTA. The president refused. The Senate was left to take the lead.[29] In this environment, Section 936 became part of the budget process, taking U.S. firms by surprise.

Senator Dole, the Deficit, and Section 936

The Senate Finance Committee chairman, Senator Robert Dole (R-Kans.), was nervous about the deficit. He had never been entirely convinced about cutting taxes in the first place. However, Dole, along with other Republican politicians, hesitated to criticize the president. The Republicans were in power, and it was important to show that they could govern. Moreover, Senator Dole had lost the party's presidential nomination to Reagan, and if he was too critical, he "could be suspected of trying to make the president look bad." However, when Reagan suggested that others should come up with their own suggestions to raise revenues, Dole was one of the few members of Congress who accepted the challenge. By the time the budget resolution was passed, he had already spent most of the year trying to draft a revenue package.[30]

The inclusion of Section 936 as one of the provisions targeted for change in Dole's revenue package originated in a series of secret meetings held between the administration and Republican and Democratic congressional leaders. Around March 1982, when it had become apparent that it would be difficult for the administration to reach a budget compromise with Congress, the president gave permission for White House Chief of Staff James Baker; Baker's assistant, Richard Darman; Stockman; Regan; and others to meet with members of Congress to try to come up with spending cuts and revenue-raising suggestions. These meetings initially were held in the strictest of privacy. Baker told Regan that he should, in fact, lie to his Treasury staff about his whereabouts when attending these meetings.[31] The group became known as the Gang of Seventeen.

Eventually, however, the Treasury staff became involved in the process. One Treasury official recalled, "Regan would come back from these negotiations with the Gang of Seventeen saying, 'I need more [revenue] but don't do something that looks too bad or that looks like raising taxes.' At some point 936 was thrown in." Indeed, though Regan personally opposed tax increases, his Treasury staff did not. And when, in April, the Gang of Seventeen broke up, the tax policy staff continued working very closely with Dole "providing him all sorts of help." For them it was an "ideal situation": they "could make very good changes in the tax law and [Dole] would take the heat."[32]

The question that comes to mind is how an obscure provision of the tax code that, when compared with other revenue-raising schemes, cost the Treasury little could become part of a revenue package at that time.[33] Indeed, Dole had wanted to "pass one or two 'big ticket' revenue raisers" rather than to get involved in too many small tax proposals that could be threatened by interest groups. However, Dole had few places to look for big revenues. The president was resolved "to keep his defense buildup sacrosanct, shelter the huge social security program from cuts in this election year, and avoid substantial tax increases or any rollback in scheduled tax decreases."[34] Dole had no choice but too look for revenue in relatively minor tax preferences (or loopholes) in the hopes that they would add up to more than $90 billion in three years. In turn, Treasury was more than happy to offer Section 936 for sacrifice.

The Gang of Seventeen produced no final agreement, but, for two months, Dole continued working on a revenue-raising package with the Treasury staff and the Joint Committee on Taxation. In late May, Dole presented a list of proposals to the Senate Finance Committee Republicans to see which ones they opposed. On 30 June committee Republicans approved a tentative plan that would meet the $98.5 billion target. According to a Treasury official, Section 936 was not among the most contentious issues for committee Republicans:

> The '82 act was largely agreed to in two and a half days of the Senate Finance Committee Republican Caucus. I was in it, we were sitting at the table, and I don't remember 936 being one of the controversies: I don't remember anybody having anything at stake with 936.

A pharmaceutical company lobbyist explained that Republican senators were indifferent to Section 936 because they represented western states: most of the biggest U.S. companies with operations in Puerto Rico at the time were headquartered in the northeast. Specifically, almost two-thirds of all of the 936 pharmaceutical and chemical companies were headquartered in Connecticut, Massachusetts, New Jersey, New York, and Pennsylvania. More than half of all of the 936 companies were headquartered in the same five states.[35]

The Republican caucus agreed to amendments to Section 936 that would have: (1) reduced the amount of passive income eligible for a federal tax credit and (2) taxed the income generated by the transfer of intangibles (patents and the like) from a U.S. parent to a possessions corporation. The second amendment eliminated the main incentive 936 offered to many companies.

On 1 July Dole, the staffs of the Finance Committee and of the Joint Committee and representatives from the Treasury presented the revenue bill to the committee Democrats. According to a Treasury official present at the meeting, after one of the counsels from the Finance Committee explained the proposed changes to Section 936, Democratic senators, who had already been contacted by Puerto Rican officials, expressed some concern over the effects of changes on the economy of Puerto Rico. Only Senator Russell Long (D-La.) mentioned that he had met with representatives from a drug company, but that the latter knew very little about what was going on and that all he could say was that "there was more to this than what meets the eye." That only one of the Democratic senators of the Senate Finance Committee had been contacted by a pharmaceutical lobbyist further illustrates the extent to which the 936 companies were relying on what they perceived to be their privileged position in society to protect their interests in Puerto Rico. It further suggests that, while Section 936 was clearly important to these companies, it never attained enough salience to become a major political issue for them because in the past they had succeeded in protecting their interests without having to mobilize. Although many of these firms had Washington offices and an independent capacity to lobby Congress, there was no indication that they had decided to mobilize regarding this issue. Moreover, important segments of the business community had begun to lobby Congress against tax increases, but the issue of the possessions tax credit was clearly treated differently by 936 companies.[36] Their confidence with respect to the possessions tax break was a response to their experiences in 1976 more than to the political environment in 1982.

Given the political environment at the time, however, there was no reason to think that Dole would change his mind about Section 936. Deficit concerns had made the senator insensitive to the companies' investment strike in Puerto Rico. Though the island's economic stability was important to the senator, he had become convinced that the companies would not leave the island even if the Section 936 benefits were dramatically cut. Dole had also been disturbed by the income-shifting practices of pharmaceutical corporations. A Treasury official explained, "Dole, in my recollection, was offended by 936; you never felt that he would give up on this."[37] In fact, the senator became so adamant that his committee's amendment to Section 936 be enacted that the proposal became known as the Dole amendment.

Ultimately, given that U.S. firms were not mobilized and that Dole refused to meet with Puerto Rican government officials, little more could have been done to prevent the committee from passing the Dole amendment. Because Democrats were not in the majority, and because they did not want to be associated with tax increases, they had not been part of the drafting of the legislation. Also, according to David H. Brockway, staff head of the Joint Committee on Taxation, everybody working on the bill knew that "the longer legislation [was] out there, the greater the probability that interests would take everything away." Thus, the committee moved quickly and secretly.[38]

At this time, well into the second (adaptive) phase of the political process, the companies recognized that relying on their structural power would not suffice to protect their interests. Specifically, the companies suddenly faced the prospect of having a big chunk of their Puerto Rico–based profits subject to federal taxation. The realization that Section 936 was close to being effectively repealed by the Senate Finance Committee finally made U.S. firms realize that they had to adapt to the new political environment and change their political strategy regarding this issue. The companies decided that they had to mobilize politically and devise ways to convince members of Congress who, like Senator Dole and the Treasury, were not sensitive to an investment strike in Puerto Rico to support the maintenance of the tax law nonetheless.

III. The Decentralization and Democratization of Congress

In 1982, however, influencing the policy process on Capitol Hill was a very different undertaking from what it had been in the early 1970s. At that time "Congress was still a rather oligarchical institution, with power concentrated in a handful of committee chairs who stood astride the policy process."[39] Indeed, as chapter 3 revealed, during the political process leading to the enactment of Section 936, the only legislator whose opinion really mattered was that of Chairman Mills.

After the congressional reforms of the 1970s, the committee chairs' power was diluted. For example, the membership of the Ways and Means Committee grew from twenty-five to thirty-seven. In this committee alone, a lobbyist now needed to secure nineteen votes. In addition, subcommittees had been created and the number of committee staff grew from twenty-four in 1970 to ninety in 1982. The Senate Finance Committee staff grew from sixteen in 1970 to fifty-five in 1982.[40] "Sunshine laws" required that committee meetings be open to the public and that committee bills be subject to floor amendments. Overall, the task of lobbying Congress became more complicated but also indispensable for the 936 companies, as the number of legislators and staff lobbyists they needed to "educate" about this issue multiplied.

After the companies realized that their investment-strike strategy would not be enough to prevent Section 936 from becoming a legislative issue and or persuade Senator Dole to drop his proposal, they decided to mobilize and engage in what they referred to as traditional lobbying techniques. These included the joining of the 936 companies and the government of Puerto Rico in a coalitional effort, the use of campaign contributions (through political action committees [PACs]), and personal presentations to members of Congress (there were no congressional hearings on Section 936 in 1982).[41]

Coalitional Efforts

On learning of the Finance Committee bill, company representatives began meeting with Puerto Rican officials in Washington to work out a plan. These meetings were attended by Washington lawyers and the companies' Washington lobbyists and tax officials. Initially, these encounters were not very satisfactory. Puerto Rican officials wanted to compromise with members of Congress. Electronics firms also believed that some sort of compromise might be needed to prevent the outright repeal of Section 936. Pharmaceutical companies felt, however, that they could prevent changes to Section 936 without having to give up any of their benefits in return. One pharmaceutical lobbyist recalled,

> In '82 we started to have these meetings at the Puerto Rico office. Some of the representatives of the government of Puerto Rico wanted to cut a deal. We did not have the votes to protect this thing, and it was probably the time to cut a deal. It is typical of our industry, being on the brink of losing something and still saying that we will only give up 5 percent.

Another lobbyist argued,

> The feeling from Puerto Rico is, "Let's cut a deal." Our perspective is, "Don't offer a compromise before you have to"—that is the feeling of some of us in the private sector.

According to Famadas, the Puerto Rican chief economist, "pharmaceuticals and Puerto Rican officials" simply had a "different perception of what was doable in Congress." He continued, "We believed that there were limits to what Congress could do for us," whereas "pharmaceuticals—individually—were used to getting their own way."

Puerto Rican officials and a few of the companies ultimately agreed (over the opposition of other individual companies) to try to get Congress to accept the cost-sharing and fifty-fifty profit split—that is, the two regulatory alternatives that the Puerto Rican government had suggested to the U.S. Treasury. It was a very weak agreement and a very weak alliance among the companies themselves and with the government of Puerto Rico. Individual companies felt that, given the opportunity, any one of them would try to cut its own particular deal at the expense of the others. Still, it was decided that the coalition's strategy would be to try to cut a deal with Treasury so that the 936 supporters could give the impression that the president himself opposed the Dole amendment. Then they would make Congress believe that if it changed as much as a comma of the Treasury–Puerto Rico agreement, Puerto Rico would go bankrupt.

Among the 936 companies, the pharmaceutical group, although not in complete accord, took the lead in lobbying.[42] And, while the pharmaceuticals also did not agree completely with the Puerto Rican government's position, the government began to work more closely with the pharmaceutical group than with any other industry. According to a Puerto Rican official, even though the case of the pharmaceuticals was the most difficult to defend, they took the position that "the worst possible case scenario for pharmaceuticals would be the best case scenario for the rest of the 936 companies."[43] If the pharmaceuticals were protected, there was no way that other industries would fare worse.

There were other important reasons for this alliance. In 1982 market interest rates were very high, and the only reason Puerto Rican banks were still making money was because of the companies' deposits (known as 936 funds).[44] Pharmaceutical deposits alone represented 80 percent of the 936 funds. Thus, according to Famadas, Puerto Rico's secretary of the Treasury felt very strongly that pharmaceutical interests needed to be especially protected.

In turn, U.S. pharmaceuticals quickly realized that they needed the help of Puerto Rican officials to protect Section 936. Company lobbyists explained that because they do not represent mass organizations, they did not have a large constituency to use to get Congress's attention. As the manager of government relations for Eli Lilly argued, "If we count all the people in the drug industry, we do not touch all the districts; we are a small employer nationwide, and that is a disadvantage." Another pharmaceutical lobbyist recalled that "936 was a difficult issue to lobby" because tax legislation, like "any international issue" or "like the inner-cities issue . . . has no real constituency." In 1982 pharmaceuticals chose to work with Puerto Rico because they realized that they needed all the help they could get. These companies were also aware that it was important for them to get as much support as possible from the people of Puerto Rico. After all, Section 936 was the U.S. government's tax policy for Puerto Rico, not for the companies. The companies' political efforts also included the use of PAC contributions and personal presentations to members of Congress.

Political Action Committees

Most recent studies of business political activities have concentrated on the study of PACs. The academic attention given to PAC contributions might be explained as a consequence of the rapid growth of business PACs since the mid-1970s.[45] In addition, there is the presumption that the readily available data make it possible for political scientists and sociologists to make observations about business's political behavior that otherwise would be much harder to make.[46] However, there are major drawbacks in assuming that the study of PAC contributions tells the story of business political mobilization. First, at the time, not all politically active firms had PACs.[47] In addition, research on PACs has concluded that they do not buy votes; if anything, PAC contributions buy access.[48] Thus, it would be wrong to assume that businesses rely on campaign contributions alone to protect their interests in Congress.

There is no question, however, that PAC contributions were an important aspect of the political activities engaged in by some of the 936 corporations during TEFRA. For example, of the pharmaceutical companies with PACs, contributions to members of the Senate Finance Committee and of the House Ways and Means Committee increased by 80 percent in the period between the 1979–80 and the 1981–82 congressional electoral cycles (see table A1).[49] However, it is important to point out that during the 1981–82 cycle, these two committees were in charge of drafting ERTA as well as TEFRA. Thus, it would be wrong to assume that pharmaceutical companies' PAC contributions were made solely to protect Section 936.

PAC contributions may have helped the 936 companies to gain access to the many members of Congress whose support they needed to protect their interests.[50] However, business's political problems were not solved by securing access to politicians; industry needed to give members of Congress reasons to support its interests—especially when the connection between U.S. investment in Puerto Rico and the members' local interests was not evident. As G. K. Wilson notes, "however great their importance in creating a favorable atmosphere," PACs "are not a method of *communicating* views."[51]

Personal Presentations to Members of Congress

Research suggests that personal communication with members of Congress has a more decisive impact on voting patterns than does contributions. Moreover, while conventional wisdom argues that most lobbying tactics (PAC contributions and/or communicating with members) merely reinforce or encourage members' policy predispositions, research suggests that lobbyists also spend a considerable amount of time trying to persuade swing votes. Personal contact with members of Congress can also be decisive when there is little information on policy alternatives.[52]

Personal contact with the legislative staff is also important. By all accounts, firms know that the members' staff and the committees' staff can exert a good deal of influence on legislative outcomes. In the case of Section 936, one lobbyist explained that because it was a very technical issue, "on a broader level you may deal with the member, [he or she] will agree with you in general, but the staff has to deal with the technicalities. If you ignore the staff they can screw [*sic*] you in the report." Thus, lobbyists have to be very careful not to hurt the egos of the congressional staffers whose support is also needed.

Accordingly, at the same time that they were trying to cut a deal with Treasury, Puerto Rican officials, along with company representatives, began to meet with members of Congress and their staff. Senator J. Bennett Johnston (D-La.) offered Puerto Rican officials the use of his technical staff to draft an amendment to the committee's package to be proposed on the floor of the Senate. Johnston, the chairman of the Energy and Natural Resources Committee, which deals with Puerto Rican issues, had traditionally shown a friendly interest in the island. According to one of his aides on the Energy and Natural Resources Committee, "Like anybody who is sensitive to Puerto Rico, Senator Johnston supports 936." However, he continued, "for the Senator it is also good politics because 50 percent of Louisiana's exports go to Puerto Rico, especially rice that Louisiana grows a lot of." Not surprisingly, the National Rice Growers Association sent a letter in support of the maintenance of Section 936. Still, a Puerto Rican official maintained that the senator would "only help Puerto Rico" if he were absolutely certain that "it will not cost him politically."

The staff at Treasury was not happy that Puerto Rican officials were trying to convince members of Congress to support the changes that Puerto Rico had been negotiating with the department. Sierra recalls that "Treasury was very upset—we had a shouting match—they complained that these were private negotiations, not to be publicized." Treasury also argued that the amendment Puerto Rican officials were proposing did "not conform with the agreement about to be entered into . . . just before the Senate proposal was put forth." The fact was, however, that some at Treasury privately supported Dole's amendment and were "stalling in taking any administrative action while the issue [was] being thrashed out on the Hill."[53]

By this time, however, U.S. firms and Puerto Rican officials had received the administration's support. During Finance's markup, Treasury officials had been told that the White House wished the department to "address these concerns [about Section 936] administratively." The day after TEFRA was reported out by the committee, Secretary Regan called a press conference and asserted that "notwithstanding our general support for the Senate Finance package, we have some reservations about certain proposals." Regan singled out the provision relating to Section 936 as a proposal the administration did not support.[54] Some of the 936 companies' lobbyists explained that the administration was particularly sensitive to the interests of the pharmaceuticals because Vice President George Bush, a former member of the board of Eli Lilly, had intervened on their behalf. Supporters of 936 even got President Reagan to call Dole, but rather than softening the senator, the strategy backfired. That the administration was going out of its way to prevent legislative changes to Section 936 only angered Dole and made him more determined to amend the tax law. As a result, Section 936 supporters' only hope of preventing the Dole amendment from being enacted was to persuade other members of Congress that the tax law should be retained.

R. Smith explains that the purpose of personal presentations is to

> show how the position favored by the advocate is also one consistent with the goals of the members—either by shaping the members' personal understandings of the consequences or by providing members with acceptable explanations of their positions.[55]

Accordingly, supporters of Section 936 devised their arguments to fit the members' particular interests. To those legislators sensitive to the interests of Puerto Rico, the companies argued that, contrary to what the Treasury thought, Section 936 was an indispensable tool for the island's economic development. The companies soon realized, however, that for "the vast majority of [U.S.] politicians, the island is a remote concern that fits uncomfortably into the American constitutional system and costs their constituents, the American tax payers, a great deal of money."[56] As one company lobbyist explained, members of Congress believed that "we should be helping the people in Alabama, not Puerto Rico."[57] As a result, according to the 936 lobbyists, legislators were most sensitive to the argument that what hurt the companies' Puerto Rican affiliates also affected the companies' ability to protect the jobs of constituents employed in their affiliates on the mainland.

Still, some influential members of Congress, including Senator Daniel Patrick Moynihan (D-N.Y.) and Congressman Charles Rangel (D-N.Y.), were interested in protecting the well-being both of their constituents and of Puerto Ricans living in Puerto Rico. According to a business lobbyist, Moynihan "understands Puerto Rico and is genuinely interested." His relationship to Puerto Rico dates back to his days as U.S. ambassador to the United Nations, when he opposed the Decolonization Committee's effort to place the island on the list of non-self-governing territories. Rangel also has a personal connection to Puerto Rico—his mother and grandmother are Puerto Rican. According to the congressman's legislative counsel, for some people, 936 "is bad tax policy," but Rangel cares about Puerto Rico "and he thinks the tax code is an instrument of social policy and social change." One lobbyist explained further,

> Moynihan and Rangel represent inner cities. Inner cities' people have major Puerto Rican constituencies. They are more aware of the economic situation and know why so many Puerto Ricans moved to New York: because of the economic situation [on the island]. They have seen firsthand why 936 has been important for Puerto Rico.

By all accounts, however, what really mattered to Moynihan and Rangel was a combination of the fact that they had Puerto Rican constituencies as well as a good number of the 936 companies headquartered in their state. By helping the residents of Puerto Rico, they came across as heroes to their Puerto Rican constituents and, at the same time, believed that they were protecting their constituents' jobs in New York.[58]

A sympathetic attitude toward business in general also explained why some members of Congress supported 936. According to a tax counsel for the Senate Finance Committee, Senator Lloyd Bentsen (D-Tex.) had always supported Puerto Rico and Section 936, "though publicly he trie[d] to be neutral."

A pharmaceutical company lobbyist elaborated, "Bentsen supported us because he understands the tax code and because he is a former businessman and knows how things work." Another example of this attitude was Congressman Philip Crane (R-Ill.) a member of the House Ways and Means Committee. According to one of his aides, Crane "has been a supporter of 936 since the beginning; he is a strong supporter of business . . . [and] does not like it when members want to tax companies to pay for their little programs; his view is that companies don't pay taxes, people do."

Some members of Congress saw no reason why they should support Section 936. Confronted with this situation, lobbyists played on the fear of mass Puerto Rican emigration. As the lobbyist for one pharmaceutical company commenting on the TEFRA effort explained,

> What do Symms [R-Idaho] or Wallop [R-Wyo.] care about 936? They, in fact, said to me "Why should I care?" I say, "I have a 747 full of Puerto Ricans. Would you like one? Because that is what you are going to get if 936 is repealed."

On 21 July, during the Senate floor discussion of TEFRA, Senators Johnston, Moynihan, Henry Jackson (D-Wash.), and Alfonse D'Amato (R-N.Y.) offered the proposal that Puerto Rican officials and a few of the firms had been working on as an alternative to the committee's amendment to Section 936. Johnston and Moynihan argued that the committee's proposal, if enacted, would have a "devastating" and "destabilizing" effect on Puerto Rico's economy.[59]

Dole responded by getting into a discussion of the perceived abuses by the 936 companies. He explained how pharmaceuticals deducted R&D costs from their taxable income and then transferred ownership of the product to Puerto Rico to claim a 100 percent federal tax credit on their profits. He then added, "A clearer case of having your cake and eating it too has seldom existed in U.S. tax law."[60] Dole also said that he was aware that Treasury was meeting with the government of Puerto Rico to reach a compromise and that he would wait to see what transpired in those meetings before making any changes to the committee's proposal. However, he argued,

> we have a mandate from the Senate on $98.3 billion in revenue. My concern would be that if, in fact, the administration, which has a little different view on section 936 than others, including myself, would make some agreement that would take a couple billion dollars away from $98.3, I would trust the administration would recommend where we would find the $2 billion and not just say, "Well, we have made the agreement and we will leave it up to Senator Dole and others on the committee in the Senate to figure out where they will get the $2 billion."[61]

Johnston and the rest of the senators proposing the amendment ultimately agreed to wait to see what resulted from Puerto Rico's negotiations with Treasury.

Before the Senate vote took place, Puerto Rican officials reached a compromise with Treasury. Reluctantly, Treasury agreed to support the adoption of the cost-sharing and profit-split rules to compute the tax-exempt income of the 936 companies. Thinking that Treasury was bound by the deal, Puerto Rican officials returned home. However, the legislative outcome was far from secure because, among other things, the staff at Treasury refused to lobby Congress on behalf of the agreement.[62] When the Dole amendment passed the Senate, U.S. firms were suddenly faced with the task of convincing House members and their staff that the amendment should be dropped from the bill. At this point in the process, the companies began more aggressively to advocate their own particular deals.

IV. Default Strategy: Fragmented Lobbying

Although 936 companies tried to coordinate their lobbying efforts with other firms and with the Puerto Rican government, a high degree of fragmentation characterized the 936 coalition's effort. First, not all firms lobbied Congress with the same intensity. Second, some firms tried to get their own particular deals enacted at the expense of Section 936.

Business's inability to work as a unit has been attributed to a variety of factors. First, cooperation is inhibited by the free-rider problem. For example, larger firms are more likely than smaller firms to mobilize to lobby the government because size allows them to "spread the costs of political action over a large volume of business," whereas "small firms would have to devote a larger percentage of their total revenues to participate in political activity."[63] Moreover, larger firms are more likely to mobilize to lobby the government because the presumption is that they have a bigger stake in the outcome of policy. More importantly, firms behaving as rational actors have an incentive to free ride because they know that they will enjoy the benefits achieved by the firms that mobilized for political action.[64]

Accordingly, some of the Washington representatives complained about the free-rider problem, which, they said, occurred between large multinational companies and small companies as well as between Fortune 500 companies. The Washington representative of a 936 company said of Merck, one of the world's largest pharmaceutical firms,

Only a handful [of companies] are going to do all the work even when part of a coalition; only a handful of reps do all the work, it's a matter of personalities. Merck, for example, has the worst D.C. office. Some reps just come here to read the trade magazines and report to their bosses the work that in effect others are doing for them.

In contrast, a Puerto Rican official recalls that during TEFRA, Johnson and Johnson (which at the time did not even have a Washington office), Baxter, and Pfizer were among the most aggressive of the pharmaceutical companies. Among the big electronics companies, "Westinghouse went where it was told to go," and General Electric was even less active.

Some companies which lacked the same intense interest in the protection of Section 936 chose to rely on the pharmacetical lobby. As a lobbyist for an electronics company who was not very active during TEFRA explained,

> Pharmaceuticals have tons of issues to deal with, which impact them, [are] of interest to them, but 936 looms as a much more important issue for pharmaceuticals than for electronics.

Business's political fragmentation may also be explained by the nature of the policy in question. In the case of Section 936, changes in the tax law affect different firms differently. During TEFRA, individual companies were very well aware that there were many ways in which the government could raise money through Section 936. Consequently, they advocated legislative solutions that would affect their firms the least, regardless of the possible negative effect on the competition. As one representative from a pharmaceutical company explained,

> My client is the [company's] tax division in New York. The committee can say I want $100 million from 936. There are five different ways to do it, and I know which one is the least painful to my company. . . . There are tons of ways to raise the money, and that is when you have your deals being cut. I always tell the staff [on Capitol Hill], "If I am going to be killed, can I choose the weapon?"

Finally, government structures also played a role in determining the character of business political participation. In the United States, business's lack of political unity has been attributed to the decentralized political power structure. At the federal level, the system of "separate institutions sharing power" with executive bureaucracies and congressional committees invites businesses to pursue their own narrow interests.[65]

Moreover, the fragmentation of the U.S. government has grown over time. Beginning in the 1960s, the breakdown of the party system gave members of Congress independent sources of support that have contributed to the further dispersion of U.S. political power. The decline of the party system combined with democratization and decentralization of Congress in the 1970s makes it even harder for businesses to determine exactly where the locus of power lies.[66] The dispersion of political power makes it more complicated for businesses to influence the government but also represents more potential opportunities to translate individual business interests into law.

Once it became apparent that they had to mobilize, U.S. firms lobbied in competition with one another because there were multiple points of potential access that they could try to influence to their advantage. Both administration officials and legislators were considering different proposals, which affected different industries differently. The White House and the secretary of the Treasury supported Section 936, while the Treasury staff did not. The companies also knew that even if some legislators supported them, they could always be hurt by the hostile Senate Finance Committee and Joint Committee on Taxation staffers who would ultimately sit down and write the bill. Finally, the administration and Senator Dole were also at odds on the issue. As the political process progressed and more actors became involved, the political outcome turned more uncertain prompting firms to advocate their own particular deals more aggressively.

On 28 July the Ways and Means Committee members, instead of producing their own bill, voted to go straight to conference with the Senate.[67] During conference it became apparent that the House conferees had failed to even "study the issues or reach a consensus before the conference began." This situation gave Rostenkowski and the other House conferees "considerable leeway to negotiate with Senate conferees." In the end, tax provisions that many senators had hoped would be softened in conference were left intact.[68] Section 936, however, was one exception where the amendment came out of conference looking better than it had in the Senate.

Interviews with company lobbyists revealed that when the Dole amendment passed the Senate and the House had gone straight to conference, U.S. firms got scared. Bills coming out of conference are generally sent to the floor under closed rule, which meant that the only hope of convincing Congress to drop the Dole amendment was in conference, giving 936 supporters only a few weeks to plead their case. Indeed, the companies' most aggressive lobbying occurred during the House-Senate conference. "We were working twenty-four hours a day. We had to change the impression that we create only five jobs, but more in the thousands," a company lobbyist recalls. At this point, pharmaceutical companies tried to increase their access by calling on their CEOs to come to Washington to do their share of lobbying and by employing Washington insiders. The companies hired Tommy Boggs, a superlobbyist. According to one lobbyist, around Washington everyone knows that "when you hire [Boggs], it means that you are serious and you are willing to spend megabucks."

During conference U.S. firms continued to lobby forcefully for their own separate deals: according to the director of government relations at American Cyanamid, "It was now widespread." Though the Puerto Rican government had reached a compromise with the Treasury, there were no guarantees that the conference committee would not adopt the Dole amendment. Rather than take that risk, almost every pharmaceutical company began to propose its own legislative alternative. Electronics companies also began to become more involved. Ballantine recalls that when the bill was already in conference, the head of General Electric's Washington office approached him "asking me to see what I could do, saying 'This matter is not only of importance to pharmaceuticals.'"

V. Less than Ideal Political Outcomes

Representative Rangel was credited with saving Section 936 during conference.[69] According to Brockway, the staff of the Senate Finance Committee and of the Joint Committee on Taxation tried to get conferees to keep the Senate version of 936 and make it more attractive for labor-intensive companies to come to the island. Brockway argued that the companies would not leave if the Dole amendment were enacted. Rather, he contended that offering a tax credit for wages would attract more investment and more employees. For Brockway "it was clear that what we were offering was better for Puerto Rico." He explains that

> Rostenkowski had no problem with that, but you could not persuade Rangel by saying, "Look at what we have. It's better for Puerto Rico." [Rangel] was representing the Puerto Rican government and the companies, and he said "I have to go with what the companies want."[70]

Ultimately, in the words of one lobbyist, "Dole got rolled," 936 "got traded for something totally unrelated," the Senate got something, and "Rangel got what he wanted." Only three conferees, Senator Dole and Representatives Sam Gibbons (D-Fla.) and J. J. Pickle (D-Tex.) voted against replacing the Dole amendment with the Puerto Rico–Treasury compromise.

On 17 August, barely a month and a half after it came out of the Senate Finance Committee, TEFRA was reported out of conference. President Reagan, believing that the package's ratio of spending cuts to revenues was three to one (it was actually one to one) instructed his staff to lobby the House and Senate to ensure its enactment.[71] TEFRA was signed into law on 3 September.

The 936 companies, however, were not happy with the outcome of TEFRA. Though Section 936 had been preserved, its benefits had been curtailed. The 936 companies had wanted to solve the transfer-pricing controversy through regulation, not legislation. They had opposed any legislative changes to the tax law because they felt that, once enacted, legislation was more difficult to change than regulation. Moreover, the enactment of TEFRA meant that for the first time there would be explicit statutory guidelines for the allocation of intangibles to an island affiliate, which up until that time had been transferred to Puerto Rico legally free of federal tax. The tax law changed from being a 100 percent tax credit on the Puerto Rican–based profits of U.S. manufacturers to a tax credit subject to the limitations of the cost-sharing and profit-split options. The companies were convinced that their federal tax bills would rise. According to the Treasury's own estimates, TEFRA was expected to reduce the companies' tax benefits under Section 936 by about 30 percent in 1984 and in subsequent years.[72]

VI. Conclusion

In 1982 the increased saliency of the tax break and the budget combined with the increased decentralization of Congress contributed greatly to the companies' political defeat. But business did not help its case by first relying on its structural power to protect its interests and then engaging in divided lobbying. The firms' reliance on their structural power was a legacy of their political success in 1976. The firms' failure to mobilize regarding this issue is particularly telling because many had an independent capacity to lobby the government and because it is likely that some possessions corporations, like many other important segments of the business community at this time, were politically active regarding other political issues. The behavior of the possessions corporations suggests that firms' strategies may vary depending on the issue because the learning scenarios differ. Finally, divided lobbying was the default strategy adopted by the possessions corporations when they realized that their structural power would not longer suffice to protect their interests in Puerto Rico.

The lessons learned by the companies in 1982 differed fundamentally from the lessons they learned in 1976. After TEFRA the companies believed that their political strategy had failed. Pharmaceuticals and electronics both felt that their political efforts, their attempted coalition with other companies and the government of Puerto Rico, PAC contributions, personal presentations to members of Congress, the hiring of insiders, and the mobilization of their CEOs were rendered ineffective because they did not mobilize in time and because when they did mobilize, they failed to pursue a coherent and cohesive lobbying strategy. As one pharmaceutical lobbyist explained,

> In '82, industry and the government of Puerto Rico were not very well organized—'82 was a mess, and you are trying to convince members [of

Congress] to keep a 100 percent tax exemption, and that was made more difficult by the inability of industry and Puerto Rico to work together.

But once the companies decided to mobilize, their fragmentation seemed all but inevitable, given the fact that even before Section 936 became part of the budget process, electronics companies and pharmaceuticals disagreed. Electronics companies felt that the pharmaceuticals' abuses were going to result in the loss of the tax law. In addition, pharmaceuticals favored the cost-sharing option, and electronics favored profit-split. Once Section 936 became part of the budget process, many pharmaceutical companies insisted that there should be no compromise with Congress and that Section 936 should be retained intact. The electronics firms and the Puerto Rican government disagreed. The latter felt that a compromise was needed to prevent the tax law's outright repeal. In addition, it appeared initially that some electronics companies had less interest in the protection of the tax law as pharmaceuticals did. In spite of these divisions, however, 936 companies still expected that a compromise would be reached with Treasury and that no statutory guidelines would have to be enacted. But when the Senate Finance Committee voted to adopt the Dole amendment, the companies felt they had no choice but to actively advocate their own particular deals. The conference committee ultimately adopted, as part of its bill, the Treasury–Puerto Rico compromise because it was the only deal that had any appearance of being favored by all parties involved—the White House, the Treasury Department, the Puerto Rican government, and some individual companies.

Rather than thinking that they had defeated Dole's attempts to eliminate the tax law, the companies viewed themselves as the real losers. After all, they had fared better in 1976, when they did not even have to mobilize to protect their interests in Puerto Rico. This time they had mobilized, and while it is difficult to isolate the consequences of their behavior from the impact of other political actors, the lesson that possessions corporations drew from this experience was that their political strategy was to blame for their loss. This lesson is important, because as long as firms believe that their behavior had an impact on the outcome, they will evaluate future political threats through the prism of this experience. The implications of this new learning for the political strategies of pharmaceuticals and electronics during the process leading to the next battle, the Tax Reform Act of 1986, is discussed in the next chapter.

CHAPTER 5

Experimenting with Collective Action:
The Tax Reform Act of 1986

They used standard lobbying techniques: they formed a coalition of companies, and pooled their funds together, and hired people who used to work
on the Hill and people who knew people in the administration, and put together a "whom do you know" network.
                    —Ronald Pearlman, Assistant Secretary for Tax Policy

When you think of what we cut back in investment in the states, and given
the [Treasury] reports, the fact that 936 survived is just amazing.
                    —David Brockway, Staff Head of the Joint Committee on Taxation

The evidence presented thus far suggests that the political behavior of business
is shaped by what it learns from prior political success. In this chapter, the ability of the 936 firms to learn from what they perceived to be their prior mistakes
explains why they decided to change their political strategies in an effort to
adapt to a political environment which continued to be characterized by deficit
concerns, a decentralized Congress, and divided government. After TEFRA, the
companies decided that time had come for them to unite to protect their interests. By the time Treasury waged its next political attack, pharmaceuticals and
electronics were ready to protect their interests more effectively. In turn, contrary to the experiences of other firms and industries, the subsystem that developed for the protection of the possessions tax break in 1982 survived the political upheaval that lead to the enactment of the Tax Reform Act of 1986.

I. Business Strategies Are Updated

The conditions that motivated the political mobilization of 936 companies during TEFRA remained relevant in its aftermath. The budget deficit remained a
major political concern, as many in Congress sought to keep deficit reduction
the priority issue on the tax-policy agenda.[1] Even though President Reagan resisted congressional pressure to raise taxes after 1982, 936 companies were
aware that efforts to reduce budget deficits could have a major impact on the
profitability of their operations.

Deficit reduction was not the primary motive behind tax reform, but the budget deficit continued to loom as an important issue during the tax-reform process. On the one hand, many members of Congress considered deficit reduction a more pressing priority than tax reform.[2] On the other hand, some legislators felt that "it was essential to increase the perceived fairness of the tax system before trying to raise revenues that would reduce the deficit."[3] Accordingly, though the tax-reform project was to be revenue neutral, reformers targeted tax preferences for elimination or drastic curtailment to achieve lower tax rates without increasing the budget deficit.

The fragmented nature of the federal government also remained an important motivation for the political mobilization by business. After TEFRA, electoral outcomes suggested that the trend toward fragmentation had continued. Although President Reagan had won reelection in 1984, the Republican Party's Senate majority had been reduced as the nation entered the fifth year of what at the time was its longest period of divided government. In the House of Representatives the GOP gained only fifteen seats, eleven seats short of the twenty-six it lost in the 1982 midterm elections. "Since the development of a stable two party system, no president had emerged from his election with a smaller portion of partisans" in Congress.[4] Thus, as it was the case during TEFRA, the congressional reforms of the 1970s, combined with the decline of party, resulted in a lack of cohesive political leadership that continued to make political outcomes difficult to predict. In the aftermath of TEFRA, the task of lobbying the government remained complicated but also indispensable for the 936 companies that wanted to protect the tax law from political tinkering.

Other factors that had contributed to the political fragmentation of business in the 1980s were also relevant after TEFRA. The tax law remained a complex policy instrument, open to numerous amendments that could be enacted to raise revenue in ways that affected individual 936 companies differently. And, as this chapter will show, during the process leading to the enactment of the Tax Reform Act of 1986, Treasury was again at odds with the White House and the relevant congressional committees on the issue of Section 936. Disagreement among government officials represented multiple points of potential access for the pharmaceutical and electronics companies to advocate their own particular interests.

By the time Treasury came up with a new proposal to eliminate Section 936 in 1984, however, the possessions corporations had already established a political organization, known as the Puerto Rico–USA Foundation (PRUSA), with the sole purpose of protecting the tax law. Unlike in 1982, during the process leading to the Tax Reform Act of 1986, individual companies mobilized early to lobby members of the administration and Congress and displayed an unprecedented degree of unity. What motivated the 936 companies to unite for political action after 1982 and maintain that unity throughout the ensuing political battle?

Within the traditional literature on collective action, Truman would argue simply that interests get organized to protect themselves against political threats to their benefits.[5] However, chapter 4 revealed, though the 936 companies felt that their benefits were threatened when Section 936 became part of the budget process, they did not organize for collective political action, as Truman would have predicted. On the contrary, their political effort was characterized by individual firms proposing their own particular deals at the expense of the common good.

Although he challenges Truman's basic thesis about group formation—arguing that by no means does collective action automatically occur even when potential members share interests—Olson agrees that it is possible for relatively small groups to be organized when a few of the larger units are willing to shoulder the cost of the organization because they have a bigger stake in the outcome of policy. Accordingly, not all the 936 companies became members of the organization created for the protection of Section 936 in 1984. Specifically, all of the pharmaceuticals and many of the largest electronics companies became members, while most of the smaller 936 companies did not.[6]

However, the argument that large firms are more likely than smaller firms to mobilize and bear the costs of organizing for the collective protection of their policy interests does not really explain why businesses decide to organize for collective action when they do. The fact that large pharmaceutical and electronics companies were more likely to organize for collective action than the smaller 936 companies does not really explain why PRUSA was organized in 1983.

To understand why businesses decide to organize for collective action at a particular juncture in time, it is necessary to look back at what they may have learned from their prior political experiences. The political strategies of the companies during the process leading to tax reform were a reaction to their experiences in dealing with the 936 issue during TEFRA. Interviews revealed that 936 companies learned three things from TEFRA. First, the realization that Section 936 had been nearly eliminated made individual companies aware of the possible costs to their operations if they did not pay serious attention to the political aspects of the tax law. Second, the companies concluded that an investment strike in Puerto Rico would not be enough to protect the tax law from congressional tinkering. And third, they believed that the reason their benefits had been curtailed was because they did not pursue a common political strategy. As explained in chapter 1, experiential learning is superstitious. Firms are likely to assume that their behavior influenced the outcome of policy in the past. They make inferences about the consequences of their actions. If firms perceive the outcome of policy to be a failure, they will take the time to reevaluate past strategies. After 1982, pharmaceuticals and electronics believed that they had lost an important political battle and blamed their political behavior for it. Because the political environment and the outcome had taken them by surprise, 936 firms decided that they had to change their strategy so that next time they could be ready to mobilize collectively before the tax law came into any real danger of elimination.

The clearest evidence of this change in strategy was the establishment of a formal organization with the sole purpose of providing collective protection to Section 936. According to Luisa Cerar, then head of the Washington office of Puerto Rico's Economic Development Administration, after the "scare of 1982 we realized that TEFRA was probably not going to be the last attack" on Section 936. Puerto Rican officials also realized that if they wanted to keep the federal tax exemption in place, the island government and the 936 companies would need to be better prepared to lobby the U.S. government. Puerto Rican leaders also felt that they could gain some influence by associating more closely with the firms because they were the actual constituents of members of Congress.

The impetus to organize also came from the companies themselves. After TEFRA, the electronics companies had an ad hoc group that disbanded when PRUSA was organized. A Puerto Rican government lobbyist recalled that "it was very hush-hush," because electronics companies were trying to devise a proposal that would "insure the policy against future attack," and they did not want the pharmaceuticals involved. Cerar ultimately brought both groups to the table, which is not surprising: the interest-group literature has noticed that competing interests sometimes need mediators, "some of them lobbyists and some of them persons in official positions," and Cerar clearly played this role.[7]

Cerar met with a few of the Washington representatives of the 936 companies that she felt comprised the main industrial sectors with Puerto Rican investments. These included the representatives of Motorola, Westinghouse, American Home Products, Baxter International, and Squibb, among others. The companies agreed that an organization created for the purpose of defending Section 936 was a good idea, and from that moment, they assumed the costs and took over the process of setting the operation up.

Cerar's initial group of companies hired a law firm to handle its affairs and, more importantly, to solicit other companies. The group specifically chose to work with a law firm that had a reputation for strength in both lobbying and technical expertise. The companies decided on Groom and Nordberg, which, in turn, brought in Peter Holmes from General Electric's Washington office to coordinate the lobbying operation. Carl Nordberg, a former international tax consultant for the Joint Committee on Taxation, became responsible for the technical aspects regarding the protection of the tax law. Nordberg basically would be in charge of representing PRUSA during negotiations with the technical staff in Congress.

It is important to note that the 936 companies' decision permanently to staff a Washington office rather than to employ the services of a law firm only when needed signifies the degree to which their political strategies for the protection of Section 936 had changed since TEFRA. That the 936 companies were willing to foot the bill for a full-time lobbyist when many companies also had their own Washington offices further indicates that they had realized that the politicization of the deficit combined with the increased fragmentation of Congress required a greater political effort to protect their Puerto Rican interests.

Groom and Nordberg sent letters to more than two hundred firms, and by January 1985 PRUSA had more than fifty members (see table 11). It its important to note that membership was not limited to pharmaceutical and electronics companies. Rather, banks and investment houses doing business in Puerto Rico were the indirect beneficiaries of the tax law and joined the foundation. Initially, annual contributions ranged from $3,000 to $25,000, depending on the size of the firm. The board of directors comprised twenty-five member companies (all

TABLE 11.   PRUSA Member Companies, 1985

Abbott Laboratories	Fluor Corporation/Daniel	Pfizer
Alberto-Culver	Construction	Phillips Petroleum
American Cyanamid	General Electric	Pittway
American Home Products	Gould	Price Waterhouse
American Hospital Supply	Grow Group	Production Graphics
Arthur Andersen	Hewlett-Packard	Corporation
Avon Products	Inland Container	Prudential-Bache
Banco Popular de Puerto	Intel	Revlon
Rico	International Playtex	R. J. Reynolds Tobacco
Baxter Travenol Laboratories	Johnson and Johnson	International
Bristol-Myers	Lenox	Richardson-Vicks
C. R. Bard	Locite	Schering-Plough
Carter-Wallace	Martinez, Odell, Calabria,	Sea-Land
Chase Manhattan Bank	and Sierra	G. D. Searle
Chesebrough-Pond's	McConnell, Valdes, Kelly,	SmithKline Beecham
Citibank	Sifre, Griggs, and	Squibb Corporation
Coca-Cola	Ruiz Suria	Sterling Drug
Colorcon	Medtronic	Sun Refining and
ConAgra	Mentholatum	Marketing
Cooper Laboratories	Merck	Superba
Crowley Maritime	Millipore	Syntex
Deloitte, Haskins, and Sells	Motorola	U.S. Surgical
Digital Equipment	Nabisco Brands	Upjohn
Corporation	O'Neill and Borges	Wang Laboratories
Drexel Burnham Lambert	Pall	Warner-Lambert
Economics Laboratory	Paradyne	U.S. Surgical
E. I. DuPont de Nemours	Pelton	West Company
Eli Lilly	PepsiCo	Westinghouse

of which had to pay $25,000, regardless of size), a tax committee, and a committee of Washington representatives. Because the companies felt that their activities should be closely coordinated with the government of Puerto Rico, the latter was authorized to appoint five non-dues-paying members. PRUSA was created specifically because the member companies felt that the coordination of their activities, the education of Washington politicians, and the political monitoring of Section 936 were necessary to protect the tax law from future attacks.

Coordination

Immediately after TEFRA's enactment, little unity existed among the 936 companies. The electronics companies felt that pharmaceuticals were abusing the system and wanted to negotiate a deal that favored the electronics industry as an insurance policy against future attack. By the same token, electronics companies felt that, given the opportunity, pharmaceutical companies would try to get their own deal. Pharmaceuticals felt the same way about the electronics and about each other. Thus, one reason why PRUSA was created was so that both pharmaceutical companies and electronic companies would know what the others were doing. With that purpose, PRUSA scheduled regular meetings with the tax officials and Washington representatives of its member companies. In those meetings, members learned of each others' interests, and a common political front would be negotiated. A number of the pharmaceutical company lobbyists interviewed argued that PRUSA served partly as a front for pharmaceuticals. One lobbyist elaborated:

> The foundation, PRUSA, was put in place [because] we wanted to have some coordination with the Puerto Rican government and because the pharmaceutical industry wanted to have the electronics companies involved. In a way, PRUSA gives drug companies some cover.

Education

In their work on interest groups, Schlozman and Tierney found that virtually every group they studied emphasized the tasks of making formal and informal contacts with policymakers and presenting them with information about complex issues and about the consequences of potential legislative decisions.[8] Accordingly, the 936 companies felt that they needed to educate members of Congress about the importance of Section 936 to both Puerto Rico and the United States. Specifically, according to the Washington representative of Baxter International, member companies felt that the education of members had to be an ongoing effort, so "that we do not have to educate people over a two-week span," when the issue came before Congress. Another reason why PRUSA wanted to educate as many members as possible was because, as Holmes explained, "Rangel does not want to defend it alone; he also needs the support of other members."

Company lobbyists argued that congressional staff turnover also represented a threat to Section 936. One company representative explained that the greatest difficulty in protecting Section 936 "is that there is such a big staff [in Congress] and there is so much turnover. Not only does the staff leave with every congressman that leaves, but staff leaves in between." Hence, PRUSA was responsible for educating not only legislators but also their continuously changing staffers.

PRUSA's overall educational activities consisted of letting members of Congress and their staff know "that there are mainland jobs that would not be here if it were not for Puerto Rico and 936"; that Section 936, as a tool for the economic development of Puerto Rico, for which it was enacted in 1976, was working; that the Treasury Department's tax-expenditure calculations were wrong because they assumed that if the tax law were repealed, the companies would not leave the island in search of other low-tax jurisdictions; and that 936's elimination would hurt the profitability of many U.S. firms. It would be especially disastrous for the pharmaceutical industry, which was the only U.S. industry that was still an international leader. It would also hurt the electronics companies, which would be at a further disadvantage vis-à-vis their Japanese counterparts, who enjoyed this kind of tax-sparing agreement with other countries.[9]

One of the methods PRUSA utilized to get its message across was commissioning studies of the tax law by public-policy research organizations. For example, in 1984 the group hired Robert Nathan Associates to study why the wage credit that Treasury proposed to replace Section 936 with was insufficient to maintain Puerto Rico's level of economic prosperity.[10]

However, Holmes explained that the best way to communicate to members of Congress and their staffers the importance of 936 to Puerto Rico was by taking them there to see the progress for themselves. According to Holmes, "some of the companies' lobbyists who have a relationship with a member [of Congress] will invite him and then PRUSA takes over." The sponsoring company paid for the trip. Though it was generally not hard to persuade members of Congress to take these trips, Holmes pointed out that "it is easier to get a member to go in the winter than in the summer." He explained that these trips served to protect the tax law because it gave the issue a human face:

> After this kind of trip you are never sure that someone like [Representative Richard] Gephardt [D-Mo.] will defend 936 on the floor or become an active defender of the section, but you know that when the issue comes before him he will have Puerto Rico and Puerto Ricans in mind.

By all accounts, these trips also had some impact on the way the congressional staff thought about Section 936. As one staff member of the Ways and Means Committee explained,

> Those trips do serve a certain educational purpose. You have lunch at a plant with people who have lined up for those jobs at these [manufacturing] plants [in Puerto Rico], and if you sit beside someone who is happy to be there and enjoys the job, it is a pretty good sales pitch.

Another staff member concurred:

> PRUSA does two trips a year for staff of the Ways and Means in groups of six to eight people. They are very effective, taking people to play golf in Puerto Rico. But in all fairness to PRUSA, they do more than play golf. They have dinners with businessmen, and there is always a conversation about 936 over dinner. It's heavy-duty lobbying.[11]

Monitoring

Finally, PRUSA was put in place to keep track of any political threats to Section 936. Many of the member companies felt that conventional trade organizations had so many issues to monitor that they could not be trusted to adequately monitor the tax issue. Moreover, in spite of the fact that many of PRUSA's member companies had Washington offices, they had too many issues to deal with; as a result, many companies have organized single-issue groups such as PRUSA. Thus, as Holmes explained, "My job is to stay on top of the issue for [the companies] and then to say to them, 'We have gotten to a point when I can't do it alone,' and then, when assistance is needed, they come through."

During the tax-reform process, the 936 companies hit the ground running. They were prepared to engage in an intensive lobbying campaign to protect the tax law even before Treasury sent its proposal to the White House. A review of the political process also reveals that when PRUSA faced its first political test, its member companies did not break ranks to advocate their own particular interests at the expense of the tax law. By contrast, the Puerto Rican government was pursuing its own distinct strategy in disagreement with many of the 936 firms.

II. The Process of Tax Reform

The 1984–86 history of PRUSA and the Puerto Rican government's defense of the tax law can be divided into three stages. First, the government of Puerto

Rico tried to stop the Treasury's proposal before it was sent to Congress, while PRUSA and its member companies directed most of their lobbying efforts toward persuading House Ways and Means Committee and Senate Finance Committee members. In the second stage, when the White House had sent its tax-reform project to Congress, PRUSA felt that it already had the votes necessary to protect Section 936 from repeal. Still, the government of Puerto Rico remained active and by this time had broadened its lobbying to include Congress. The Ways and Means Committee reform package ultimately contained only minor changes to Section 936. In the third stage, individual companies continued their lobbying, this time of the Senate Finance Committee members to get them to eliminate the changes adopted in the House. Although the companies succeeded in the Senate, the amendments were put back in during conference. Overall, however, the 936 companies were satisfied with the outcome of the Tax Reform Act of 1986. PRUSA members felt that lobbying so early in the process had protected the tax law from any real danger and that the organization had been very effective in keeping them working together.

Stage I

In his January 1984 State of the Union address, President Reagan announced that he was going to ask the Treasury Department to engage in a comprehensive revision of the tax code. Reagan had wanted to beat the Democrats to the punch because he erroneously believed that they were going to use tax reform as a campaign theme.[12] Treasury Secretary Donald T. Regan, however, took seriously the president's request and began working on a tax-reform plan with the help of his assistant secretary, Ronald Pearlman, a lawyer; Charles McLure, an economist and Pearlman's deputy; and a small group of economists, representatives of the IRS, and members of the Reagan White House. In November 1984 the Treasury unveiled its tax reform proposal for "Fairness, Simplicity, and Economic Growth." This proposal was known as Treasury I and was circulated with the purpose of getting the public's reaction. The idea was that the Treasury would modify the proposal and then resend it to the White House. It would then be revised and submitted to Congress.

According to Birnbaum and Murray, the theory behind Treasury's initial tax plan was that "all income should be treated equally by the tax system, regardless of where it comes from, what form it takes, or what it is used for." For Pearlman and McLure, this approach meant that "the tax code should be returned to its original purpose, which was to raise revenue for the government, not to engineer the economy and promote social change."[13] The two tax experts went after every possible tax break, even proposing to repeal the same investment incentives that President Reagan had signed into law in 1981. Thus, it is not surprising that Treasury I contained a proposal to repeal Section 936. Pearlman explained, "Our initial judgment" to eliminate the possessions tax credit "was not a 936 prejudice":

> Our initial attitude was that the tax code is not the place for economic incentives. The goal should be to tax income at the lowest possible rate and still have government revenues. We asked ourselves, "What kind of tax policy is best for the nation, not just Puerto Rico?"

To ease the possible shock to the Puerto Rican economy, Treasury I stipulated that Section 936 was to be replaced with a temporary scheme of limited tax credits based on a diminishing percentage of the federal minimum wage (i.e., a wage credit), culminating in the complete elimination of any federal tax preference for Puerto Rico. According to Treasury's estimates, implementation of this measure would result in approximately $3.7 billion of additional revenue within a five-year period.[14]

Immediately after the Puerto Rican government heard about Treasury I, it began to plan its own strategy to protect Section 936. The island government hired Richard Copaken, a partner in the law firm of Covington and Burling. Copaken convinced the Puerto Rican government that he had access to administration officials and that they could be persuaded to stop the proposal before it was sent to Congress. Copaken suggested that the way to save Section 936 was to appeal to the Reagan administration's national-security interests.[15] With that strategy in mind, the Puerto Rican government proposed to use the tax law to help President Reagan's Caribbean Basin Initiative (CBI).

In 1981 CBI had been presented as the administration's revolutionary economic solution to the political instability of the Caribbean and Central American region. However, the program had not worked as expected. The idea had been to increase U.S. imports from these countries to help develop their economies. By early 1985, however, CBI countries were complaining that the program could not work because they needed an investment program, not a trade plan.[16] Thus, on 2 January 1985, during his inaugural message, the governor of Puerto Rico offered to make $700 million of the 936 companies' profits deposited in the Puerto Rican Government Development Bank available for investments in the CBI countries on the condition that Section 936 was not eliminated.[17] The idea was to use the 936 funds for low-interest loans to companies building twin plants. Under the plan, a company would build one plant in a CBI country to take advantage of the cheaper unskilled labor and would locate a complementary plant in Puerto Rico for the more complicated, final assembly.

The 936 companies, particularly pharmaceutical firms, did not like this strategy. First, they opposed the idea of tying Section 936 to investments in the Caribbean. As in 1982, some of the 936 companies felt that the tax law could be saved without having to offer a compromise in return. Second, businesses did not like to be told where to invest. As one economist who participated in the process recalled,

> I attended a few meetings with PRUSA and with the representatives of [the] 936 companies, and they felt they were getting their arms twisted to do investments for political reasons and that they would lose money as a result.

Nonetheless, he continues, some "individual companies grudgingly went along with the CBI idea." By March 1985, the governor of Puerto Rico reported that SmithKline Beecham and Johnson and Johnson were pursuing twin-plants projects in Grenada.[18]

PRUSA and the rest of its member companies chose a different approach. Some individual companies with access to the White House lobbied directly. As one pharmaceutical company representative explained in an interview, "There are political appointees and lifelong bureaucrats, and it depends whom you go to, but if you are not lucky with them you go to the boss's boss at the White House, and that is what we did in 1986." Another lobbyist explained that while "it is hard to say what effect these meetings" with White House officials have, they "at least make them think twice. So rather than them only hearing one side of the story [in this case the Treasury's side], we bring in another perspective."

Most research suggests, however, that generally, Congress is the primary target for most pressure-group activity.[19] Accordingly, most PRUSA members intensive lobbying took place in Congress for two basic reasons. First, the 936 companies believed that it was nearly impossible to influence the Treasury staff and, therefore, did not want to waste the time. As the lobbyist from Baxter International explained, "Treasury has a tendency to wall itself off—they just don't listen to reason." Second, Holmes explained, "We directed our educational operation to those who were going to make the ultimate decision"— members of Congress. Specifically, Holmes continued, PRUSA targeted House Ways and Means Committee members because "they looked at the issue first, they took the first crack at the issue."

Access gained through PAC contributions becomes relevant at this time. During the 1985–86 election cycle, PAC contributions by PRUSA pharmaceutical companies to members of the House Ways and Means Committee and Senate Finance Committee totaled close to half of the total contributions of all 936 companies who were also PRUSA members ($462,860) (see table A3). Thus, it is likely that through the pharmaceutical companies and other 936 companies who also had PACs, PRUSA enjoyed the access it needed to plead its case with members of these two committees. But access is also gained through the long-term relationships developed after years of interaction. For example, Holmes felt that a great deal of the access he enjoyed came as a result of his prior work at General Electric. He said, that campaign contributions "are important, they give you access, [but] I probably have the contacts and access I have in Congress because of the relationships I developed when I worked for GE. It is important to have the relationship so you can communicate."

The Puerto Rican government and PRUSA evidently were pursuing two different strategies. The island government was offering the CBI-936 connection to save the tax law. Most of PRUSA's companies felt that the CBI strategy was not needed and believed that a united strategy directed at Congress would suffice to protect their interests. The Puerto Rican government, however, felt that the twin-plant proposal would get enough support from members of the administration and the White House that Treasury would be forced to drop its proposal to eliminate Section 936.[20] Consequently, the Puerto Rican government paid very little attention to Congress at this time. However, as PRUSA had expected, although several individuals in the State and Commerce Departments and in the National Security Council showed some interest in the twin-plant idea, tax reform remained Treasury's domain, and that department was not at all interested.[21] As a Treasury economist working on the issue recalled, "The CBI thing was completely unserious; with a few million dollars a year they wanted to save a $2 billion tax expenditure." There was no backing down on the department's proposal to eliminate the tax law.

Yet even if the government of Puerto Rico and the companies were pursuing different strategies, the behavior of the latter contrasted sharply with their initial political response to the events leading to TEFRA. In 1984 the companies had a lobbying strategy in place before the issue made it to Congress and contacted members of the administration and Congress at a time when many other experienced business lobbyists were confident that tax reform had no hope of being enacted.[22] Moreover, neither the island government nor PRUSA ever gave the impression that they would accept any changes to Section 936. No one came forward with suggestions for amending Section 936.

By January 1985 it was still not clear whether the administration would aggressively pursue tax reform. "The White House showed no clear sign of interest in the proposal, and the chorus of complaints from special interest groups discouraged even the Treasury secretary."[23] Then came the announcement that Regan and White House Chief of Staff James Baker would trade places—Baker would become treasury secretary, with a mandate to get Congress to pass tax reform, while Regan would take his place at the White House. Announcement of the swap gave new hope to the prospect for tax reform. Baker had a reputation for getting what he wanted, and the administration was sending the message that it cared enough about tax reform to put its main man in charge.

Baker brought Richard Darman with him as deputy treasury secretary.

Though initially critical of Treasury I, Darman came to believe that it had been "a brilliant, if inadvertent, strategic move," because "to avoid the worst," special-interest lobbyists would "have to settle for something less onerous" without necessarily threatening the reform effort.[24] Both men concluded, however, that Treasury I had to be amended to make it more politically acceptable before it could be supported officially by the White House.

According to Pearlman, during Baker's revision of the tax package the reformers became convinced that, whether or not Section 936 was a tax loophole incompatible with the goals of tax reform, the tax law was not working for Puerto Rico. The reformers concluded that a wage credit would offer an incentive for U.S. firms to establish manufacturing operations on the island at a much lower cost to the U.S. government. Pearlman recalled,

> In stage II, when we talked about 936 specifically, we also discovered, based on Treasury data, that it was not offering Puerto Rico what it was supposed to. We found that 936 was a capital incentive, that companies had gone to Puerto Rico, especially drug companies, and established highly automated plants; the outcome is very high profits for these companies when really not much is going on [in Puerto Rico].

According to the companies, even though Treasury had not yet reviewed how the new cost-sharing and profit-split regulations were working, the department's staff had convinced Pearlman that they were not enough to correct abuses by the 936 companies. As chapter 4 revealed, the Treasury staff had opposed cost sharing and profit split because the staffers felt these provisions kept the tax law overly generous.[25] In 1982 the White House pressured the Treasury staff to reach a compromise with Puerto Rican officials. But after TEFRA, Treasury continued with its criticism of Section 936.

Treasury's criticism was not altogether unreasonable. The staff at Treasury still expected the companies' tax bills to go up after TEFRA, and the companies initially agreed that this would be the case, which is why they considered the outcome of the process in 1982 a serious political loss. However, with the help of tax lawyers, the companies were able to continue to profit substantially from Section 936. Tables 12 and 13 illustrate the extent to which the companies continued to reduce their federal tax bills as a result of Section 936. The Treasury staff was keenly aware of the fact that through successful tax planning the companies had minimized TEFRA's impact.

By the time Treasury II was sent to the White House on 23 April, it was clear that Section 936 had not been saved by the Puerto Rican government's CBI proposal. Treasury II sought to eliminate Section 936 and replace it with a permanent wage credit against federal taxes consisting of 60 percent of the minimum wage plus 20 percent of wages paid in excess of the minimum wage, up to four times the minimum wage. The measure proposed a five-year grandfather clause for the existing corporations operating under the rules of Section 936. According to the Treasury, implementation of this proposal would result in approximately $1.4 billion of additional revenue within a five-year period.[26] In the interim, although the Puerto Rican government continued to attempt to convince the administration to leave Section 936 untouched, it also began to work more closely with PRUSA to secure enough support from legislators so that by the time the president sent his tax reform proposal to Congress, Section 936 would be out of danger.

While it was not common knowledge at the time, the truth was that the administration was not entirely convinced by Treasury's proposal to replace Section 936 with a wage credit. Copaken had contacted Michael Deaver, the deputy chief of the Reagan White House, who had just recently announced that he was resigning his government job to begin his own lobbying firm. Deaver was later convicted of perjury regarding the accusation that he had violated laws prohibiting the lobbying of government officials within a year of leaving office when he lobbied on behalf of the governments of Canada and Puerto Rico and

TABLE 12.   U.S. Firms Reporting a Tax Savings under Section 936, 1982–85 (in percentage points)

	1982	1983	1984	1985
American Hospital Supply	14.7*	14.3*	20.0*	—
Avon Products	—	3.0*	—	—
Baxter Laboratories	13.9*	13.6*	20.0*	—
Carter-Wallace	15.7*	15.1*	7.5*	7.4*
Eli Lilly	3.9*	5.1	6.4*	8.0*
Hubbell	—	—	0.7	3.9*
Johnson and Johnson	6.8*	8.1*	9.8*	11.0*
Medtronic	19.1*	16.5*	18.7*	30.0*
Merck	3.7	4.4*	3.8*	6.9*
Millipore	12.1*	12.2*	12.1*	15.6*
Pall	14.4*	14.1*	14.7*	16.2*
PepsiCo	—	—	1.2	5.6*
Schering-Plough	15.5*	15.9*	11.5*	15.2*
SmithKline	—	—	18.4*	17.6*
Sterling Drug	3.8*	3.4*	4.2*	4.8*
Upjohn	35.6*	26.6*	19.3*	14.7*
U.S. Surgical	—	—	6.3	10.7
Westinghouse	11.2*	23.5*	15.4*	11.1*
Federal Statutory Tax Rate	46%	46%	46%	46%

Source: 10-K reports, 1982, 1983, 1984, 1985.

(—) Information not available or no tax savings reported.

*Indicates that the possessions tax break was the most important factor reducing federal taxes.

the Korean Broadcasting Corporation. However, according to James McDonough, who has gone over the testimony at the trial, when Deaver called Darman in May to check on what the White House was thinking about Section 936, Darman said that "Reagan, Bush and the National Security Council all favored keeping Section 936." Darman testified that the "wage credit proposal enjoyed little support among the high Reagan officials." The twin-plant idea, according to Darman, looked interesting but was still too "sketchy."[27]

Why would the administration support the maintenance of Section 936 at the same time that it had vowed to reform the federal tax code? Based on interviews with Treasury officials, it seems that Puerto Rico's strategic importance in the Caribbean conflicted with Treasury's proposal—that is, the island's image as a showcase of U.S. economic growth and development and Puerto Rico's importance to national security (at the time the island housed the largest U.S. naval base and remained the world's best naval training area) could be put at risk by Treasury's proposal. In addition, according to Ed Rollins, a member of the White House staff, pharmaceutical companies had also actively tried to influence the White House, which may have helped to secure its support for the maintenance of the tax law.[28] Either way, however, the fact was that, at the time, the White House did not want to make any more changes to the tax proposal before it was sent to Congress. And, as the companies had predicted, no amount

TABLE 13. Tax-Free Puerto Rican Earnings as a Percentage of Consolidated after-Tax Earnings, 1982–85

	1982	1983	1984	1985
American Hospital Supply	32.0	31.0	43.5	—
Avon Products	—	6.5	—	—
Baxter Laboratories	30.2	30.0	43.5	—
Carter-Wallace	34.1	32.8	16.3	16.0
Eli Lilly	8.5	11.0	13.9	17.4
Hubbell	—	—	1.5	8.5
Johnson and Johnson	14.8	17.6	21.3	23.9
Medtronic	41.5	35.8	40.6	65.2
Merck	8.0	9.5	8.2	15.0
Millipore	26.3	26.5	26.3	33.9
Pall	31.3	30.6	31.9	35.2
PepsiCo	—	—	2.6	12.1
Schering-Plough	33.6	34.5	25.0	33.0
SmithKline	—	—	40.0	38.2
Sterling Drug	8.2	7.3	9.1	10.4
Upjohn	77.3	57.8	41.9	31.9
U.S. Surgical	—	—	13.6	23.2
Westinghouse	24.3	51.0	33.4	24.1

Source: 10-K reports, 1982, 1983, 1984, 1985.

(—) Information not available or not tax savings reported.

of lobbying could get Treasury to back down from its proposal to eliminate the tax law. Once in Congress, the outcome of the process could go either way, which is why the companies had been trying to secure the votes needed to protect the tax law even before it was sent to the legislature.

PRUSA had been particularly active in organizing trips to bring members of Congress to the island. In April Senators Russell B. Long (D-La.); J. Bennett Johnston (D- La.), George Mitchell (D-Maine), and Patrick J. Leahy (D-Vt.) went to Puerto Rico on a trip sponsored by PRUSA. The group also sponsored a trip by four tax advisers to members of the Senate Finance Committee. Individual companies sponsored the trips of Democratic House Majority leader Jim Wright (D-Tex.) and three House Ways and Means Committee members, Bill Frenzel (R-Minn.), Carroll Campbell (R-S.C.), and Barbara Kennelly (D-Conn.). By May a total of eight senators and fifteen representatives had visited the island. According to Holmes, by the time the White House sent the tax package for House consideration, PRUSA had already secured all of the votes it needed to protect Section 936 in the House Ways and Means Committee.

Stage II

On 28 May 1985 the tax package was sent to Congress. It was now up to the chairman of the House Ways and Means Committee, Dan Rostenkowski (D-Ill.), to keep the reform effort alive. In turn, "the chairman's prestige depended on passage of some sort of tax reform."[29] As chapter 4 demonstrated, Rostenkowski previously had done poorly. First, Congress had passed the Republican version of the ERTA in 1981. Second, unable to get his committee members to agree on a revenue-raising package, the House Ways and Means Committee had voted to go straight to conference with the Senate on the TEFRA bill in 1982. "Rostenkowski needed a big win to establish himself and his committee as legitimate legislators."[30] Thus, when President Reagan, in a nationally televised speech in May 1985, outlined his tax-reform proposal, Rostenkowski enthusiastically endorsed the plan.

Without committing himself to any of the changes proposed by the administration in Treasury II, Rostenkowski immediately began working with his committee on his own tax-reform bill. Although PRUSA felt it already had the votes to protect Section 936, Rostenkowski's position on the tax law was not clear. In fact, there were reports in the Puerto Rican media that suggested that the chairman actually did not look favorably on Section 936.[31] However, according to Rangel's legislative counsel, "Rostenkowski needed nineteen votes, and he asked [the members of the Ways and Means Committee], 'What do you need to vote for this bill?'" Among other things, Rangel chose to protect Section 936 in exchange for his support for tax reform. Rostenkowski then divided the committee into task forces to focus on specific aspects of tax law. Each task force had to come up with a specific amount of dollars in tax revenues. Not surprisingly, to Rangel's task force fell the responsibility for any changes made Section 936. According to Holmes, "Rostenkowski told Rangel, "I need 300 million from 936 in five years."" The chairman left to Rangel's discretion how to come up with that amount.

Although the outcome of tax reform was still uncertain and PRUSA continued actively to lobby Congress, it was clear from the outset that Rangel was working to make sure that the committee did not support Treasury II's recommendation to eliminate Section 936 and replace it with a wage credit. But Rangel's work in defense of Section 936 did not stop there, as he was also trying to secure the support of legislators who were not members of the House Ways and Means Committee.

Contrary to conventional wisdom, research on Congress suggests that legislators' main concerns are not necessarily "how to vote but what to do with [their] time, how to allocate [their] resources, and where to put [their] energy."[32] Moreover, as explained in chapter 4, research on the impact of PAC contributions has concluded that money does not buy votes. Based on these findings, in their study of the relationship between contributions and members' behavior, R. L. Hall and Wayman concluded that money buys a sympathetic legislator's time. In other words, contributions buy access to sympathetic legislators, who, in turn, lobby their colleagues on the group's behalf.[33]

Since TEFRA, Rangel's fund-raisers in Puerto Rico, attended by the officials of the U.S. companies located there, had become the most important sources of funding for his campaigns. During the 1985–86 cycle, 936 companies' PACs who were also members of PRUSA contributed a total of $27,070 to his reelection bid (see table A2). Accordingly, judging from Rangel's attitude during the hearings on tax reform, it was clear that he was acting as the companies' representative in Congress. The following is a hearing excerpt of Congressman Rangel asking the witness representing PRUSA, Jerry Myers, vice president and administrative officer of American Hospital Supply Corporation, and the witness representing the Pharmaceutical Manufacturers' Association (PMA), Gerald J. Mossinghoff, about the activities of the 936 firms on the mainland:

> *Mr. Rangel:* How many headquarters would those firms have? Would it be 75 headquarters?
> *Mr. Myers:* Yes.
> *Rangel:* And would, generally speaking, they be located in 75 different congressional districts?
> *Myers:* Well, there are some duplications, but probably as many as 40 to 50.
> *Rangel:* And so there shouldn't be any question that we should expect 40 or 50 members to understand the problems that you are facing with 936?

Myers: Right. And as I said at the outset, our 75 members employ over 2.5 million people in the United States.

Rangel: So that means that beyond the 40 or 50 congressional districts, that you would have plants probably scattered throughout the 50 states?

Myers: Yes, indeed.

Rangel: And these plants probably have a lot of voters working there. I don't see why we have the problem, but if you could share with me where the headquarters are and where the plants are. If you haven't got the names of the members, we will be able to provide them for you.

Myers: We have those names and I would be pleased to share our list with you.

Rangel: It would be very helpful. I assume that the pharmaceutical [industry has] less of a problem in order to establish where the plants are located.

Mr. Mossinghoff: We know where they are, sir.

Rangel: And I assume you know what members represent well the interests of those employees where those plants are?

Mossinghoff: Yes, sir.[34]

Indeed, it was clear that Rangel intended to use those lists to convince other members of Congress that it would be in their interest to reject Treasury's proposal for the repeal of Section 936.

Not all of the members present at the Ways and Means hearings on Section 936 were as accommodating to the companies as Rangel. Under questioning, however, supporters of Section 936 were united in their opposition to any compromise that would entail the elimination or radical modification of Section 936. For example, Representatives Barbara Kennelly (D-Conn.) and J. J. Pickle (D-Tex.) asked the witnesses to suggests changes to Section 936 that would result in increased revenues for the Treasury and more jobs in Puerto Rico. Supporters of the tax law argued that any changes to Section 936 would only result in the companies leaving Puerto Rico in search of more favorable tax jurisdictions outside the United States, a reduction of revenue to Treasury, and an increase in Puerto Rican unemployment.[35]

During the Puerto Rican delegation's testimony, Representative Frank Guarini (D-N.J.) expressed his concern with the deficit and the issue of fairness:

The focus isn't really on Puerto Rico. It is on the pharmaceutical companies down there that aren't paying any taxes that we thought we had struck a bargain with some two years ago, and they had gotten around by their bookkeeping process to have us sustain the same tax loss that we had sustained before. And we now have a $200 billion deficit facing our Nation, and that is a mutual concern to all of us, because we are all in this boat together. . . .

I understand the importance of 936. But yet, we want to have a sense of awareness on the part of the companies that are using this that it is at the expense of the wage earner in the United States. Someone has to pick up that, and the middle working man in the United States—if you want to call him "Joe Six-Pack" or a fellow in New York City or somewhere else—is having that tax burden put on his back, because the companies that are operating down there are not paying their fair share of taxes.[36]

To offset this kind of remark, Mossinghoff argued that a 1984 Joint Committee on Taxation study "showed that our members' companies paid the highest effective tax rate of all industries at 32.9 percent." He continued, "So, there is no question about pharmaceutical firms paying their fair share despite the tax advantages they get in Puerto Rico."[37]

Regarding the electronics companies, Myers argued that Section 936 concerned U.S. firms' international competitiveness. He argued that the tax law was especially important for the "U.S. high tech semiconductor and computer firms" that are "locked in a competitive struggle with Japanese counterparts." He explained that the Japanese government utilizes this kind of tax arrangement to give an advantage to its multinationals in places like South Korea, Singapore, Ireland, and Malaysia. Were Congress to take away Section 936, it would put the U.S. electronics industry at an even greater disadvantage.[38]

Another example of business unity came from the chairman of the Generic Pharmaceutical Industry Association (GPIA), William F. Haddad, who also served as vice chairman and CEO of Danbury Pharmacal. Like the representatives of PMA, PRUSA, and the Puerto Rican delegation, Haddad refused to even consider any changes to Section 936. He began by explaining that he probably was "public enemy No. 1 of the Pharmaceutical Manufacturers Association." In fact, he said, "I think this is the first time that we have ever sat down together on an issue." But, he argued, Section 936 was also important for generic drug firms, and it was important that GPIA's support be made public. GPIA's support was significant because, as Rangel pointed out, the generic drug firms make low-cost medicines available to "our poor and our aged citizens."[39]

By the end of July, Rostenkowski announced publicly that there existed a consensus among his committee members for the maintenance of Section 936 but that the tax law might still be subject to some modifications.[40] Ways and Means Committee staffers now began pressuring supporters of Section 936 to offer a compromise that would take away some of the excessive tax benefits from some of the pharmaceutical companies. PRUSA and its member companies refused, and the government of Puerto Rico, by now very sensitive to the companies' position, refused as well. No alternatives would be offered.[41]

At the same time there was a change in Treasury's attitude. Roger Mentz, a lawyer by training who had come in early in 1985 as the department's assistant secretary, believed that the department's staff was wrong about Section 936. During an interview, Mentz explained,

> I was sensitive to the issue because I used to work for Warner-Lambert and other 931 and 936 companies. I basically agreed [with the government of Puerto Rico] that a wage credit would not be applicable for a highly sophisticated economy like Puerto Rico's. . . . The wage-credit was a stupid idea. Puerto Rico is a high-tech economy, and wage credit would work in Bangladesh and Zaire but not in Puerto Rico. It just did not fit with the Puerto Rican economy, particularly one that is so based on 936.

Still, in September, when Treasury staffers suggested to Mentz that they should eliminate the cost-sharing option because it was too difficult to administer, he agreed. The staff had argued that cost sharing encouraged companies to shift as much as possible of their intangible income to the island affiliate and thus gave rise to disputes between the individual companies and the IRS. Again, however, PRUSA rejected this proposal and, according to Mentz, "the companies got Rangel to support them." By the same token, after being assured of congressional support, the government of Puerto Rico also refused to negotiate with the Treasury on the issue of cost-sharing.

Once it was decided that 936 would be retained, Nordberg and Brockway ultimately had to negotiate on some of the minor changes to the tax law that would result in the $300 million in revenues that Rostenkowski had initially requested. Though it was clear that 936 supporters would not offer any alternative to the tax law, it was important to give the impression that they were willing to sit down at the table. As pointed out in chapter 4, the companies knew that keeping congressional staffers happy was as important as persuading members of Congress because the staffers write the bill. Accordingly, Brockway explained that "on the provisions where there was no vote," businesses that did not like to sit down at the table with the staff "were screwed." He continued, "The idea of this bill was that someone was going to get screwed—someone in the business community was going to get hurt. . . . The key was to be sitting at the table." Thus, according to Brockway, supporters of Section 936 were able to secure a good deal because they were willing to talk with the staff. These dealings were facilitated by the fact that only Nordberg negotiated on behalf of the 936 companies, which had given him the authority to represent them. The basic structure of Section 936 was to remain intact, however, and congressional staffers knew this.

PRUSA then continued to work to secure the support of other legislators and the few House Ways and Means Committee members whose support was not yet assured. For example, on 12 September 1985 PRUSA sponsored a breakfast meeting where sixty-two House members agreed to sign a resolution authored by Rangel calling for a rejection of Treasury's plan to replace Section 936 with a wage credit. On 15 September Gephardt, a member of the House Ways and Means Committee, visited the island on a trip sponsored by a 936 company. Gephardt, one of the original proponents of tax reform, had opposed Section 936. Once he visited the island, however, his opposition seemed to weaken, although he still did not forcefully support 936.

Finally, on 15 November, the committee Democrats agreed on a tax-reform bill.[42] On 3 December the Democrats' version of the bill was passed by the full committee by a vote of twenty-eight to eight. Still, passage by the full House remained uncertain. "Republicans—feeling cut out as Ways and Means Democrats caucused, believing Baker and Darman had ignored them while attending to Rostenkowski, and opposing reform anyway—were seething."[43] President Reagan unsuccessfully tried to reassure his partisans that any problems would be fixed in the Republican Senate. According to Bill Frenzel (R-Minn.), "The phrase 'the Senate will fix it up' is the moral equivalent of 'I'll respect you in the morning.'"[44]

On 11 December dissatisfied Democrats joined in with Republicans to defeat a rule to allow floor debate on the bill. With only 14 out of 182 House Republicans voting in favor of allowing House consideration of the tax bill, the rule was defeated 223 to 202. Only when President Reagan assured Speaker of the House Tip O'Neill (D-Mass.) that at least fifty Republicans would vote for the rule did the congressman agree to bring the bill back to the floor. On 17 December, both the rule and the Ways and Means tax bill passed the House.

Stage III

Though Section 936 had been saved, with minor changes, not all of the 936 companies were satisfied.[45] The House version of the tax bill amended Section 936 to force companies that used the cost-sharing method to pay an annual royalty fee to their parent firms. But the amendment went beyond Section 936 because it was also made to Section 482 of the Internal Revenue Code. The new provision stipulated that royalty payments for the use of an intangible be commensurate with the income arising from that intangible. As a result, if an intangible whose ownership had been transferred to a foreign affiliate and/or a 936 company (i.e., any corporation not subject to current U.S. tax) increased in value, the annual royalty payment had to increase as well.

According to a pharmaceutical lobbyist, during PRUSA's negotiations with the Joint Committee on Taxation, "Brockway offered the 'superroyalty' because he had always been bothered by the drug companies' use of 936." In turn, she continued,

> Carl Nordberg was so concerned with saving 936 that, when the "super-royalty" was offered as a compromise by Brockway to save 936, [Nord-berg] forgot that we operate everywhere, and it was a decision that he did not consult with the companies [because] he had the leeway to negotiate for us, and he committed himself to that.

According to Brockway, once they learned of the "'superroyalty,' the companies freaked out." Consequently, even as the prospects for tax reform decreased considerably during the Senate's consideration of the project, a "Section 482 Royalty Group," made up of some individual 936 companies, was formed to try to get the superroyalty provision deleted from the bill.

Tax reform, however, seemed doomed in the Senate. The Senate Finance Committee chairman, Robert Packwood (R-Ore.) had not shown as much enthusiasm for the cause of reform as had Rostenkowski. In addition, a group of senators began to pressure the Finance Committee and the White House to reduce the deficit first, using taxes if necessary. On 4 March 1986 fifty senators, including seven members of the Senate Finance Committee, sent a letter to the president asking him to delay action on the tax bill until a deficit-reduction package was enacted.[46]

Many Finance Committee members had also made it clear that they were reluctant to eliminate many of the existing tax breaks. All in all, few senators in the committee were committed to tax reform. So controversial was the Finance Committee's markup of the tax-reform bill that on 18 April Packwood decided to suspend it. To save tax reform, Packwood and his staff director, William Diefender, decided to propose reducing tax rates far more dramatically than had been previously proposed. After working secretly with six other committee members and Brockway and his staff, on 24 April Packwood finally released his tax-reform proposal, known as Packwood II.[47]

In the meantime, some 936 companies representing themselves were busy lobbying senators for the elimination of the superroyalty provision. However, what was most remarkable about this effort was that none of the 936 companies that lobbied individually (as opposed to lobbying for PRUSA) offered any compromise at the expense of Section 936. Officially, PRUSA also joined in the effort against the superroyalty, but again, Section 936 was not to be touched. (The Puerto Rican government was not involved in this particular effort.) But while the tax-reform proposal reported by the Senate Finance Committee on 29 May did not contain the superroyalty provision, it was put back in during conference.

Finally, on 22 October 1986 President Reagan signed the tax-reform bill into law. The act transferred about $120 billion in tax liability from individuals to businesses and substantially reduced individual rates to 15 percent and 28 percent and corporate rates to 15 percent, 25 percent, and 34 percent.

III. Success of Experimental Response

Most of the studies of the Tax Reform Act of 1986 point to the fact that the enactment of tax reform always seemed improbable if not impossible.[48] One of the reasons why such was the case was that reducing the income tax drastically would require the elimination of so many business loopholes that it seemed impossible that the business community would allow reform to go forward. In the end, however, not all business groups came out losers. For example, Martin has shown that early corporate supporters whom President Reagan had courted to help promote his tax-reform agenda were its major beneficiaries. This group included high technology and a number of small-business and service-sector groups.[49] But according to White and Wildavsky, for those businesses that lost, the process revealed first that many never really thought that tax reform would be enacted; they were therefore taken by surprise when the project became unstoppable in the Senate.[50] Second, businesses were divided on the issue of tax reform. For example, Birnbaum and Murray found it puzzling that "many powerful interest groups lined up in opposition to reform never joined forces to defeat it." According to Darman, "they were brought down by the narrowness of their vision."[51]

By contrast, the 936 companies did better than other business groups and better than they had done in 1982. Contrary to their behavior during TEFRA, in 1986 the companies prepared early to engage in an aggressive lobbying campaign that was characterized by a high degree of unity. In spite of the fact that they were unsuccessful in getting the superroyalty provision stricken from the tax bill, the 936 companies that were part of PRUSA's effort to protect Section 936 were extremely happy with the outcome. These firms felt that Section 936 had never really been at risk because they were able to get the votes they needed to convince members of the Ways and Means Committee to reject Treasury's proposal before it was sent to Congress for consideration. The final changes made to Section 936 were minimal, and, even with the superroyalty provision, Congress expected to raise only $300 million within a five-year period from the changes made to Section 936. This figure compared favorably with the $3.7 billion and the $1.4 billion, respectively, that Treasury I and Treasury II had expected to raise from Section 936. Moreover, even Brockway agreed that the explanation of the superroyalty provision had been left too vague and open to easy challenges by the 936 companies.[52] Finally, regarding Copaken's idea to make $700 million of 936 companies' profits deposited in the Puerto Rican Development Bank available for investment in the CBI countries, the companies argued that "they had not been party to that agreement" and felt no responsibility in its regard.[53]

IV. Conclusion

Remarkably, PRUSA was one of the few business groups that did not lose as a result of the 1986 tax-reform process. In the words of Brockway, "the fact that 936 survived is just amazing." But a closer look at the process reveals that, contrary to the experiences of other industries, the subsystem that developed between pharmaceutical and electronics firms and Congressman Rangel after 1982 survived the political upheaval of 1986. As a member of the committee whose vote Rostenkowski needed, Rangel was willing and able to protect the tax break from broad criticism and to lobby other members on the companies' behalf. Rangel was not the only one to do so. All policymakers who wanted and were a position to protect their interests did so.[54] The companies contributed effectively to the protection of their tax interests by preparing early to engage in an aggressive lobbying campaign that was characterized by a high degree of unity. Their political strategy was based on what they had learned from their experiences in 1982. In turn, the success of their experimental collective-action strategy in 1986 would guide the companies' behavior when a new political battle over Section 936 unfolded as part of President Clinton's first budget proposal to Congress in 1993.

CHAPTER 6

Learned Response to a New Political Environment: The Omnibus Budget Reconciliation Act of 1993

Experienced political operatives misjudged the situation [because] we always try to fight the last war.
—Pharmaceutical Company Washington Representative

The companies' 1986 success explains why they initially pursued a common political strategy when President Clinton included the elimination of the Section 936 income credit and its replacement with a wage credit as part of his first budget proposal to Congress. By this time, however, the political structure of the issue had changed. First, by early 1992 Senator David Pryor (D-Ark.) had become the pharmaceutical companies' nemesis when he used his chairmanship of the Senate's Special Committee on Aging to publicize the fact that no other industrialized country subsidized this industry as much as did the United States. Second, the perceived pharmaceutical-company abuses of the Section 936 rules became more public after the General Accounting Office (GAO) published a damning report. Third, pharmaceutical companies were labeled villains by the incoming Democratic administration, which campaigned on the promise of health-care reform.[1] Fourth, organized labor wanted President Clinton to keep his campaign promise to eliminate incentives for companies to go overseas. And fifth, Puerto Rico's new prostatehood governor was not an aggressive supporter of Section 936.

Given this new political environment, it is surprising that the electronics and other more labor-intensive companies remained in a coalition with the pharmaceuticals for as long as they did. In retrospect, some of the companies felt that they should have tried to negotiate their own deals earlier, for it was only when it became inevitable that the bill to eliminate the income-tax break would pass the House Ways and Means Committee that they began to break ranks. It is clear, however, that the initial reaction of the entire membership of PRUSA was an automatic response guided by prior experiences. When firms win in the political arena, they are less likely to reevaluate past behavior in light of new political circumstances. Hence, consistent with the learning view, 936 companies believed that their political success in 1986 was a consequence of their political strategy, and they simply repeated it in 1993. The companies' subsequent fragmentation was the default strategy adopted by the electronics and other labor-intensive companies once they realized that the coalition strategy with the pharmaceutical companies was not as effective as in 1986.

I.   A New Political Environment

Since 1989 pharmaceuticals—which remained the major beneficiaries of Section 936 and continued to manufacture most of their blockbuster drugs for the U.S. market in Puerto Rico—had been under political attack for the prices charged for drugs.[2] Then, in 1992, Senator Pryor proposed the "Prescription Drug Containment Act." According to a White House official close to the issue, "Senator Pryor felt that the drug industry was gouging the elderly and was also getting support from the federal government in the form of Section 936." Hence, his proposal negated Section 936 benefits to drug companies that raised their prescription drug prices higher than the level of inflation.

According to one of Pryor's aides, the process began when the senator became chairman of the Special Committee on Aging:

> Just before his heart attack, Senator Pryor asked us to start thinking about mechanisms to control drug costs. He held hearings on the issue in 1989, and they resulted in a law to control drug prices for Medicare recipients. [But] the companies [made] up the discount by cost shifting . . . like charging HMOs more, for example. So, we had to start thinking of other ways, [and] we looked at tax breaks.

After studying the issue, the committee staffers found that pharmaceuticals got special tax treatment in four areas: marketing and advertising tax credits, research and development, orphan drugs, and Section 936. But, Pryor's aide continued, "936 was the most advantageous of the four." The committee staff knew about 936 as a tax incentive to Puerto Rico, but they were all surprised when they concluded that it served the pharmaceuticals more than it benefited the island. Incidentally, the Treasury Department staff had been making the same argument for the past fifteen years. But the Senate committee report went beyond the Treasury's argument that the tax break was a tool for escaping federal taxation. The committee staff declared that Section 936 "contributed to the [pharmaceutical] industry's already overflowing coffers," argued that the price of prescription drugs outpaced the rate of inflation, and cited a labor study that concluded that the tax break was no more than an incentive for U.S. companies to transfer mainland jobs to Puerto Rico.[3]

"The Mother of All Tax Breaks"

Senator Pryor thus came up with idea that Section 936 benefits should be eliminated for companies that raised their drug prices higher than the rate of inflation. He held a press conference and sent a "Dear Colleague" letter in which he highlighted the support of eleven senators and of groups such as the American Association of Retired Persons, the Children's Defense Fund, and the AFL-CIO. Then, on 11 March 1992, the senator proposed his legislation as the first amendment to a Democratic tax bill. He explained that for many years politicians had believed the pharmaceutical industry when it argued that it "needs these big profits to pay for the costs of researching, development, and marketing." Pryor argued that the time had come to hold pharmaceutical companies accountable for their tax-free profits in Puerto Rico in light of the fact that the price of drugs in the United States was 40 to 60 percent higher than in other industrialized countries.[4] He proposed that the money saved by the elimination of what he referred to as "the mother of all tax breaks" be used to pay for an extension of the two-year, 100 percent self-employment health-insurance tax deduction contained in the tax bill under consideration.[5]

During the ensuing debate it became clear that, as it had been the case since the 1970s, some policymakers believed that Section 936 was U.S. policy for Puerto Rico, while others believed that Section 936 was a corporate tax subsidy. For example, Senator Daniel Patrick Moynihan (D-N.Y.) argued against Pryor's amendment by explaining that Section 936 was not only about pharmaceutical companies but about the Puerto Rican economy. He suggested,

> It would be a great mistake, in my view, to take this, to not deal with the issue when it ought to be dealt with in the context of the status of the people of Puerto Rico. Section 936 is part of the arrangements we offer for economic development in possessions of the United States. It is their due. They do not have many rights as possessions, as it were. But we gave it to them in the 1920s. To take Section 936 away now in this context, without consultation or a hearing, is not something I would want to see my country do. Nor, I think, would other senators want to do so.[6]

A number of senators contacted previously by the Pharmaceutical Manufacturers' Association, PRUSA, and many individual drug firms also argued against the amendment. For example, Senator Jesse Helms (R-N.C.) said that he had been contacted by two companies in his state, and he would not want to risk hurting their profitability. Moreover, he argued that price controls were "unconstitutional."[7] And in one surprising turnaround, Senator Bill Bradley (D-N.J.) also came to the defense of the of the pharmaceutical companies. He argued,

If 936 is the problem, then I suggest the distinguished Senator from Arkansas introduce a bill to deal with 936. If health care costs is the problem, then deal with all health care costs, deal with hospital costs, deal with physicians costs, and not just pharmaceuticals.

Pharmaceutical costs are only 7 percent of all health care costs in this country. If you are going to deal with only 7 percent of the problem and ignore 93 percent, they you have not really begun to come to grips with what the real problem is.

So I strongly hope that we will reject this amendment and that, instead, we will keep our pharmaceutical industry strong and healthy, generating jobs, generating patents, generating trade surpluses for the United States and most importantly, delivering the drugs that will lengthen the lives of American consumers.[8]

The senator's behavior was remarkable given that fact that he had never represented the companies' position during previous attacks on Section 936 in 1982 and 1986. In fact, Bradley, widely considered the intellectual father of the Tax Reform Act of 1986, had proposed the elimination of the possessions tax break as part of his own version of the tax-reform bill. But in 1992 things were different for the senator. In 1984 he had won reelection with sixty-five percent of the vote, but in 1990 he won by a scant three points. He said that "it was a terrible blow" that made him more receptive to his constituents' interests.[9] These constituents included pharmaceutical companies, one of the biggest employers in New Jersey.[10] A Senate Finance Committee aide explained, "It must have been painful for Senator Bradley to defend 936 because he does not like doing this for the companies, and he would not have done it three years ago." However, it would not be long before Senator Bradley would find himself again defending the interests of the pharmaceutical companies in his state.

The debate over Pryor's amendment lasted for ten hours: thirty senators addressed the amendment during floor debate, highlighting their concerns for the escalating costs of health care and making Section 936 a well-known issue. After the debate, the possessions tax credit ceased to be a relatively obscure and complicated tax break for U.S. companies doing business in Puerto Rico. And while pharmaceutical companies fended off that attack, it was serious enough that some of the firms feeling particularly vulnerable to charges of price gouging—including Johnson and Johnson, G. D. Searle, and Bristol-Myers Squibb, among others—voluntarily decided to limit the rate at which they raised their prices.[11]

After his amendment was defeated, in an effort to give more publicity to the issue, Senator Pryor asked the GAO (the research arm of Congress) for a study about the benefits of Section 936 to pharmaceutical companies. In May 1992 the GAO report was released. It revealed that for some companies the tax savings per employee amounted to more than $70,000. For example, in 1989 Pfizer had five hundred employees in Puerto Rico, it paid them an average salary of about $25,000, and its tax savings per employee were estimated at $156,400.[12] According to an aide to the chairman of the Senate Finance Committee, Lloyd Bentsen (D-Tex.), the senator and others who had traditionally been "sympathetic towards the Commonwealth of Puerto Rico and very sympathetic to Section 936" were "shocked" by the level of benefits. Again, Treasury had been reporting the pharmaceuticals tax savings per employee since publishing its first report on the possessions tax credit in 1978.[13] This time, however, the Treasury staff had an unrelenting ally in Pryor.

Candidate Clinton

To help him in his efforts to make Section 936 an element of the public agenda, Pryor enlisted the support of his friend the Democratic presidential candidate, Bill Clinton. Clinton had made the need to rein in health-care costs and reform the system an integral part of his campaign. And in September 1992, during a major health-care speech at the Merck Pharmaceuticals headquarters, Clinton took the opportunity to endorse "Senator Pryor's proposal to end special breaks for companies that do not keep the cost of traditional, already established drugs with inflation."[14] According to PRUSA, which was closely monitoring the presidential race and was keeping its members informed of any new developments, it was common knowledge that Clinton was referring to the Section 936 tax subsidy. For this reason, PRUSA's members were also keeping a eye on the Puerto Rican elections. The companies wanted to make sure that no matter what happened on the mainland, they could continue to count on the support of Puerto Rican politicians. But status politics on the island were also making Section 936 an election issue in Puerto Rico.

"No Taxation, No Representation"

In the months prior to the November election, PRUSA's executive committee met with the gubernatorial candidates from Puerto Rico's two leading political parties, the Popular Democratic Party (pro–commonwealth status) and the New Progressive Party (prostatehood). PRUSA was concerned that the prostatehood candidate for resident commissioner, Carlos Romero Barceló, a former governor, had become an outspoken critic of Section 936.[15] Barceló had fought for the preservation of Section 936 in 1982 but was now arguing that the tax break impeded Puerto Rican statehood. As explained in chapter 3, Puerto Rican political elites had always associated Section 936 with the commonwealth status. By contrast, if the island were to become the fifty-first state, the tax credit would be automatically repealed, since Puerto Rico would be subject to federal taxation in exchange for political representation. Barceló's reasoning was that as long as Section 936 existed, Puerto Ricans would continue to support commonwealth status.[16]

Barceló's animosity toward the pharmaceutical companies was evident, and PRUSA was concerned that the prostatehood candidate for governor, Pedro Rosselló, felt the same way. But according to PRUSA's chief lobbyist, Peter Holmes, "Rosselló assured PRUSA that the prostatehood party would defend 936 vigorously until Puerto Rico became a state." In other words, Rosselló assured PRUSA's leadership that, if elected, he would not promote the elimination of Section 936 as a means to hurt the presumed economic attractiveness of commonwealth status to Puerto Rican voters. A company representative explained that the companies needed to be sure of Rosselló's support because

> when members of Congress meet with me they know that I represent a special interest. When members meet with the governor of Puerto Rico, even if he does not have much political clout, there is a deference shown to him because he represents the public interests . . . the interests of the Puerto Rican voters who elected him.

Not everyone shared this opinion of the Puerto Rican delegation. Some firms argued that Puerto Rican governors were "pompous" and "always brought a big entourage" that served no practical purpose. Still, PRUSA believed that if Clinton were elected, as long as the Puerto Rican leadership supported Section 936, the new administration would be "receptive." According to Holmes, the expectation was that, "because Clinton had been a governor of a poor state," he would have "an appreciation of the importance of incentives to encourage economic development."

Organized Labor and Section 936

In addition to Senator Pryor's incessant criticism of the drug companies, their prices, and Section 936, other factors coincided to broaden the impact of the tax law and increase the saliency of the issue in Washington. In 1988, American Home Products (AHP), maker of Advil and Anacin, opened a new plant in Puerto Rico. Two years later, the company closed its plant in Indiana and laid off 775 workers, most of them members of the Oil, Chemical, and Atomic Workers Union (OCAW). The union argued that AHP had broken a Puerto Rican law that prohibited U.S. firms from opening plants in Puerto Rico if it resulted in mainland workers losing their jobs. The union brought suit against AHP and charged that Puerto Rican officials had participated in this fraud. The union decided also to investigate whether there were other cases of runaway plants and in 1991 asked the Midwest Center for Labor Research (MCLR) to examine the situation. The resultant MCLR study argued that there were indeed twenty-five examples of plant closures in the United States in which Section 936 had been the motivating factor.[17] In 1992 a class-action suit was filed on behalf of former AHP workers in Indiana, New York, Pennsylvania, and New Jersey. In July of that year the suit was settled out of court when the company agreed to pay $24 million to the workers.

In spite of the fact that Puerto Ricans, who are U.S. citizens, resented labor's categorizing of the transfer of jobs from the mainland as an "example of a third world country trying to steal American jobs," the union persisted.[18] In turn, PRUSA argued that OCAW did not take into consideration the fact that these companies had restructured their worldwide operations, not only those in Puerto Rico and the mainland. For example, in 1988 Allergan, a manufacturer of eye-care products with two plants in Puerto Rico, not only closed its plant in Irvine, California, but also eliminated three hundred jobs worldwide. By 1991, however, the company had created only fifty new jobs in Puerto Rico.[19] OCAW admitted that the MCLR report contained some errors, but the union became a strong supporter of the "runaway plants" bill proposed by Representative Fortney H. "Pete" Stark (D-Calif.). The bill never became law, but its purpose was to strengthen the process by which plant closings on the mainland were monitored.

When Clinton won the November 1992 presidential election, labor wanted him to keep his campaign promise to limit tax breaks that encourage companies to go overseas.[20] According to a White House official, while "President Clinton was not sure that Section 936 should be made part of the issue of jobs going overseas, it was on labor's agenda." But, "during the transition, President Clinton was also being pressured to eliminate Section 936 by Senator Pryor and Barceló." At that time, the context of the discussion was how to pay for health-care reform and how the revenues from Section 936 could be used to pay for Medicaid in Puerto Rico. In the end, however, deficit reduction would enable the staff at the Treasury Department to target Section 936 for elimination once again. But the efforts of Pryor and organized labor would pay off, because by the time the president's deficit-reduction project was sent to Congress, Section 936 had become associated with the perceived abuses of U.S. pharmaceutical companies and with runaway plants.

Campaign Promises

Of Clinton's many campaign promises, cutting the deficit in half by the end of his first term would become the most important. Clinton initially tried to follow his goal to close the "'investment gap' between the United States and its global competitors" by proposing a public investment program.[21] But it was reduced to a modest economic-stimulus plan. Clinton's promise of health-care reform was also postponed, as the deficit hawks in his administration—Leon Panetta, director of Office of Management and Budget and former chairman of the House Budget Committee, and Alice Rivlin, Panetta's deputy and former director of the Congressional Budget Office—convinced Clinton to give priority to deficit reduction. Democrats in Congress also sent the message that deficit control should be emphasized above all else. And Republicans had vowed not to let the president forget his promise to cut the deficit in half.[22]

Once the president and his staff decided the balance between spending cuts and tax increases to meet the goals of deficit reduction, the Office of Management and Budget and the agencies had to come up with the cuts and the Treasury had to come up with the tax revenue. An aide to new Treasury secretary, Lloyd Bentsen recalled, "It was not easy." They had to "raise $250 billion over five years, and there was a lot of pressure to take that number that had been handed to you from above and to put flesh in those bones." He continued, "the problem is that [the White House] hands out numbers with a lot of don't's and little do's." And the president wanted the Treasury staff to find money for things like a new "investment tax credit and the $500 tax credit per child." It would not be long before Section 936 would be targeted for revenues.

II. The Companies' Learned Response

A member of the Treasury staff working on the international tax provisions recalls that after the Tax Reform Act of 1986 "there were not many glaring tax loopholes. There was nothing left to close and not [have it] be called a tax increase." He explains that by 1993 the possessions tax break was among the top five largest corporate tax expenditures; hence, "it was inevitable that 936 would be on the table." In addition, he says that the staff members felt a general animosity toward the pharmaceuticals and sought to "exploit the latent split in the ranks of the companies." To take advantage of this potential rift, the staff began to work on a wage credit to replace the existing Section 936 income credit—a proposal that would hurt the capital-intensive pharmaceuticals more than it would hurt the electronics and other labor-intensive firms. The staff at Treasury knew that the capital-intensive pharmaceuticals would prefer the existing Section 936 because they enjoyed a federal income credit against their Puerto Rican profits. If the income credit was replaced by a wage credit, companies that had few employees would not be able to take advantage of the tax provision as much as labor-intensive firms. While some pharmaceuticals were large employers in Puerto Rico, the industry is not, as a rule, labor-intensive. By contrast, electronics have relatively higher labor costs and could presumably still take advantage of a wage credit.

Contrary to Treasury's habit of dealing only with Puerto Rican officials, this time the department encouraged companies to discuss how the proposal would hurt them. A member of the department's staff recalls that "the PRUSA delegation wanted no changes. That was their basic position. I could not get them to begin having discussions." However, individual companies did contact Treasury: "I got a call from every single lobbyist: Pepsi, Coke, Baxter, Lilly." Some of these companies also opposed any changes, but others were sending the message that while they "did not want a public break with PRUSA," they were willing to talk. Moreover, "some of the companies did not want to rely on PRUSA for information and were very effective at staying in touch." But while the staff at Treasury "kept inviting the companies" in an effort to get them to turn against each other, "the most aggressive lobbying was done by PRUSA," so no negotiations took place.

The companies' behavior was remarkable given the tainted reputation of the drug companies and the fact that the newly elected governor of Puerto Rico was lukewarm in his defense of Section 936. In fact, in private conversations with the Treasury staff, it became evident that the governor was also willing to explore alternatives that would continue the benefits for the labor-intensive companies at the expense of the pharmaceuticals. PRUSA was aware of this situation and advised the government against "prematurely negotiating" the issue with the administration, suggesting instead a fight in Congress. As it had been the case in 1986, PRUSA was confident that it could convince members of Congress to leave Section 936 alone, thereby avoiding a compromise with Treasury.

A number of factors explain the companies' behavior at this time. First, the interests of the companies had remained constant. As tables 14 and 15 show, the companies continued to benefit from Section 936 and to manipulate their worldwide investments to maximize their tax-free profits. Consequently, the companies saw no reason to tinker with the tax break. In fact, one of Treasury's persistent complaints was that after 1982 the companies had managed to get around the increased regulation enacted as part of TEFRA. They had continued to profit from their Puerto Rican operations, and Treasury had not seen a significant increase in revenues. Moreover, new developments also contributed to the continued attractiveness of the tax break for U.S. firms. For example, the Tax Reform Act of 1986 included an alternative minimum tax (AMT) developed by James Baker and Richard Darman, who realized that even with the passage of tax reform, the remaining tax loopholes could still enable large firms to escape taxation.[23] AMT required corporations whose federal tax liability was low to pay a federal tax by an amount stipulated by Congress. But AMT did not apply to the income earned by a possessions corporation, meaning that U.S. firms required to pay a minimum tax payment on profits repatriated to or earned in the U.S. mainland did not have to include their Puerto Rican profits in their calculations.[24] Finally, after many corporate tax breaks such as the investment tax credit were eliminated as part of the Tax Reform Act of 1986, the tax credit in Puerto Rico became even more important. As indicated in table 14, between 1986 and 1992 the possessions tax credit remained the most important factor in reducing many of the companies' federal tax liability. Table 15 shows that the companies continued to structure their international operations to take advantage of the tax break. Accordingly, neither capital- nor labor-intensive firms wanted to negotiate with Treasury simply because they preferred 936 to a wage credit.

The fact that the companies had continued to benefit from the income-tax credit does not suffice to explain their behavior at this time, however. After all, the same group of companies had been benefiting from the tax law for many years, and their political behavior had varied a great deal. The companies explain that in 1993 the decision about whether to negotiate with Treasury was a gamble. A pharmaceutical lobbyist elaborated that the "alternatives are to compromise or gamble. It is like going to Atlantic City: Do you take your winnings if you are ahead, or do you let them ride?" The fact that the decision to negotiate with Treasury was considered a gamble reflects the degree of uncertainty lobbyists felt about the political process. It also suggests that at the same time

TABLE 14. U.S. Firms Reporting a Tax Savings under Section 936, 1986–92 (in percentage points)

	1986	1987	1988	1989	1990	1991	1992
American Home Products	—	—	—	5.7	4.6	6.0	—
Bristol-Myers Squibb	—	—	—	5.0*	5.6*	7.9*	8.7*
Carter-Wallace	10.1*	10.2*	7.0*	6.0*	5.8*	5.8*	5.6*
Digital Communications	2.8*	3.9*	4.8*	7.2*	10.1*	10.0*	10.0*
Eli Lilly	9.2*	10.7*	4.4*	4.1*	5.1*	4.7*	7.0*
Hubbell	6.4*	5.9*	5.3*	5.8*	6.2*	6.2*	6.3*
Johnson and Johnson	25.8*	8.6*	7.0*	9.7*	9.1*	7.8*	9.6*
Marion Merrell Dow	—	—	—	—	—	4.0	—
Medtronic	20.3*	17.3*	10.7*	9.6*	9.1*	8.7*	8.5*
Merck	6.6*	6.3*	3.7*	4.6*	4.3*	5.1*	5.1*
Millipore	15.9	11.1*	8.6*	9.4*	17.7*	8.0*	9.8*
Pall	18.7*	13.2*	7.6*	7.7*	4.4*	3.3*	5.3*
Schering-Plough	15.4*	11.7*	9.2*	9.0*	8.4*	7.5*	6.8*
Sterling Drug	6.4*	—	—	—	—	—	—
Timberland	55.0*	23.5*	21.0*	37.0*	34.0*	18.2*	15.7*
Upjohn	19.9*	15.2*	9.1*	9.4*	9.1*	12.5*	11.0*
U.S. Surgical	13.6*	13.7*	10.0*	9.2*	7.8*	9.0*	12.9*
Westinghouse	12.2*	7.8*	—	—	—	—	—
Federal Statutory Tax Rate	46%	40%	34%	34%	34%	34%	34%

Source: 10-K reports, 1986, 1987, 1988, 1989, 1990, 1991, 1992.

(—) Information not available or no tax savings reported.

*Indicates that the possessions tax break was the most important factor reducing federal taxes.

that Washington lobbyists have become more savvy, the political process has also continued to become more uncertain. Hence, in 1993 the companies were united in their decision not to negotiate with Treasury because they relied on their past experiences to deal with an uncertain political environment. The companies believed that their collective refusal to negotiate during the process leading to the Tax Reform Act of 1986 had resulted in the maintenance of the tax break at that time.

Moreover, while it might be argued that firms made a conscious decision not to negotiate, interviews revealed that their behavior was not the result of a reassessment of past strategy or an adaptation to the new political environment. Rather, another lobbyist simply explained that "in general the mode was to defend 936." Another lobbyist agreed: "At the beginning of every dispute, one of the things we should do is always do a review of assets to see if we have what it takes to get what we want." He explained that in 1993 the companies did not take the time to evaluate their position; rather, "we were united at the beginning because it was the strategy that had worked before." The response that had succeeded in 1986 clearly was being automatically invoked.

It should be noted that not all of the companies were united in the belief that a no-negotiation strategy was the most appropriate at the time. One lobbyist explained that some companies "did read the situation correctly, but they did

TABLE 15.   Tax-Free Puerto Rican Earnings as a Percentage of Consolidated after-Tax Earnings, 1986–92

	1986	1987	1988	1989	1990	1991	1992
American Home Products	—	—	—	16.7	13.5	17.6	—
Bristol-Myers Squibb	—	—	—	14.7	16.4	23.2	25.5
Carter-Wallace	21.9	25.5	20.5	17.6	17.0	17.0	25.5
Digital Communications	6.0	9.7	14.1	21.1	29.7	24.4	29.4
Eli Lilly	20.0	26.7	12.9	12.0	15.0	13.8	20.5
Hubbell	13.9	14.7	15.5	17.0	18.2	18.2	18.5
Johnson and Johnson	56.0	21.5	20.5	28.5	26.7	22.9	28.2
Marion Merrell Dow	—	—	—	—	—	11.7	—
Medtronic	44.1	43.2	31.4	28.2	26.7	25.5	25.0
Merck	14.3	15.7	10.8	13.5	12.6	15.0	15.0
Millipore	34.5	27.7	25.2	27.6	52.0	23.5	28.8
Pall	40.6	33.0	22.3	22.6	12.9	9.7	15.5
Schering-Plough	33.4	29.2	27.0	26.4	24.7	22.0	20.0
Sterling Drug	13.9	—	—	—	—	—	—
Timberland	—	58.7	61.7	—	—	53.52	46.1
Upjohn	43.2	38.0	26.7	27.6	26.7	36.7	32.3
U.S. Surgical	29.5	34.2	29.4	27.0	22.9	26.4	37.9
Westinghouse	26.5	19.5	—	—	—	—	—

Source: 10-K reports, 1986, 1987, 1988, 1989, 1990, 1991, 1992.

(—) Information not available or no tax savings reported.

not have the power to change the strategy." As a result, a critical mass of firms doing business in Puerto Rico followed the same strategy, and Treasury officials could not get any company to negotiate seriously.

While the companies were keeping abreast of new developments regarding the tax break, they essentially did not reassess their strategy in spite of the fact that the political environment in 1993 differed markedly from 1986. This time Section 936 had been made part of the public agenda by a broader group of government actors. Pharmaceuticals were under attack in the Senate for their level of benefits, all of the companies doing business in Puerto Rico under the rules of Section 936 were being criticized by House members and organized labor for their presumed runaway activities, and the Puerto Rican prostatehood administration was less than forthcoming in its defense of the existing tax break because it was associated with the opposition party. But while the companies may seem oblivious to the new political environment in Washington, their behavior at the time is consistent with the prevalent view of lobbying.

Business lobbyists are experienced individuals who know the political process, pursue their clients' interests through a variety of channels, and do not rely on trade organizations or issue groups (such as PRUSA) to keep them abreast of new developments.[25] At the same time, however, lobbyists are not always sure of how to advance their clients' interests under the conditions of political uncertainty in which they repeatedly find themselves. Accordingly, in 1993 it was one thing for pharmaceutical, electronics, and other companies with operations in Puerto Rico to keep up with developments relevant to Section 936 and quite another to reassess their united strategy of no negotiation even though they knew that their interests were seriously threatened by a new political environment. Feeling that the decision to negotiate was a gamble, a critical mass of firms did not negotiate simply because refusing to compromise had worked in 1986. After all, what need did firms have to come up with their own counterproposal if they expected their strategy to succeed? As the political process progressed, however, the companies began to adapt to the new political environment, and as in 1982 the default strategy would be divided lobbying.

III. The Budget Process

In February, during his State of the Union Address, President Clinton unveiled the largest deficit-cutting plan in history. He proposed to cut the deficit by $493 billion in four years, $247 billion in spending cuts and $246 in tax increases. The plan would raise $7 billion from Section 936. The changes to Section 936 included the elimination of the 100 percent credit on income and its replacement with a 65 percent credit on wages paid.[26] There was no doubt that the proposal was meant to hurt the capital-intensive pharmaceutical companies more than the labor-intensive companies. The *New York Times* reported that Wall Street was predicting that the proposal to change Section 936 would be costly for pharmaceuticals:

> Pfizer would have to absorb a 13.9 percent decline in earnings the first year . . . while Upjohn's earnings would fall 13 percent. Next would be Bristol-Myers, with a potential decline of 9 percent, followed by Merck, Schering-Plough, Eli Lilly and American Home Products, all off 6 to 7 percent.[27]

Reacting to the president's proposal, Pfizer, AHP, Merck, and Bristol-Myers hired the services of the Chicago law firm of Winston and Strawn, where former House Ways and Means Committee member Beryl F. Anthony was now a partner. Anthony was also a "friend of Bill," and his wife was assistant secretary of the Treasury for legislation. This action did not mean that the companies had broken ranks with PRUSA; rather, they had decided to employ the services of a Washington insider to help them in the general effort to retain the income credit.

The Debate Moves to Congress

On 18 March House Democrats approved a budget resolution that contained President Clinton's recommendations for tax increases and spending cuts virtually unchanged. After the budget resolution passed, it was now time for the chairman of the Ways and Means Committee, Dan Rostenkowski (D-Ill.) to examine Clinton's tax plan.[28] Rostenkowski wanted to give Clinton what he wanted and promised to work hard to pass the administration's tax provisions. The committee held hearings on the issue, and from the testimony and discussion it became evident that the controversy over runaway plants and Pryor's GAO report had managed to place Section 936 at the top of the agenda. While some committee members associated Section 936 with Puerto Rico's economic well-being, many saw it primarily as a tax break for U.S. firms that was robbing mainland Americans of their jobs and making pharmaceutical companies rich at the expense of U.S. mainland taxpayers. This situation clearly presented a problem for all companies benefiting from Section 936 because, as Representative Charles Rangel (D-N.Y.) pointed out, "the popularity of pharmaceuticals was falling down below the popularity of even members of Congress."[29]

During the hearing, representatives from the Puerto Rican prostatehood administration tepidly defended Section 936 and pointed out that Congress should consider enterprise zones for Puerto Rico. By contrast, the mayor of San Juan, a member of the procommonwealth party, forcefully defended Section 936 and criticized the administration's wage-credit proposal.[30] Representatives from OCAW and from the United Rubber, Cork, Linoleum, and Plastics Workers union both testified in favor of the administration's changes to Section 936. The latter came on behalf of union workers at the Acme Boot Company in Clarksville, Tennessee. The company had announced plans to begin laying off workers January 1994. According to the union, the situation in Clarksville was yet another example of a runaway plant. Both witnesses also expressed their support for two new bills cosponsored by Representatives Stark and Tim Romer (D-Ind.) that would deny the tax benefits of Section 936 to runaway plants. The night before the hearings began, the CBS Evening News ran a segment about the Acme Company. Rangel said that he found it problematic that the CBS piece referred to Puerto Rico as a foreign country, but in the hearings Treasury Secretary Bentsen responded that a tax break of "$70,000 per employee" needed to be "reassess[ed]."[31]

Representative Nydia Velázquez (D-N.Y.) and the National Puerto Rican Coalition testified on behalf of Puerto Ricans living on the mainland who were concerned about what would happen to their families living on the island. The companies were represented at the hearings by PRUSA, the Emergency Committee for American Trade (representing sixty Fortune 500 firms), the Puerto Rican Manufacturers' Association, and the Puerto Rico Private Sector Coalition (representing twenty-nine island organizations). During their testimony the companies sought to present a united front. PRUSA's representative argued that the administration's wage-credit proposal did not recognize that Puerto Rico should be able to attract both capital- and labor-intensive firms. These witnesses attempted to convince the committee members that Section 936 was not about a tax credit for U.S. companies in general or pharmaceuticals in particular but about the economy of Puerto Rico; that if the administration proposal were enacted, the companies would leave Puerto Rico, and hence the tax revenues from the elimination of the income credit would never be realized; that to assume that if the companies left Puerto Rico they would relocate on the U.S. mainland would be a mistake; and that "if productive employment opportunities are not made available for the Puerto Rican people, their only alternative may be welfare or migration to the mainland."[32]

After the hearings, the companies continued to maintain a united front, and PRUSA offered no alternative to the administration's proposal. No doubt the companies' unity was under considerable strain as they were forced for the first time to lobby an unsympathetic Puerto Rican administration at the same time that they lobbied the Clinton administration and the U.S. Congress. At this time New Jersey–based Johnson and Johnson began circulating a plan for a "Mainland Grassroots Initiative in Support of Section 936." The memo suggested, among other things, a television and radio public-relations campaign and emphasized that the "message must have a Hispanic flavor" to "stir emotion in the mainland Hispanic community."[33]

The companies then learned that the Puerto Rican governor had made a counterproposal to the Clinton administration during a governors' meeting in Washington, D.C. The governor suggested the elimination of the income credit and its replacement with a 100 percent wage credit and a 10 percent credit for new capital investments. Like the administration's proposal, the governor's was clearly designed to benefit the labor-intensive firms and offered very little to the capital-intensive firms, especially when compared to the existing income credit.[34] The proposal was declared "dead on arrival" at Treasury, but it prompted the CEOs of two pharmaceutical firms and two electronics companies to fly to Puerto Rico for a meeting with the governor. According to a participant, during the meeting, the CEOs of Abbott Laboratories, Bristol-Myers Squibb, Medtronic, and Millipore urged the governor "to take a more active position in support of the [existing Section 936] and to modify his own proposal in order to develop broader-based support among the companies." In other words, these companies wanted the governor to support the maintenance of the income credit. Two weeks later, on 27 April, the governor appeared before the Senate Finance Committee and for the first time strongly defended the existing Section 936. He also unveiled yet another proposal that attempted to satisfy both capital- and labor-intensive firms.[35]

That same day, Moynihan and his wife, Elizabeth, had a private dinner invitation from the Clintons. The senator took the opportunity to repeat to the president the argument that he had made during the debate over Pryor's amendment a year before—essentially, that Section 936 was more than just a corporate tax break and that it could bring serious consequences for the U.S.–Puerto Rican economic and political relationship. Moynihan also suggested that a drastic change in tax policy could lead Puerto Ricans to vote for statehood in an upcoming plebiscite. The president could not let the Senate enact the administration's proposed changes to Section 936.[36] Clinton, however, did not change his mind about Section 936 at this time. According to an administration official, "the White House viewed the tax break as a tax provision for the U.S. companies, and [since] the drug companies were fighting health-care reform, [they] did not have much access with the administration."

IV. Default Strategy: Divided Lobbying

As the Ways and Means Committee was coming close to a vote and it was becoming increasingly clear that its members were going to adopt the president's plan unchanged, the first public break with PRUSA materialized. On 10 May Allergan began to circulate a proposal that provided for an enhanced wage credit and no income credit. At this point, the companies' united front began to deteriorate rapidly. Labor-intensive companies began to meet among themselves and with the Puerto Rican administration. PRUSA lobbyists and capital-intensive firms were not invited to these meetings. A lobbyist for a medical-products firm recalled that initially, "we did not push for a wage credit, but as the threat became more serious, we became smart." Because their 1986 experience had been a success, PRUSA members initially repeated their united strategy unreflectively and automatically. But the political environment had changed since the tax-reform debates, and firms were finally realizing that their strategy was not working as effectively as before. Labor-intensive firms explained that they suddenly realized that they were being brought down by the pharmaceuticals, which created fewer jobs and had no real defense for the level of their profits in Puerto Rico. (Another GAO report released in July but whose content was common knowledge earlier estimated that in 1989 all pharmaceuticals combined had 18,011 employees in Puerto Rico; electronics had 21,256; scientific instruments, 8,483; and apparel, 19,611.)[37] Accordingly, the labor group began to lobby for a better wage credit than the one offered by the administration. The fate of Section 936 was slowly becoming a zero-sum game. The labor group was proposing the elimination of the existing Section 936 income credit favored by the pharmaceuticals in exchange for an enhanced wage credit.

Pharmaceuticals tried to argue that the quality of the jobs they created in Puerto Rico was not being recognized. A pharmaceutical lobbyist explained,

> For example, let's say Sara Lee has 5,000 employees, and it pays them minimum wage. Pfizer has 1,000 and it pays them $40,000. How do you say that Pfizer jobs are no good and Sara Lee's jobs are? We were always on the defensive, and we looked silly saying, "We are here to defend [a] $100,000 [tax credit] per job."

Moreover, pharmaceuticals argued that not all of them were small employers in Puerto Rico. Yes, their tax benefits per worker were greater than those for other firms, but some pharmaceuticals also employed a lot of people in Puerto Rico. For example, Johnson and Johnson employed 3,354 workers, compared to General Electric's 3,555.[38]

The companies ultimately could not prevent the committee from voting in favor of the administration's deficit-reduction plan, which, in addition to the proposed changes to Section 936, also included a provision against runaway plants.[39] Two weeks later, on 27 May, the House voted on the deficit-reduction bill. The president narrowly won, 219 to 213.[40] For weeks Rangel, who could not mount a credible defense for Section 936 in light of the equivocal behavior of the Puerto Rican administration, had been saying to the companies, "If you want to stop this, you have to go to the Senate side, where party unity is not so strong, and try to protect it." The time had come: the debate would now move to the Senate Finance Committee under the chairmanship of Senator Moynihan. Senator Bradley and Senator Pryor were also members of the committee, in which Democrats had only an eleven to nine majority.

PRUSA Decides to Negotiate

As the battle moved to the Senate, the Puerto Rican Manufacturers' Association and some individual companies began to mobilize the New York Puerto Rican community. The companies had also contacted state and local officials with large Puerto Rican constituencies, prompting New York Mayor David Dinkins and Governor Mario Cuomo to write letters urging the Senate to modify the House version of the tax provision.[41] At this point, however, it seemed that PRUSA could do nothing to prevent some companies from turning against each other. A lobbyist for the organization explained,

> We said to the companies, "Go and argue your position, but don't do it at the expense of others." Within the labor-intensive umbrella, Allergan, Sara Lee, and Baxter broke ranks. Allergan in a very public way started to openly criticize the income credit and produce its own reports arguing that it was a waste.

On 2 June PRUSA had an "emergency" meeting of its board of directors.[42] For the first time since Clinton proposed the elimination of Section 936, PRUSA decided officially to offer a compromise plan that included both an income- and a wage-credit option (the latter would now be referred to as the economic-activity credit). In other words, faced with the possibility that the income credit could be eliminated entirely, PRUSA's executive committee decided to change its no-negotiation strategy and offer instead a plan that sought to maintain a balance between the new interests of the labor-intensive firms and the capital-intensive firms. A few days later, however, as Bradley's staff was being briefed on PRUSA's counterproposal, rumors began to circulate that while Moynihan might be open to new suggestions, Pryor adamantly opposed the maintenance of an income credit.[43] Pryor had persisted in his attack on the tax break and two days before the president's State of the Union Address had introduced his own bill to eliminate the Section 936 income credit and replace it with a 40 percent wage credit.[44]

As these events took place in the Senate, the White House was trying to deal with the reaction of the Congressional Black Caucus to the president's decision to withdraw Lani Guinier's nomination as assistant attorney general. In an effort to make amends, the White House invited the members of the caucus to meet with the president. Wanting to make a statement, the caucus voted to refuse the invitation.[45] The White House then decided to invite three members of Congress who were Puerto Rican, represented Puerto Rican constituencies, and had been trying to meet with the president. According to one White House official, the members were invited because "we did not want it to look like the president was rejecting minorities." During their meeting with the president, Representatives Velázquez, Luis V. Gutiérrez (D-Ill.), and José Serrano (D-N.Y.) told the president that while they had voted for the deficit-reduction plan, they did not support the changes to Section 936. Specifically, they did not want the income credit to be eliminated entirely. By all accounts, the members reminded Clinton that the passage of the budget-reconciliation bill in the House had been secured by only three votes. This time the president promised that he would retain some of the tax credit.[46] Publicly, however, the White House gave no indication that Clinton had changed his mind about Section 936.

All Politics Is Local

Back in the Senate, as the different companies continued to promote their own versions of an income and economic-activity credit, Bradley and Pryor were trying to negotiate a solution. Moynihan had decided to let the two senators come up with a compromise. But Bradley, who was representing the interests of the pharmaceutical companies in his state, refused to allow the elimination of the income credit. According to one of the insiders hired to help the pharmaceuticals, Pryor ultimately agreed to a compromise because the White House intervened at last to "help calm down" the senator. On 18 June the Senate Finance Committee voted to support a deficit-reduction bill that included a reduced income credit from 100 percent to 60 percent in 1994, decreasing by 5 percent each subsequent year until it reached 40 percent in 1998. The bill also included an economic-activity credit of 95 percent of wages and fringe benefits, a percentage of depreciation, and a share of taxes paid to the Puerto Rican government. The Senate committee bill did not include a runaway provision.

Bradley was highly criticized for his role in the Section 936 issue. For example, the same day that the Finance Committee voted to send its version of the reconciliation bill to the Senate floor, the *Wall Street Journal* published an editorial arguing that Bradley, the "tax reformer," had worked behind the scenes to protect a tax break that was only meant to help New Jersey pharmaceutical companies with operations in Puerto Rico and that had to be paid with "a 10 percent surcharge on capital gains." "This virtuoso maneuver," continued the editorial, "sums up the logic of the emerging Senate tax bill: Puerto Rico needs to keep low taxes but America doesn't."[47] A member of the Treasury staff who had worked on the wage-credit proposal argued that "it was a complete exercise of political power that [the companies] managed to get Bradley to become completely stubborn. He was willing to bring the bill down." One of Bradley's aides defended the senator, saying, "the companies do not have as much influence [over Bradley as] Senator Pryor or as the reports on TV say." On the other hand, the aide continued, "the largest employer in the state is the pharmaceutical industry, so it is legit [for the senator] to ask 'If I do this to 936, how would it affect our state?'" On 25 June, minutes after 3 a.m., Vice President Al Gore cast the tie-breaking vote in favor of the Finance Committee's version of the deficit-reduction plan. Not a single Republican voted for the measure. Only after the Senate vote did Clinton finally publicly endorse the new version of the tax law.[48]

The Companies' Lobbying Effort Continues

The time had come for the Conference Committee to harmonize the House and Senate versions of the mammoth reconciliation bills. It was expected that the most controversial issue would be the broad energy tax (based on heat content or British thermal units [BTUs]) proposed by the administration and passed by the House but eliminated in the Senate and replaced with a 4.3-cents-per-gallon gas tax. The BTU tax was expected to raise $72 billion, while the gas tax was expected to raise $23 billion. Hence, to find money to cover the differences between the House and Senate versions, it was predicted that Section 936 could also become a contested issue.[49]

While the Puerto Rican government maintained that the Senate version of Section 936 had been a victory, none of the companies were satisfied, and they continued to lobby members of the conference committee. In July the *National Journal* reported that the controversy over Section 936 "had Washington lobbyists ringing their cash registers," as more individual companies began to hire lobbying firms to promote their particular interests.[50] And, as in 1982, the last time the companies had engaged in divided lobbying, CEOs came to Washington to pressure members of the Conference Committee in person. On 12 July the CEOs of Abbott Laboratories and Johnson and Johnson met with Rostenkowski to urge him to hold the reduction in the income credit at 60 percent. Two days later the CEOs of G. D. Searle, Baxter, Motorola, Sara Lee, and Warner-Lambert, all Illinois-based companies, also met with members of Congress from their districts and offered suggestions as to how to improve the economic-activity credit. Allergan, General Electric, Pepsico, U.S. Surgical, and Westinghouse, among others, continued to propose yet another version of the economic-activity credit at the expense of the income credit.[51]

In the end, the Conference Committee adopted the Senate Finance Committee's version of Section 936.[52] The new provision was expected to raise $3.8 billion and contained both an income credit and an economic-activity credit.[53] On 5 August the House passed the Conference Committee's version of the Omnibus Budget Reconciliation Act of 1993 by a vote of 218 to 216. Representatives Gutiérrez, Velázquez, and Serrano voted for the bill. The next day the Senate approved the measure by a vote of fifty-one to fifty, with Gore again casting the tie-breaking vote. On 9 August, the following Monday, drug stocks took a hit as Wall Street analysts lowered their earnings estimates for the industry as a result of the changes to Section 936.[54]

Everyone Is Dissatisfied

The companies were not happy with either the political outcome or the political strategy. Pharmaceuticals had only been able to salvage part of their income credit, and the labor-intensive companies felt that the final version of the economic-activity credit was not as good as it could have been. Some labor-intensive firms felt that they should have negotiated earlier for a better wage credit. As a medical-products company representative explained, in retrospect, "the pharmaceuticals had lost the public-relations battle," and the labor-intensive firms failed to react to it in time. Some of the pharmaceuticals also felt that they should have been more open to negotiation rather than maintaining their "no deals" attitude throughout most of the process. Conversely, some firms argued that had the companies kept their unity throughout the process, they would have gotten more. But the behavior of the Puerto Rican prostatehood administration made it hard for the companies to work together. Ultimately, many companies believed that the 1993 legislation signaled the end of PRUSA. Two provisions now separated the labor-intensive and capital-intensive firms. And, as a pharmaceutical company representative explained, "once you have a wage and an income credit, you might as well disband."

V. Conclusion

The behavior of U.S. firms doing business in Puerto Rico during the process leading to the enactment of the Omnibus Budget Reconciliation Act of 1993 lends support to the learning view proposed in this study. Faced with a fluid and uncertain political environment, the companies initially responded unreflectively. They relied on the same united front and no-negotiation stance that they believed contributed to political success in 1986. In spite of the fact that they were faced with a new political environment, the labor-intensive firms did not reflect on how they were being hurt by their association with the drug companies; and the latter refused to negotiate with the Treasury staff or the Ways and Means Committee. In the words of one pharmaceutical lobbyist, "if [we] had ascertained the political situation, [we] would have behaved differently." He continued, "experienced political operatives misjudged the situation [because] we always try to fight the last war."

Whether a different political strategy by the companies would have led to a different outcome is of course difficult to tell. The pharmaceuticals and

Section 936 were being targeted by the administration, the Treasury staff, the Puerto Rican leadership, organized labor, and influential members of Congress. At the same time, the administration needed to figure out ways to raise revenue for deficit reduction, and the tax break had become one of the largest corporate tax expenditures. And yet, in her work on tax policy, Martin has shown that "state actors are catalysts in mobilizing interests and coalitions" between business in an effort to acquire "legitimation." Specifically, in exchange for business support, administration officials are willing to accommodate the interests of those firms with whom they have established communication.[55] In 1993 Treasury wanted to favor the labor-intensive firms at the expense of the pharmaceuticals. So it is conceivable that had the labor-intensive firms negotiated with Treasury officials early on, they could have succeeded in protecting their interests more effectively.

CHAPTER 7

Conclusion: Learning, Influence, and the Transfer of Knowledge

The organization seeks to avoid uncertainty by following regular procedures and a policy of reacting to feedback rather than forecasting the environment.

—Cyert and March (1963, 113)

The study of politics is currently shaped by an emphasis on institutions.[1] The
state's role in formulating domestic policy has been explained as a factor of policy legacies and in formulating foreign policy as a factor of historical learning.[2]
Political scientists have also produced empirical evidence of the impact of past
experiences on the political preferences and behavior of economic institutions.
Examples include studies of U.S. business's political responses to consumer
and environmental regulation, its organizational disposition in the 1970s, and
its understanding of its interests during the health-care debate in the early
1990s.[3] These studies suggest that the time, money, and effort firms spend pursuing political objectives and the type of strategy they adopt is a factor of past
experiences. In this book I have detailed the process by which firms learn from
past success and failure and provided empirical evidence from a case study over
a twenty-year period.

I. Learning and Political Strategies

The approach proposed in this book builds on the theoretical works of David
Truman, Charles Lindblom, James March, Cathie Jo Martin, Herbert Simon,
and others to explain business's strategic behavior in the political arena. I argue that business learning, dominant issues, and government structures are important factors shaping business political behavior. The essence of experiential
learning is that actors accumulate experiences of various kinds, which they in-
voke when dealing with current challenges under conditions of uncertainty.
The fundamental basis of political action thus becomes an unreflective type of
behavior drawing on the lessons learned from prior experiences. Centered on
attempts to protect an important tax break for business, the possessions tax

battles provided an appropriate case for examining the value of the business learning approach. The costs of failure to protect the tax break were clear to business, as my field interviews revealed, and the evidence presented demonstrates that even when business seems to be sure of its preferences, it does not necessarily know how best to advance them regardless of the superior structural and economic resources at its disposal. Uncertainty about the outcome encourages firms to be attentive to politics. But because firms operate in a fluid and complex political environment with multiple interests to pursue and because companies gather more information than they process, they also experience uncertainty about which strategy is most likely to maximize their influence.[4] As a result, firms' initial reaction to political threats to their interests reflect their internal biases and is more a response to prior experiences than to current political events.

In the prevailing view of lobbying, corporations employ the same repertoire of tactical options to promote and protect their interests as do other interest groups. They contact members of Congress, appointed officials, and other lobbyists; engage in fund-raising activities; direct PAC contributions; and try to mobilize public opinion in an effort to maximize their influence.[5] Yet dominant theoretical and empirical evidence suggests that critical determinants of business influence are more precisely its structural power to cause unemployment, its decision to mobilize, and, when it does, the extent to which its political effort is fragmented or united.[6] Firms are implicitly aware of these choices, especially since the explosion of organized interest activity over the past thirty years, because they share a common political past and culture. As Vogel points out, "the efforts of particular industries and firms to achieve their political objectives do not take place in isolation."[7]

How firms decide which strategy to pursue among the existing alternatives has been a central theme of this book. The study was divided into four major political events, but the number of observations that I sought to explain were six: business's various responses to political attacks to its interests. This historical and multiple-observation case-study approach suggests that business strategies vary a great deal over time and throughout the political process, depending on the relative impact of learning, salient issues, and government structures. In response to political threats to relatively constant interests, firms may rely on their structural power, as the companies in this study did in 1976 and during the initial phase of 1993; they may operate as an issue-based interest group, as they did in 1986 and during the initial phase of 1993; or they may pursue their own narrow, individual interests, as they did during the adaptive phases of 1982 and 1993. Each time an effort was made to verify that the behavior the companies described during the interviews coincided with public officials' perceptions of business political strategies. The tendency of a critical mass of firms to use past experiences to guide their political behavior was indirectly corroborated by the government officials who participated in the different tax battles.

The behavior of the companies in this study varied so much, especially from 1982 to 1993, that it might be argued that firms change their strategies at random. But what at first glance appears to be haphazard behavior is, on closer look, a clearly discernible pattern. This pattern can best be understood if the learning view is incorporated. At each political juncture the companies' initial understanding of new political realities was shaped by their political experiences in the preceding period. Their political strategies were guided by what they had learned from prior successes and failures. When firms perceived their past behavior to have succeeded, they repeated it. When they perceived their past behavior to have failed, they experimented with a different strategy. When the political environment to which they had to respond proved different from the circumstances encountered in the preceding period, firms changed their strategy in an effort to adapt. But whenever they tried to respond to a new political environment during the adaptive phase of the political process, firms inevitably engaged in divided lobbying. In the absence of an agreement on anything else, firms reverted back on an individualized strategy, paying little regard to the interests of business as a group.

Beginning in 1973, labor attacks on U.S. multinationals made the taxation of foreign income a dominant political issue. To protect their interests, companies doing business in Puerto Rico relied on the implicit threat of an investment strike on the island. There is no evidence to suggest that the companies based their strategy on past legislative successes. It is likely, however, that their behavior was grounded on the knowledge that they had never had to mobilize for the protection of their federal tax interests in Puerto Rico. As the political process progressed, the taxation of multinationals ceased to be a dominant political issue, and a powerful committee chairman had the freedom to be sensitive to the incentives presumably needed to encourage American investment in Puerto Rico. There was no need for the companies to change their strategy of relying on their structural power to cause unemployment in Puerto Rico. During the initial phase of the political process leading to the TEFRA in 1982, the companies repeated the behavior that they perceived to have succeeded in 1976. But the firms' reliance on an investment-strike strategy proved ineffective, as Section 936 was targeted for elimination when budget deficits became the most important factor influencing tax legislation. Uncertainty about the outcome and the process was heightened by a now decentralized Congress in which the companies could no longer rely on sympathetic committee chairs to protect their interests. Issue transformation and shifting government structures required the companies to update their political strategies.

During the adaptive phase of the process, companies doing business in Puerto Rico decided to mobilize for political action and engaged in fragmented lobbying. The resulting legislation reduced firms' flexibility to manipulate their federal tax liabilities through the use of Section 936. Whether firms could have secured a different outcome in 1982 had they engaged in collective action is difficult to tell. But firms make inferences about the impact of their behavior on the outcome of policy, and 936 companies believed that they lost a significant portion of the break because of their failure to mobilize early in the process and their unwillingness to unite for political action.

After TEFRA the companies realized that a looming budget deficit and decentralized committee structures represented a dangerous threat to Section 936. Their ability to learn from prior experiences led the companies to unite. When the next political attack materialized during the process leading to the Tax Reform Act of 1986, the companies initially remained true to their commitment for collective action. The companies had no need to change their political strategy during the adaptive phase of the political process because from the beginning it seemed that their collective strategy would suffice to protect their Puerto Rican benefits. This political strategy does not provide a complete explanation for the maintenance of Section 936 in 1986, yet firms were convinced that their unity had been key to their victory. Hence, in 1993 they initially repeated their collective-action strategy because they believed it would prove to be as successful as it had been before. But this time the political environment differed remarkably. During the adaptive phase of the process, the companies realized that the collective strategy was hurting rather than helping them in their efforts to protect their Section 936 benefits. As in 1982, the companies were forced to reject their initial strategy in favor of their default strategy, divided lobbying.

All of the strategies employed by business were to some extent complementary. Whether U.S. firms were relying on their implicit threat to cause unemployment or mobilizing for political action, the ultimate message was structural. Hence, when the companies mobilized during the second phase of 1982 and in 1986 and 1993, the message that they were trying to convey was that they would be forced to leave Puerto Rico if the benefits of the possessions tax credit were reduced or eliminated. The companies mobilized to convince policymakers that if the industry could no longer operate profitably in Puerto Rico, the island's role as the showcase of democracy in the Caribbean, the jobs of constituents employed by affiliates on the mainland, or U.S. national-security interests during the cold war would be at risk. In 1976 and during the initial phase of 1982 U.S. pharmaceutical and electronics firms assumed that policymakers would be aware of the incentives businesses need to invest. By contrast, during the adaptive phase of 1982 and in 1986 and 1993, companies were forced to become familiar with the particular interests of policymakers, devise valid arguments, and formulate an active strategy to convey them.

II. Political Power and the Meaning of Learning

Given firms' ability to learn and adapt to new political environments, why does experience not guarantee victory in the political arena, especially when interests remain relatively constant? As discussed in chapter 1, politically active firms "stay close to their particular business."[8] However, firms' political preferences are not necessarily clearly identified. Firms' interests and goals are not easily delineated because organizations "do not have simple, consistent preference functions, [and they] exhibit internal conflict over preferences."[9] As a result, even if firms pursue interests relevant to their business operations, their preferences cannot be reduced to an easily identified concern with profits. Their political behavior also cannot be predicted by assuming a profit motive because firms may not even be aware of the economic impact of politics.[10] In their classic, *American Business and Public Policy,* Bauer, Pool, and Dexter tried to predict the behavior of firms on the basis of a profit motive and were surprised to find that business was indifferent to the political process. They concluded, however, that the cost and benefits of legislation were not as clear to business as the authors had originally presumed. But even when economic concerns are clearly important, firms may not know how to translate their interests into policy positions. Martin shows that willingness to explore new policy alternatives and participation in policy networks also shape firms' policy preferences.[11] An important aspect of the political battles regarding the possessions tax break is that even when profits are clearly at stake and firms are aware of their political preferences, their political strategies are not readily formulated.

This study makes a distinction between the formulation of business preferences and the formulation of a strategy to advance those interests, finding that firms do not necessarily know how best to advance clearly defined interests. Firms in this study were aware of the costs and benefits of the possessions tax credit. Even in 1976, when their interests were first challenged by the legislative process, most of these firms had been investing in Puerto Rico for quite some time and had been fighting the Internal Revenue Service's efforts to reduce the level of tax-free profits through regulation. The companies' interest in the possessions tax credit remained relatively constant for more than twenty years. If anything, the importance of Section 936 was heightened with the enactment of the Tax Reform Act of 1986, which eliminated other important tax breaks, such as the investment-tax credit. But no matter how much experience the companies acquired by defending the tax break, their political strategies had to be reformulated because while firms are capable of learning from past experiences, doing so does not guarantee that they will be victorious in the future. Accordingly, the firms in this study won in 1976 and 1986 but lost in 1982 and 1993. As their political fortunes fluctuated, so did the lessons they learned from the particular experiences. It is important to note that these firms were mostly large firms that had developed their own independent capacities for political activity. This fact makes it even more remarkable that in spite of their superior economic resources, no amount of experience could help the companies be sure of which political strategy to adopt when their interests were threatened. Still, success or failure depended in part on how well or poorly their perception of the political context matched the actual context in which they were implementing their strategy.

It might be argued that firms can never be certain of victory because they learn wrong lessons. But that did not seem to be the case for the firms in this study. What reason did they have to mobilize in 1982, if prior experience indicated that their structural power to cause unemployment would suffice to protect their interests? Was it a mistake to organize for collective action when relying on their structural power alone and their fragmented lobbying had failed to protect their interests in 1982? What other lesson could they have drawn from their experiment with collective action in 1986 other than that it was a successful strategy for the protection of their interests?

There are a number of reasons that explain why learning from past experiences does not guarantee victory in the political arena. First, organizational learning does not concern outcomes but processes.[12] The right lessons can be drawn from past experiences and will become part of an automatic-response system. But the past political environment is not necessarily the best source of information about the future. New political issues and/or shifting government structures destroy policy subsystems and strain old political alliances. In 1982 the combination of exploding budget deficits and a decentralized Congress led to a new political environment. In 1993 by the time Section 936 became part of the budget process, it had been redefined as a tax break for the cash-rich, price-gouging pharmaceuticals and an incentive for firms to transfer jobs out of the U.S. mainland. The political system does not lend itself to much predictability, and the firms could not prepare for the extent to which a new political environment could render old political strategies ineffective. Their immediate response to new political threats to their interests was, however, consistent with previous strategic choices.

The learning approach I propose conforms with the contemporary view of lobbying. The proliferation of business representation in Washington suggests that most firms have learned that they must pay attention to the political process. Today firms' surveillance activities are encoded in their organizational memory.[13] This learning is long term and is not easily subject to change. In some cases, firms try to get as much information as they can about political issues even before they have a big stake in the political outcome. For example, Genentech, a biotechnology company, became a member of PRUSA in 1993. The company's Washington representative explained that it needed to keep track of new developments regarding Section 936 because Genentech was "considering a second investment in Puerto Rico." After the events of 1993, the company decided to place its new manufacturing facility in California and resigned from PRUSA. But in addition to their surveillance activities, firms still must decide which strategy to pursue once they become aware of possible political threats or opportunities.[14]

Learning by firms is frequently described as comprehensive rather than issue based—that is, firms and industries learn not only from their particular experiences but also from the experiences of others.[15] The experiences of firms in this study suggest, however, that it would be a mistake to assume that firms are black boxes or that their response to political threats to their various interests is the same across the board. The empirical evidence from the possessions corporations indicate that the decisions about whether firms should mobilize, lobby on behalf of their own particular interests, or engage in collective action were based largely on the particular experiences of the immediate past.

The reluctance of U.S. firms to mobilize in 1976 and during the initial phase of the debate in 1982 in spite of the Treasury Department's and Congress's threat to the possessions tax credit is particularly telling. The failure to mobilize at this time appears exceptional because a number of studies depict a business community that had begun mobilizing by the early 1970s in response to the political defeats suffered as a consequence of the activities of public-interest groups. The Business Roundtable was created in 1972, and by 1980 more than 80 percent of Fortune 500 companies had their own public affairs offices.[16] But like the case of the pharmaceutical and electronics firms regarding the possessions tax credit, business political history is filled with numerous examples in which firms were more inclined to interpret the new political environment through the prism of their particular experiences than to learn from the experiences of other industries regarding other issues.

Significant legislative setbacks also characterized the years prior to the upsurge in business's political mobilization. Notable examples include legislation regulating the activities of automobile manufacturers (the National Traffic and Motor Vehicle Safety Act of 1966 and the Clean Air Act amendments of 1970), textile manufacturers (the Flammable Fabrics Act of 1967), and the coal industry (the Federal Coal Mine Health and Safety Act of 1969). These laws were important because they imposed considerable costs on these industries. In particular, they were an unmistakable upset for the auto industry, which at the time was thought to be "one of the nation's most visible and powerful industries."[17] In addition, the Tax Reform Act of 1969 increased the federal tax burden of many industries by eliminating breaks such as the investment-tax credit and reducing the depletion deduction for gas and oil. In spite of these clearly observable defeats, Vogel asserts that by and large the business community remained guided more by its own specific political experiences than by the legislative setbacks of other firms and industries.[18] He explains,

New issues, along with new interest groups, were emerging, [but] business neither anticipated these political changes nor understood how to respond to them. . . . [E]ach segment of the business community continued to view Washington politics through the lens of its trade associations; each industry remained preoccupied with its own immediate concerns.[19]

Likewise, the increase in the level of business's political activity does not automatically translate into uniformity of tactics and strategies. For example, establishing a PAC was seen as an indication of the new political emergence of the business community in the 1970s.[20] Yet by the early 1980s, only 34 percent of the Fortune 1000 industrials and the top nonindustrial firms had established a PAC. Of the Fortune 500 alone, only a little more than half had established PACs.[21] This phenomenon suggests that while learning by firms is generally depicted as comprehensive, it is also bounded by their particular political experiences (past successes and failures) and circumstances (sharing a particular issues niche or belonging to the same trade association, interlocking directorate, or alliance).[22] In this study, experiences specific to individual firms explain much about the dynamics of their strategic choices and provide a key to understanding the processes by which they repeat or experiment with new political strategies.

III. Learning across Issues

What about learning across issues? Can the experiences of firms regarding one issue translate into learning across the board? To what extent are different issues guided by different learning scenarios for the same firm? Firms' learning and adapting abilities regarding other issues of importance to them is another topic that the literature needs to address. In spite of the evidence suggesting that different issues are characterized by different policy-making structures, there is a tendency to black-box business firms.[23] That is, the penchant in the literature has been to treat business as if one issue dominates its political behavior across the board. But at any given time, many political issues are important to firms, and these issues have different policy-making structures, different histories of success and failure, and, consequently, different learning scenarios.

　　Research on the political behavior of private interests suggests that strategies in any one issue are formulated in relation to strategies pursued on others.[24] The distinctiveness of the possessions tax credit does not allow us to address the extent to which strategies overlap, but this study suggests that firms do not necessarily approach all issues in a like manner. The companies interviewed isolated the formulation of their strategies regarding the possessions tax break from other issues. Past experiences regarding the possessions tax break were the primary source of information. And experiences regarding other issues were rarely invoked as intervening in the formulation of their Section 936 strategies. The fact that individual companies were busy with many other issues contributed to their tendency to rely on past experiences regarding Section 936 to formulate their strategy, especially during the process leading to the Tax Reform Act of 1986.

Another factor which may impede learning across issues is the organizational structure of the firm. Section 936 did not appear to be as important for some other firms as it was for pharmaceutical companies. These seemingly uninterested companies had subsidiaries and divisions for which the tax break was one of the most important issues, however. One example is General Electric. In the early 1990s the company had nineteen people working at its Washington office and it was active regarding the tax break because the issue was important for its Electrical Distribution and Control Division. The primary responsibility for following the developments regarding Section 936, however, fell on the company's tax lawyer for this division, based in Plainville, Connecticut. She explained,

> 936 is extremely important for us. We have been in Puerto Rico since the 1950s. . . . GE's businesses are all very different. Each division is a stand-alone Fortune 500 company, and you can't make a generalization about what issue is the most important for the entire company. . . . I always got involved because [the possessions tax credit] is a very technical issue, and the Washington office does not have a tax expertise.

Hence, it seems likely that large companies with many divisions and multiple issues of importance would have separate learning scenarios depending on the issue. This claim is supported by research suggesting that there is a great deal of specialization among Washington business representatives.[25]

Since some of the companies in this study lacked large Washington offices, it would be reasonable to expect that the smaller the Washington operation, the less specialization by issue. But smaller offices also showed a great deal of specialization. In the case of pharmaceuticals, the head of the office or someone at the top of the hierarchy was likely to be most involved with Section 936, although the structure of the different offices varied. For example, in the early 1990s, Merck's Washington, D.C., office had a staff of five. The person who dealt with Section 936 was the executive director of government relations. Pfizer had a four-person office, and again, the executive director of government relations dealt with Section 936. Overall, however, these offices had many heads, depending on the issue. Moreover, as one lobbyist explained, while at first glance Merck and Pfizer seemed to have small Washington offices, "what matters is their budget and their ability to hire outside consultants." Outside lawyers and consultants are not going to make the decision on whether to work with other firms, however, and are likely to follow strategic instructions provided by their clients.[26]

Even smaller offices with smaller overall budgets showed specialization. The 936 lobbyist at another pharmaceutical firm explained, "We have two lobbyists—one handles health-care issues, and the other handles trade and tax issues, among many other things." She continued, "We work as a team, but we split the issues." If they need each other's help, they ask for it, but the principal expert on any single issue is the lobbyist assigned to it. They choose the issues on which to concentrate based on what they think will be salient during the year. "In general, there are about twenty issues. . . . Some may come up [in any given year], but in the long run the same issues keep coming up." Again, this description implies that within the organization, issue management and consequently learning are to some extent specialized. That learning is likely to occur is evident because as the lobbyist explained and research indicates, most political issues have prolonged histories.[27]

Finally, the situation was similar for Medtronic, a multinational manufacturer of medical technology with a relatively small Washington office. In the 1980s and early 1990s, the company had two lobbyists and one assistant in Washington. One lobbyist dealt with Section 936 and Medicare, and while she reported to the head of the office, the latter specialized in patents. The 936 lobbyist worked closely with the company's treasurer, for obvious reasons, and she had a close working relationship with Representative Rangel. Accordingly, another factor contributing to specialization is the lobbyists' ability to contact key lawmakers regarding a particular issue.[28]

If the possessions tax break was clearly not very important to the firm or any of its subsidiaries or divisions, it either free rode or behaved as follower.[29] Again, lack of importance provides yet another reason for learning scenarios to differ depending on the issue. Finally, on many issues, concerns overlap.[30] Hence, for multiple issues that are not highly differentiated, learning might be more easily transferred from one issue to another, and the strategic learning scenarios are likely to be more complicated than for highly specialized issues.

Pharmaceuticals' experiences regarding other issues corroborate the occurrence of learning and illustrate the claim that learning may not be easily transferred across highly differentiated issues. For example, for many years the market for prescription drugs has been highly regulated in the United States. In fact, it is the most regulated prescription-drug market in the world. Since the 1960s companies have had to meet Food and Drug Administration (FDA) criteria on product safety and efficacy before a new drug can be marketed. The activities of firms trying to pressure the FDA and/or members of Congress to approve new drugs has been documented.[31] Hence, it would appear that pharmaceutical firms were knowledgeable about the importance of lobbying to the profitability of their operations. But in the initial phase of 1982, these same firms, which had been benefiting from the possessions tax credit for twenty years, did not mobilize for political action when their interests were initially threatened. While many of these firms had their own Washington offices and an independent capacity to monitor and lobby the U.S. Congress, there was no evidence that they had mobilized regarding this issue even as the Senate Finance Committee was marking up legislation. Moreover, it is possible that these firms mobilized regarding other tax issues that were being debated at the time, but the lessons they had learned in 1976 guided their behavior regarding the possessions tax credit.

The situation reversed itself in 1993. To protect Section 936, these companies initially relied on the learned collective-action strategy that had worked in 1986, and PRUSA took the lead in lobbying, but regarding other issues the companies simply had no strategy in place. A 1993 article published in the *Public Relations Journal* argued that the industry was not prepared to respond to the Clinton administration's attacks on firms' pricing and marketing behavior. While drug prices had previously been criticized, the industry had become used to keeping its business practices private and communicating exclusively with the medical and investment communities. The article explains that "even if the drugs [discovered] worked and saved people money in the long run, pharmaceutical companies had no real communications strategy to deal with the public backlash over rising prices." A pharmaceutical company director of public relations explained,

> Spending $600 a year on drugs to treat prostate enlargements is a great bargain if you consider the trauma and cost associated with surgery to treat the same problem. . . . However, many people who wouldn't blink an eye at a $20,000 hospital bill, all or most of which is paid by insurance, will have real problems with paying for medicines out of their own pockets, especially if that's the only medical cost they have.[32]

Prior to Clinton's election, the Pharmaceutical Manufacturing Association ran some ads. But when Clinton used vaccines as an example of price gauging and criticized the industry for profiting at the expense of children, the industry did not respond and "seemed unable to pull together" behind a strategy. Fueled in part by President Clinton's criticism, the press published damning stories about the industry, which remained silent. By the time pharmaceuticals got together to respond with an organized advertising and grassroots letter-writing campaign, its reputation had been tarnished and its stock prices went down. In the end, the companies regretted not responding earlier to the attacks but learned that having a collective communications strategy in place to deal with the price issue should be an integral part of their political strategy.[33] Pharmaceutical companies ultimately were lucky because, other than denouncing their behavior, the Clinton administration did not devise a good political strategy to sell its health-care-reform proposal to the American public and to Congress.[34]

A more detailed and exhaustive study of the impact of learning across issues is undoubtedly needed. However, the behavior of the companies in this study and the brief discussion of experiences of pharmaceutical companies regarding drug approval and pricing and marketing issues suggests that the learning view does provide a helpful framework for understanding how experienced Washington representatives of economically resourceful firms respond to a highly uncertain political environment.

IV. Implications

Does the political behavior of business explain political outcomes? A number of recent historical studies have emphasized the degree to which business's political behavior varies over time and across issues.[35] These findings suggest that we cannot choose a single theoretical framework to explain the behavior of business—that is, structural, interest-group, or fragmented. This study reinforces the argument that the structural power of business firms is not absolute and that firms will employ a variety of strategies in an effort to maximize their influence. While business is more powerful than most other social groups in society, its influence is not guaranteed, even as its political behavior has become more sophisticated. Two observations are germane. On the one hand, the tendency of business to fragment gives the state a great deal of autonomy. On the other hand, even when firms are united, there is no guarantee of victory. And businesses aligned with the White House cannot be sure of victory because in our system of separate institutions and shared responsibilities, not even the president is guaranteed victory.[36] This observation is important because the interest-group literature presumes that business "will be a politically powerful actor only to the extent that it is capable of mobilizing as a politically unified force."[37] Countless studies seek to prove business unity to make inferences about its influence.[38] But the exercise of power is more complicated, and business firms seem to know it. Not only does business have a natural tendency to fragment, but it also knows that collective action is not the only recipe for success. It is not that business firms are irrational; they simply cannot be sure which strategy to pursue under conditions of uncertainty.

The study of business influence will benefit from a greater emphasis on how firms learn across issues. Case studies are limited to the extent that they present evidence about particular issues. But they help develop grounded theories, providing an excellent opportunity to understand the micromechanisms that drive political processes. However, not every case study will advance theory. Longitudinal case studies encompassing multiple observations reflect the reality that most political issues have long histories. The Puerto Rican tax break is a useful case study because of its impact on the profitability of the largest U.S. corporations and because the political battles surrounding it over the past twenty-five years confirm that companies experiment with various political strategies and have a tendency to fight the last war when initially threatened.

This book's title posed the question of whether business learns from its political experiences. As a study in the relationship between society and the state, this book emphasizes the importance of dominant issues and government structures. The main message, though, is that business's political behavior is a dynamic phenomenon. Business actors in the political arena take into account previous experience, especially when confronted by uncertainty. In addition, business actors attempt to adapt to current circumstances but do so only belatedly. This pattern of instinctive and adaptive conduct can be fully understood only by looking at business's political behavior as a learning process.

Epilogue: Small Business Job Protection Act of 1996

In August 1996, as part of its Small Business Job Protection Act, Congress enacted a partial repeal of Section 936 to pay for small-business tax breaks. The small-business tax relief was enacted to ameliorate the impact of the increase in the minimum wage from $4.25 per hour to $5.15.[1] The new law stipulated that companies already doing business under the rules of Section 936 could continue to claim a partial federal credit for ten years. New firms, however, are not eligible for the tax credit.

After 1993 U.S. firms had continued to have an interest in the preservation of the possessions tax provision. In 1996, ten companies alone—Abbott Laboratories, American Home Products, Baxter International, Eaton, General Electric, Heinz, Intel, Johnson and Johnson, Motorola, and Sara Lee—had a total of forty-six factories in Puerto Rico. But when it became apparent to the companies that the tax break was once again being targeted for repeal, they engaged in fragmented lobbying. Throughout the political process leading to the enactment of the minimum-wage legislation, the companies were divided into two camps, the labor-intensive and capital-intensive firms. The rift between the companies is no doubt partly explained by their experiences in 1993. As discussed in chapter 6, after the enactment of the Omnibus Reconciliation Act of 1993, the companies realized that working in a coalition of pharmaceuticals and electronics had not been the most effective strategy to pursue in a new political environment. But in 1996, the companies were responding primarily to the fact that Section 936 was no longer a single tax break benefiting both electronics and pharmaceuticals. Rather, Section 936 had been converted into two tax breaks, a wage credit for the labor-intensive firms and a reduced income credit for the capital-intensive firms. Accordingly, the preferences of the companies had changed after the 1993 legislation since some companies clearly benefited from the income credit and others benefited from the wage credit. Hence, while neither pharmaceuticals nor electronics was happy with the 1993 law and many blamed their political strategy for their loss, they did not change their strategy of lobbying separately for the wage and income credit because the new tax break had effectively divided the companies into two camps. This situation contrasts sharply with the companies' stable policy preferences in the twenty-year period covered in this book.

When Section 936 began to be targeted for elimination in 1996, the Clinton and the Puerto Rican prostatehood administrations, working separately, lobbied to keep the wage credit. However, Republican members of Congress fixed on both the wage and the income credit as corporate tax breaks, which they referred to as corporate welfare.[2] The chairman of the House Ways and Means Committee, Bill Archer (R-Tex.) initially also resisted the pressure of "fiscal conservatives" to eliminate Section 936 along with billions of dollars worth of corporate tax breaks.[3] But the new chairman of the House Budget Committee, John R. Kasich (R-Ohio) was relentless. In the administration, Labor Secretary Robert Reich had also been publicly calling for the abolition of corporate tax expenditures as early as 1994 and had mentioned the possessions tax break as a good candidate for elimination.[4] Finally, both the Cato Institute, a conservative Washington think tank, and the Democratic Leadership Council's Progressive Policy Institute also targeted Section 936 as an example of corporate welfare.[5] Not surprisingly, the Washington press reported that U.S. firms were complaining that the possessions tax break had "become the poster boy of corporate welfare."[6] In the end, when members of Congress began to look for revenues to pay for tax breaks for small businesses hurt by the rise in the minimum wage, Section 936 became the most likely target. The phaseout of Section 936 signified the end of one of the oldest and most complicated federal tax provisions.

Political Action Committee (PAC) Contributions to Members of Congress

TABLE A1. Total PAC Contributions by 936 Pharmaceutical and Chemical Companies to Members of the Senate Finance and House Ways and Means Committees, 1979–84

	1979–80	1981–82	1983–84
Abbott Laboratories	6,498	14,250	12,050
American Cyanamid	3,700	5,000	1,750
American Home Products	400	1,950	1,700
Baxter International	1,650	5,350	14,400
Boc	—	—	400
Bristol-Myers	4,700	11,350	7,825
E. I. DuPont de Nemours	—	—	900
F. Hoffman–La Roche	2,400	4,250	5,650
Johnson and Johnson	5,200	11,950	15,500
Eli Lilly	5,450	16,800	16,761
Merck	4,250	5,600	7,350
Pfizer	24,200	27,050	21,950
Sandoz Pharmaceuticals	300	2,575	1,150
Schering-Plough	3,900	6,300	10,250
G. D. Searle	2,900	2,000	1,500
SmithKline Beecham	5,300	12,950	15,650
Sterling Drug	900	1,000	300
Upjohn	1,150	2,550	2,000
Total	72,898	130,925	137,086

Source: Federal Election Commission.

TABLE A2. Total PAC Contributions by PRUSA Members to Congressman Charles Rangel, 1985–86

Abbott Laboratories	1,150
American Cyanamid	1,000
American Home Products	2,270
Avon Products	1,250
Baxter Travenol	2,150
Bristol-Myers	750
Coca-Cola	1,000
E. I. DuPont de Nemours	500
General Electric	1,500
Johnson and Johnson	1,900
Eli Lilly	500
Medtronic	250
Merck	500
Motorola	1,000
Nabisco	1,000
PepsiCo	800
Pfizer	1,300
R. J. Reynolds Tobacco	450
Roche Products	800
Schering-Plough	1,000
SmithKline Beecham	3,500
Upjohn	1,000
Warner-Lambert	500
Westinghouse	1,000
Total	27,070

Source: Federal Election Commission.

TABLE A3. PRUSA PAC Contributions to Members of the Senate Finance Committee and House Ways and Means Committee, 1985–86

	1985–86
Abbott Laboratories	27,050
American Cyanamid	5,800
American Home Products	9,220
Avon Products	14,435
Baxter Healthcare	11,200
Bristol-Myers Squibb	11,950
Coca-Cola	28,800
Crowley Maritime	30,575
E. I. DuPont de Nemours	12,750
General Electric	53,350
Hewlett-Packard	5,450
Intel	2,850
Johnson and Johnson	23,950
Eli Lilly	21,750
Medtronic	750
Merck	5,025
Merrill Lynch	138,007
Motorola	25,750
Nabisco	16,750
Pepsico	14,100
Pfizer	42,365
RJR Nabisco	32,850
Schering-Plough	11,000
SmithKline Beecham	23,600
Warner-Lambert	3,500
Westinghouse	21,750
Total	594,577

Source: Federal Election Commission.

Notes

Chapter 1

1. Bauer, Pool, and Dexter 1972; G. K. Wilson 1981; Berry 1997; Vogel 1989.
2. Heinz et al. 1993, 59.
3. Bauer, Pool, and Dexter 1972.
4. Martin 1991, 1995.
5. Cyert and March 1963.
6. According to Bauer, Pool, and Dexter, there was little political activity by businesses during the reciprocal trade fight of 1953–55 even though many economists had predicted that this issue would be of importance to U.S. firms. The authors concluded that business was indifferent to the political process because the "immediate pay-off" of the policy was not "evident" (1972, 398–99). Since the benefits of the possessions tax credit were evident to U.S. firms, failure to mobilize when their policy interests were at stake would suggest that firms were making a deliberate strategic choice.
7. Statement by tax lawyer for pharmaceutical companies, interview by author, Washington, D.C., September 1997.
8. See 10-K Reports for Eli Lilly (1973), Motorola (1976), and Merck (1984).
9. See 10-K Report for G. D. Searle (1975), Upjohn (1993), Johnson and Johnson (1989–94).
10. Pulliam 1993.
11. See, for example, Canellas 1985.
12. Steinmo 1993.
13. Heinz et al. 1993, 249, 251.
14. Mucciaroni 1995; Vogel 1989.
15. Lindblom 1977, 179–82.
16. Bauer, Pool, and Dexter 1972, pt. 5; Hansen 1991, 12; R. Smith 1984.
17. Truman 1971; Hansen 1991, 12; R. Smith 1984.
18. Olson 1968, 146; Moe 1980, 191–99.
19. Yoffie 1987, 43–60.
20. G. K. Wilson 1992.
21. Salisbury 1984; Yoffie 1987.
22. Mahon and Post 1987.
23. *The New Webster's Comprehensive Dictionary of the English Language.* 1987, 562.
24. Cyert and March 1963; Levitt and March 1988, 319; March and Olsen 1984, 745.

25. Walker 1991, 53. The argument that the political behavior of institutions should be examined separately from interest groups was first made by Salisbury 1984.

26. Walsh and Rivera Ungson 1991, 61; Cyert and March 1963.

27. Martin 1995, 907, 902.

28. Collins 1981; Martin 1994; Vogel 1983; G. K. Wilson 1990, 281; G. K. Wilson, personal communication with author.

29. Cyert and March 1963, 112.

30. Scott 1992, 110; March and Olsen 1976; Walsh and Rivera Ungson 1991, 61.

31. Levinthal and March 1993, 101.

32. Cyert and March 1963; March and Simon 1958; March and Olsen 1984. The concept of learning proposed in this study is similar to Martin's (1995) policy legacies in the general sense that past experiences guide firms' political behavior in the future. However, this study's concept varies from the concept of policy legacies because the emphasis is on how learning leads firms to act unreflectively and automatically to advance defined interests. By contrast, Martin is concerned with how policy legacies influence firms' formulation of their interests.

33. J. Q. Wilson 1995, xx. For similar views on lobbying, see Schlozman and Tierney 1986; Salisbury 1990.

34. Feldman and March 1981.

35. Cyert and March 1963, 35.

36. March and Simon 1958, 173.

37. This approach to organizational learning incorporates the two dominant views of institutional learning found in the political science literature. For example, on the one hand, Levy (1994, 283) argues that learning may increase the "degree of confidence in one's beliefs" without necessarily resulting in a change in policy. On the other hand, Heclo and P. Hall's view of learning is tied to policy change (Hall 1993; Heclo 1974). Likewise, Martin (1995, 902) acknowledges that as a determinant of firms' preferences, policy legacies can lead business to either reject or welcome new policy solutions.

38. Cyert and March 1963, 81; March and Olsen 1976;Heinz et al. 1993, 358–60; Martin 1995.

39. Heinz et al. 1993.

40. Mucciaroni 1995; Vogel 1989.

41. Lowi 1964, 709. See also Baumgartner and Jones 1993.

42. Baumgartner and Jones 1993, 6.

43. Ripley and Franklin 1987, 8; Browne 1990.

44. Heclo 1978; Baumgartner and Jones 1993, 8.

45. Sanders 1988, 382.

46. Baumgartner and Jones 1993, chap. 10.

47. Ibid.; Gais, Peterson, and Walker 1995.

48. Dodd 1986.

49. Mucciaroni 1995; Salisbury 1979; Vogel 1983; G. K. Wilson 1982.

50. Baumgartner and Jones 1993, 14.

51. Polsby 1968.

52. While American Samoa, Guam, the U.S. Virgin Islands and certain Pacific islands are also U.S. possessions, Puerto Rico accounts for more than 90 percent of the tax ex-

penditures associated with the possessions tax credit (U.S. Government Accounting Office 1993).

53. I thus follow the methodological logic formulated by King, Keohane, and Verba 1994, 52–53.

54. Companies represented in these interviews include Abbott Laboratories, American Cyanamid, American Home Products, Baxter International, Bristol-Myers Squibb, General Electric, Genentech, Hewlett-Packard, Johnson and Johnson, Eli Lilly, Medtronics, Merck, PepsiCo, Pfizer, Warner-Lambert, and Westinghouse.

Chapter 2

1. Statement of John J. Shea, House Committee on Ways and Means, Hearings on Revenue Act of 1918, 65th Cong., 2d sess., 1918, 1:442–57; see also House Ways and Means Committee, *Report 767*, 65th Cong., 2d sess., 1918.

2. U.S. Treasury Department 1979, 15.

3. *Congressional Record,* 67th Cong., 1st sess., 1921, 5275–85.

4. At the time, all U.S. possessions, with the exception of Puerto Rico and the Philippines, had a mirror tax system—that is, their residents were taxed according to the U.S. Internal Revenue Code with the revenue collected retained by the possessions. Under the Foraker Act of 1900, the U.S. Congress granted Puerto Rico and the Philippines the power to enact their own taxing authority.

5. See House discussion in *Congressional Record,* 67th Cong., 1st sess., 1921, 5275–85. It is not clear from the discussion whether the provision originated in the U.S. Treasury or the House Ways and Means Committee. However, there is mention in both the House and Senate discussions that the U.S. Treasury as well as Commerce Secretary Herbert Hoover supported the measure.

6. U.S. Treasury Department 1980, 7n. 2.

7. *Congressional Record,* 67th Cong., 1st sess., 1921, 5279.

8. See Senate discussion in *Congressional Record,* 67th Cong., 1st sess., 1921, 6488–94, 6546–549.

9. Puerto Rico, the Philippines and Guam became U.S. possessions as a result of the Spanish-American War of 1898. American Samoa came under U.S. control in 1899. The U.S. Virgin Islands were purchased from Denmark in 1917.

10. U.S. Treasury Department 1980, 9.

11. U.S. Treasury Department 1978, 10.

12. Lewis 1963, 87–88. Lewis also points out that some of the first books written about Puerto Rico appraised new business opportunities in the island. Julius W. Pratt has also noted that "just after the war of 1898 ended, the Washington Bureau of Statistics reported a large number of inquiries, 'chiefly from great producing business centers,' as to the opportunities for American capital and skill to develop the resources of the island" ("American Business and the Spanish-American War," *Hispanic American Historical Review* [May 1934], quoted in Quintero Rivera 1974, 105).

13. Arturo Morales Carrión (1983, 165) refers to this period as the "era of flattering statistics." For example, in 1901 the value of all shipments of goods to and from the United States and other foreign countries was $17,502,103; by 1910 this figure had in-

creased by 400 percent to $68,595,326. Sugar exports valued at $4,715,611 in 1901 increased to $18,432,446 in 1909.

Though the price of sugar dropped after the 1920s, sugar production remained profitable because both the Fordney-McCumber Tariff of 1922 and the Hawley-Smoot Tariff of 1930 were highly protectionist (T. R. Clark 1975, 107).

Absentee ownership was not characteristic only of the sugar industry. For example, by 1930 absentee ownership had reached 60 percent for sugar production, 80 percent for the tobacco industry, 60 percent for public utilities and banking, and 100 percent for the shipping business (Lewis 1963, 88).

14. Lewis 1963, 88–90.

15. Carr 1984, 61. Two New Deal Agencies, the Puerto Rican Emergency Relief Organization and the Puerto Rican Reconstruction Organization, spent $1 million per month in Puerto Rico; they provided some food assistance and public-works jobs but left untouched the basic problems of the island's underdeveloped economy. See also T. R. Clark 1975, chap. 5.

16. U.S. Commerce Department 1979, 17.

17. The party's roots lay in the island's pro-independence movement. However, the party leadership felt that to give priority to the political-status issue would cost them the support of voters concerned about the potentially disastrous economic effects of independence. See Morales Carrión 1983, chap. 13.

18. Carr 1984, 65.

19. U.S. Commerce Department 1979, 17.

20. PRIDCO is now the Economic Development Administration (FOMENTO).

21. U.S. Commerce Department 1979, 18.

22. Carr 1984, 74. Private investment had played some part in the first phase of the economic program. PRIDCO had offered buildings for lease by private businesses and had opened an office in New York to promote investment in Puerto Rico. However, in 1944 Tugwell failed to sign a bill passed by the Puerto Rican legislature providing tax exemption for manufacturing investment on the island.

23. Unless otherwise noted, this discussion is taken from U.S. Treasury Department 1983, 23–24, and Pantojas-García 1990, chap. 3.

24. *Detroit Free Press,* 10 May 1953, as quoted in Taylor 1954, 363.

25. The act sought to limit old firms' ability to qualify for new grants. In 1960 this prohibition was relaxed to allow existing industrial units to expand and, with the permission of the governor of Puerto Rico, to be allowed new full industrial exemptions.

26. The exemption could be extended by allowing a business to postpone the start of its tax exemption period up to four years from the beginning of its operations date. Elective partial exemptions also extended the length of the exemption. Moreover, because exemptions were granted for individual items, every time a company expanded or began production a new item, the company was eligible for a new exemption grant.

27. U.S. Commerce Department 1979, 19

28. U.S. Treasury Department 1983, 33; Carr 1984, 75, 205.

29. Lewis 1963, 169–70.

30. U.S. Commerce Department 1979, 7, 33–37.

31. By 1982 the Puerto Rican minimum wage equaled that of the U.S. mainland.

32. U.S. Treasury Department 1978, 31. For example, between 1973 and 1976, the

number of establishments in the apparel, textiles, and leather industries had decreased from 601 to 520 (U.S. Commerce Department 1979, 26).

33. Carr 1984, 14; Pantojas-García 1990, 121.

34. U.S. Treasury Department 1979, 19–20. The banks in Guam would simply pass the funds into the Eurodollar market. Canadian CDs were also attractive; although their interest was not from a possession source like Guam, if the deposit was made in Canada and denominated in U.S. dollars, it was also free of Canadian, U.S., and Puerto Rican taxes (Holbrook 1977).

35. Sierra 1973, 310. For other mainland publications with tax-planning suggestions, see Rudick and Allan 1952; Mihaly 1963; Griggs 1971.

36. Mihaly 1963, 97. The author goes on to say that there are IRS regulations to prevent this kind of arrangement. However, he underlines the fact that this is an added benefit to tax-free investment in Puerto Rico because IRS guidelines dealing with "income shifting" are "relatively permissive."

37. U.S. Treasury Department 1978, 19, 21.

38. Mihaly 1963, 98.

39. U.S. Treasury Department 1978, 21. As chapter 3 will show, the U.S. Treasury found that the 1963 and 1968 regulations did not reduce the practice of "profit shifting." In fact, the U.S. Treasury argues that "nowhere has the application of Section 482 been more controversial than to transactions between a U.S. parent and its possessions corporations" (U.S. Treasury Department 1978, 18).

40. Moreover, in spite of being under investigation by the IRS, U.S. firms doing business in Puerto Rico had an advantage in setting their intercompany pricing policies. According to Section 482 of the IRS code, "transfer prices" should equal "arm's-length prices." One way to determine the arm's-length price is to use the price that unrelated firms would pay for identical or similar products in the same circumstances. In the majority of the cases in Puerto Rico, however, there was no a "comparable independent transaction" that could have been used to determine the arm's-length price because island subsidiaries were set up to supply "distinctive" products to the parent (Griggs 1971, 376–78). For example, prescription drugs are generally manufactured by only one company. Such being the case, U.S. firms seem to have had a great deal of flexibility and autonomy in deciding what the arm's-length price of their products should be.

Also, technically speaking at least, if the U.S. firms transferred the inventory and intangible property to their subsidiaries at the time of their inception, the subsidiaries would not have to make arm's-length payments to the parents (Holbrook 1977, 18). The U.S. Treasury did not buy this strategy: IRS agents saw it as income shifting of the worst kind. The problem was that the strategy was legal.

41. G. P. Wilson 1993. For an important review of the literature on the relationship between taxes and the profits of multinational corporations, see Caves 1996, chap. 8.

42. Until the Tax Reform Act of 1986, the United States was generally considered a high-tax area.

43. G. P. Wilson 1993, 202

44. In 1984 Congress decided to permit companies to seek additional years so that they could have a maximum of fourteen years of effective market exclusivity. In exchange, the law also enacted provisions to help speed up the process to get generics on the market after the expiration of the patent (see Hamilton 1984; Rich 1984).

The life of a drug, however, might also be shortened by the relatively fast replacement of old drugs, which is characteristic of the pharmaceutical industry. A study of the age of the two hundred most prescribed drugs in the United States in 1966 indicated that studies that show product life of more than nine years might be "exaggerated somewhat" by a few drugs that were on the market for more than twenty years (James 1977, 24).

45. G. P. Wilson writes,

> Although manufacturing costs have been increasing recently, they are small for most drugs compared to the estimated $200–350 million required to get a drug through R&D and regulatory approval. Likewise, manufacturing costs pale in comparison to the foregone revenues when patents expire. For blockbuster drugs, with peak sales approaching a billion dollars a year, the lost revenues from delaying a product launch can be staggering. (1993, 202)

46. U.S. Treasury Department 1978, 21.

47. Even now, when pharmaceutical firms consider establishing a presence in a foreign market as a result of potential price breaks for establishing their operations in a specific country or to take advantage of favorable economies of scale, one of the managers G. P. Wilson interviewed maintained that "there are [still] big bucks in taxes and these other considerations must be quite large to offset the tax benefits" (1993, 208). For more on the continued importance of taxes for pharmaceutical firms, see Thurston 1988, 12.

48. U.S. Commerce Department 1979, 142.

49. One reason why the possessions tax credit was more important than the investment-tax credit for this group of firms is that while pharmaceuticals are capital intensive, they are not heavy industry. As one tax lawyer suggested, there is "big difference between the capital expenses of a pharmaceutical company and Alcoa" (the world's largest integrated aluminum company), for example. The capital investments of pharmaceuticals are proportionally less than the capital investments of heavy manufacturing and, accordingly, it follows that companies would vary in their ability to take advantage of the possessions tax break (a 100 percent tax credit on income) and the investment tax credit (a 10 percent tax credit against the costs of capital investment). For additional discussion on how particular industries benefit differently from various corporate tax breaks, see Martin 1991.

50. U.S. Commerce Department 1979, 43.

51. Gover 1993, 58

52. G. P. Wilson 1993, 201. One reason why manufacturing costs are higher for semiconductors than for pharmaceuticals is the upgrade costs. Semiconductor producers have to upgrade their manufacturing equipment to keep up with innovation, which results in a higher cost of goods sold. Pharmaceutical facilities are costly, but their upgrade costs are notably less (G. P. Wilson 1993, n. 17).

53. Ibid., 208–13.

54. U.S. Commerce Department 1979, 157.

55. Ibid., 153.

56. U.S. Treasury Department 1978, 39–43. Treasury arrived at this figure by dividing the total tax expenditure per industry for 280 possessions corporations (the combined book income of these companies representing fourth-fifths of the book income of all possessions corporations) by the total number of employees.

Chapter 4 will show that Treasury figures on tax revenue foregone have been a source of controversy. U.S. firms argued that these estimates are based on the unrealistic assumption that were the tax break eliminated, the companies would stay in Puerto Rico and pay federal taxes. The point here is, however, that pharmaceuticals were by far the largest beneficiaries of the possessions tax break.

Chapter 3

1. Gilpin 1975; Krasner 1978.
2. Culhane 1972, 113.
3. Lenhart 1971, 1486. Labor recommendations to repeal the tax deferral and foreign tax credit were embodied in the Foreign Trade and Investment Act 1972 introduced by Senator Vance Hartke (D-Ind.) and Representative James A. Burke (D-Mass.) on 28 September 1971. Though the bill was never enacted, it represented one of the most serious congressional attacks on foreign direct investment (Culhane 1972, 108–19).
4. While individual members of Congress and public-interest groups such as Ralph Nader's Tax Reform Group and Common Cause were pressuring Congress for a comprehensive reform of the tax laws, the AFL-CIO exerted the most aggressive pressure for a review of the federal tax treatment of foreign profits of U.S. multinationals.

In addition to making the taxation of U.S. multinationals an element of the public agenda, labor's aggressive campaign prompted other public studies on the issue, including those undertaken by the U.S. Tariff Commission, Commerce Department, Treasury Department, and State Department on the impact of multinationals on the U.S. economy and their compliance with U.S. tax laws. Congressional hearings on the issue were held also by the House Foreign Subcommittee on Foreign Affairs in 1969 and by the Foreign Economic Policy Subcommittee of the Joint Economic Committee in 1970 (Lenhart 1971; Culhane 1972).

5. Statement of Jay W. Glasmann, U.S. House of Representatives, *Panel Discussions before the Committee on Ways and Means, On the Subject of General Tax Reform,* 93d Cong., 1st sess., 1973, pt. 11, 1702, 1792.
6. Ibid.
7. Pastor 1980, 56–57.
8. Casellas n.d., 4.
9. See table 8.
10. The Commonwealth of Puerto Rico was established in 1952. Commonwealth status is meant to define the political and economic relationship between the United States and Puerto Rico, but its meaning is ambiguous, and the status of Puerto Rico is more clearly defined by what it is not than by what it is. Under this status, Puerto Rico is not a state or an independent nation. The creator of the commonwealth status, the Popular Democratic Party, defines it as a "free associated state" in which Puerto Ricans have chosen to be "associated with, but not form part of, the United States" (Carr 1984, 4). Under the commonwealth status, Puerto Ricans are represented in Washington by an elected resident commissioner who can speak but cannot vote on the floor of the House. The commissioner may, however, vote in committees on which he or she serves.
11. "Salvador Casellas" 1977, 10. In addition, unless otherwise noted, this part of the narrative is based on an interview with Casellas.

12. In 1926 a congressional investigation found evidence of tax evasion facilitated by employees of the Internal Revenue Bureau. In response, the House established the Joint Committee on Internal Revenue Taxation (now Joint Committee on Taxation) in 1929. The committee, made up of five Senators and five House members, was to assist in revenue legislation by gathering data and to "gain a 'closer insight' into the problem of the administration of the tax laws (a euphemism for preventing corruption in the Internal Revenue Bureau)" (Manley 1970, 307). According to Manley (1970, 307–25), the committee staff's most valuable function is linkage. After discussing tax legislation with the members of the Ways and Means, "the staff, and more prominently the Chief of Staff, crosses the rotunda and explains the bill to the Finance Committee." Moreover, staff members are sometimes thought to be more competent than the Treasury staff members in drafting revenue measures. Finally, the committee also holds quasi-hearings for lobbyists to present their position, thereby working as a link between the revenue committees and lobbyists.

13. "Salvador Casellas" 1977, 14.

14. It is not clear whether representatives from the business community had been allowed to sit in during a closed markup of legislation or whether the committee was operating publicly. According to Fenno (1973, 106), it was not unusual for "clientele groups" to be allowed to participate in private committee deliberations.

15. As quoted in Casellas n.d., 8–9.

16. Hernández Colón 1974, 2, 13.

17. Ibid., 14–15.

18. As quoted in Casellas n.d., 8–9.

19. Fenno has argued that in addition to reelection, House members are concerned with acquiring influence within the House and with enacting good public policy. In fact, he found that the most important reasons why members of the Ways and Means Committee pursued membership were (1) influence within the House, (2) making good public policy, and (3) getting reelected (Fenno 1973, 1–5). Likewise, Manley found that members of Congress believed that their membership on Ways and Means was of "little value in their districts" (Manley 1970, 87). This result is not surprising given that committee members were generally chosen from safe districts. Thus, it is likely that Mills sought to protect Puerto Rico's economic growth by retaining and even enhancing the incentives for U.S. companies to invest in Puerto Rico because he thought it was the best policy at the time.

20. House Committee on Ways and Means, "Tax Reform Act of 1975," *Report 94-658,* 94th Cong., 1st sess., 1975, 254.

21. Packenham 1973.

22. By the 1950s, the economic and social transformation of Puerto Rico was being heralded as a miracle by the U.S. press and academic community (see, e.g., "Tax-Free Puerto Rican Profits Depository Cited," *New York Times,* 2 April 1959, 43; "Humphrey Praises Puerto Rican Gains," *New York Times,* 3 December 1959, 13; "Puerto Rico Cited in U.N. as a Model: U.S. Recommends Methods of Operation Bootstrap to Under-Developed Lands," *New York Times,* 30 March 1961, 1; and "Puerto Rico's Road to Progress Is Described as a Dubious Model: Puerto Rico Gain Held Impressive," *New York Times,* 24 April 1961, 45. Moreover, island administrators were being invited to international forums to share their economic-development strategies.

The U.S. government was also exploring ways in which to adapt the lessons learned from the island's industrial-incentives program to U.S. foreign technical and economic assistance policy. In 1961 a *New York Times* story explained how in 1960 alone, as part of its technical assistance program, the International Cooperation Administration invited 1,500 "economic officials and students . . . from such countries as Morocco, Nigeria, Indonesia, Israel, Greece, Haiti, Belgium, Jamaica, Ireland, and others" to learn about the island's economic-development program. ("Puerto Rico's Economic Progress Attracts World's Attention," *New York Times,* 1 February 1960, 35).

The Kennedy administration was also eager to use Puerto Rico as a development model and diplomatic bridge between Latin America and the United States (Carr 1984, 317). "The Puerto Rican experience," wrote Arthur Schlesinger Jr., "was an important source of ideas behind the Alliance [for Progress]" (1965, 700; see also 697–726). In addition, a former head of Puerto Rico's Economic Development Administration, Moscoso, was appointed coordinator of the alliance.

For examples of academic works and commentaries, see Baer 1959; Lewis 1955; Perloff 1953, 44–54; Galbraith and Solo 1953.

23. Carr 1984, 316.

24. Manley 1970, 150, 380, 207, 124–26.

25. Ibid.

26. Strahan 1990, 13.

27. U.S. House of Representatives, Committee on Ways and Means, "Tax Reform Act of 1976," *Report 94-658,* 94th Cong., 1st sess., 1975, pp. 254–55.

28. A tollgate tax was imposed on dividends paid out of Puerto Rican–source income to headquarters in the mainland. Casellas explains that once he reached an agreement with U.S. officials, he felt bound to impose the 15 percent tollgate tax. Interestingly, U.S. firms did mobilize against the Puerto Rican tollgate tax, arguing that it was unconstitutional. CEOs of major U.S. firms with Puerto Rican affiliates met in New York with Governor Hernández Colón to try to persuade him to veto the tax. The CEOs argued that they would leave Puerto Rico if the tax were imposed. In a memo to the governor, Casellas argued that the companies would not leave and implied that if the tax were vetoed, he would resign. Much to the surprise of U.S. firms, the tollgate tax ultimately was enacted and signed into law by the governor (see also Schoene 1983).

29. For a more detailed discussion of the differences between Section 931 and Section 936, see U.S. Treasury Department 1979, 16–23.

30. Holbrook 1977, 25.

31. Ibid., 24; *Caribbean Business,* 1 October 1974; *Caribbean Business,* 1 July 1975.

32. Holbrook 1977, 24–25.

33. "Tax Reform" 1974, 181–93.

34. Balz 1974b, 913.

35. Balz 1975, 1235, 1237. See also Joint Committee on Internal Revenue Taxation, *Committee Members' Selections of Proposals for Consideration in the First Phase of Tax Reform,* 94th Cong., 1st sess., 1975, Committee Print.

36. Balz 1976, 329; "Washington Update" 1976, 1157.

37. In their book about the many channels through which multinationals can shift funds to minimize taxation, Robbins and Stobaugh explained that

regardless of what industry a multinational enterprise finds itself in, optimization has its costs. At the outset, out-of-pocket charges arise from the additional personnel, time, communication interchange, and computer facilities required to do various things. These things include making an accurate description of the system, gathering the required information, formulating an appropriate policy, and monitoring the transactions within various units involved. (1973, 170)

38. Lindblom 1977, 175.

39. Vogel 1989. Some of these firms had extensive political experience in collective action dating back to the 1960s (Martin 1994).

Chapter 4

1. Strahan 1990, 137.

2. Some of the new tax benefits enacted as part of ERTA included accelerated cost-recovery allowances for physical investment, a more liberal investment-tax credit, and more liberal tax leasing provisions (U.S. Treasury Department 1983, 50; see also "Restructuring of Puerto Rico Tax Aids Debated" 1981). Incidentally, TEFRA restricted these new provisions.

3. In a *Business Week* report on the tax law, a drug industry analyst argued that the "increased tax-free earnings from Puerto Rico" had actually "masked the pretax slippage of pharmaceutical company profits in the past few years" ("Closing in on Puerto Rico's Tax Haven" 1978, 156). Indeed, according to a Treasury official, one extreme example of this case was G. D. Searle: in 1981, the company reportedly had losses in all of its affiliates except Puerto Rico.

4. "Closing in on Puerto Rico's Tax Haven" 1978, 156.

5. As the companies explained, it is hard for Treasury to keep a secret for very long, since all correspondence between the department and the public is accessible under the Freedom of Information Act.

6. Section 936 was expected to reduce the federal tax expenditure associated with the possessions corporations by $10 million in 1977. In 1976 the tax expenditure of Section 931 had been estimated at $285 million in 1977. However, this figure had been estimated before possessions corporations were required to report their Puerto Rican earnings. When the tax-return data became available as a result of a filing requirement enacted in 1976, the tax expenditure estimate was revised from $285 million to $634 million (U.S. Treasury Department 1978).

7. U.S. Treasury Department 1980, 45.

8. Ibid.

9. U.S. Treasury Department 1978, 55–56.

10. In 1979 Treasury reported that between 40 and 50 percent of the tax expenditure associated with Section 936 continued to be attributable solely to the pharmaceutical industry. About 20 percent was attributed to the electronics industry. The tax expenditure per employee for pharmaceuticals was calculated to be about three times the actual compensation of a Puerto Rican employee, while the tax expenditure per employee for electronics was around 1.25 times the actual compensation. When ranked according to the tax expenditure per employee, the top six 936 companies had tax savings per employee in excess of $100,000. The next seventeen companies had tax savings per employee of

$50,000. Together, these twenty-three companies alone accounted for 39.6 percent of the total federal tax foregone and only 4.2 percent of total employment created by 936 companies (U.S. Treasury Department 1979, 56, 66).

11. Scholes and Wolfson 1992, 25.

12. U.S. Treasury Department 1983, 19. For a discussion of Section 482, see chap. 2, sect. 3.

13. A contract manufacturer can only declare tax-exempt income for a percentage of labor costs and raw materials; the income from the intangible belongs to the contractor.

14. "Restructuring of Puerto Rico Tax Aids Debated" 1981, 1054–55.

15. The discussion of what transpired during these meetings is based on interviews and a transcript of the meetings made available by a participant.

16. The number of investment agreements between the Puerto Rican government and foreign investors decreased from 136 in 1980 to 83 in 1981 and 97 in 1982 (U.S. Treasury Department 1983, 20). Yet it is possible that U.S. firms were not being honest about their investment strike in Puerto Rico. A number of possible explanations exist for the companies' investment strategies at this time. Their investment activities may have been impacted by the economic slowdown on the mainland or the reduction in pharmaceutical-company profits, or fewer new products were designed or patents discovered that would justify the establishment of new manufacturing operations in Puerto Rico. Alternatively, the political uncertainty surrounding Section 936 may have, in fact, reduced the island's attractiveness as an investment site. This explanation would suggest that 936 companies were serious about engaging in an investment-strike strategy until the uncertainty was eliminated. If such was the case, the political strategy of relying on a threatened investment strike in 1976 differs from the actual investment strike in the early 1980s. However, while the investment strategies of the companies appear to have changed during the initial phase of the process leading to TEFRA, 936 firms were nonetheless relying on their structural power to communicate their interests to U.S. policymakers. They expected policymakers to make the connection between changes to Section 936 and possible adverse impact to Puerto Rico and the U.S. companies without engaging or organizing an explicit political effort. In this sense, the firms' reliance on an investment-strike strategy essentially differed from the fragmented lobbying and collective-action strategy they would engage in the future.

17. Under the cost-sharing rule, a U.S. parent would be permitted to transfer certain manufacturing intangibles (specifically patents, inventions, formulas, processes, designs, patterns, and know-how), as long as: (1) the island affiliate had a significant business presence in Puerto Rico (the significant-business-presence requirement would be satisfied if more than 25 percent of the value of the product was added by the Puerto Rican affiliate and at least 65 percent of labor costs were incurred in the island affiliate); and (2) it shared a percentage of the cost of research and development in the form of a cost-sharing payment made by the island affiliate to its parent. If these two conditions were met, then the intangible would be treated as belonging to the Puerto Rican affiliate, which would be entitled to all of the income arising from that product. Though this option would not increase the parent's taxable income, it would reduce the amount of R&D that the U.S. parent could deduct from its tax liability.

Under the fifty-fifty profit-split rule, the island affiliate and the U.S. parent could split their combined taxable income attributed to the products produced "in whole or in part" in Puerto Rico. As a result, 50 percent of the profits of the product would be subject to U.S. tax, and 50 percent would be exempt from U.S. tax. This option would permit the 936 corporation to obtain part of the return on all intangibles related to the Puerto Rican product. The business-presence requirement for profit split would be the same as for cost sharing.

For a detailed discussion of these options, see Doernberg 1989, chap. 3; Government Development Bank of Puerto Rico 1982.

18. According to a Joint Committee on Taxation report prepared by its staff and the Senate Finance Committee staff with the cooperation of the Treasury, possible amendments and/or alternatives to the tax credit included eliminating Section 936; reducing the amount of passive income (i.e., interest income) exempted from federal tax; taxing income attributable to the transfer of intangibles; and/or replacing the 100 percent tax credit for income with a wage credit—that is, a tax credit "equal to a fixed amount of wages paid to employees of the possessions corporations" (Joint Committee on Taxation, *Description of Possible Options to Increase Revenues,* 97th Cong., 2d sess., 1982, Committee Print, 110–12). In theory, a wage credit would encourage labor-intensive industries rather than capital-intensive firms to invest on the island.

19. White and Wildavsky 1991, xv.

20. Strahan 1990, 137.

21. Although there has been much disagreement about the deficit's economic implications, the concerns included its possible raising of interest rates, slowing of output and growth, causing inflation, and resulting in future generations having to pay much higher taxes and receive fewer services in return (White and Wildavsky 1991, chap. 2).

22. Strahan 1990, 125.

23. White and Wildavsky 1991, 80.

24. The former chairman of the Ways and Means Committee, Al Ullman, had lost his House seat to a Republican in the November 1980 elections.

25. White and Wildavsky 1991, 183. See also T. B. Clark 1981b, 1714.

26. T. B. Clark 1981b, 1712; 1982b, 271.

27. T. B. Clark 1982b, 269.

28. T. B. Clark 1981a, 1972. In his study of the politics of the Ways and Means Committee, Strahan argues that after the committee's restructuring in the mid-1970s, it became more "conflictual," with "frequent amendment or rejection of committee bills by the full House." The events of the early 1980s only confirmed that the "committee could no longer manage its traditional function of balancing particular interests of members and clientele groups with fiscal concerns or other broader policy goals" (Strahan, 1990, 1; see also Rudder 1983).

29. "Tax Increases Meet Deficit Reduction Target" 1982, 5.

30. White and Wildavsky 1991, 119, 248. See also "Tax Increases Meet Deficit Reduction Target" 1982, 5.

31. Regan 1988, 176–84.

32. As quoted in White and Wildavsky 1991, 251.

33. In June 1980 Treasury reported that the tax expenditure for Section 936 for the 1978 tax year was $840 million (U.S. Treasury Department 1980, 34). In terms of how much money would be raised by enacting changes in the tax law, Section 936 ranked twentieth out of twenty-seven revenue-raising proposals considered by Dole and others

(T. B. Clark 1982d, 579; see also "Tax Increases Meet Deficit Reduction Target" 1982, 33; T. B. Clark 1982b, 268).

34. T. B. Clark 1982b, 268.

35. FOMENTO n.d.

36. T. B. Clark 1982a, 355, 389; 1982c, 896–901.

37. Some lobbyists suggested other reasons to explain why Dole opposed 936. For example, the Washington representative of a pharmaceutical company explained, "us cynics think that Dole believed that he had been a greater supporter of Puerto Rico than Bush and Reagan, but in the Puerto Rican primaries the Puerto Rican people did not go for him." However, it seems that Dole was genuinely shocked to learn of the drug companies' profits. Moreover, he was targeting the drug companies rather than Puerto Rico.

38. In spite of the fact that many companies had mobilized against the effort to raise taxes, Dole kept the business community in the dark. According to one business lobbyist, nobody knew "what was coming until it was in the [Finance Committee] report" (quoted in White and Wildavsky 1991, 251). By contrast, 936 companies failed to mobilize regarding the possessions provision even though their tax lawyers and Puerto Rican officials knew that it had become part of the budget process and that Dole was serious about the cutbacks.

39. Tierney 1992, 209.

40. See Sundquist 1981; Rieselbach 1986; T. B. Clark 1982c, 899.

41. The literature on collective action generally defines traditional lobbying methods as an inside strategy as opposed to a public strategy. The latter would include a public-relations campaign to try to shape public opinion or encourage members of the public to communicate their opinions to politicians.

Lobbyists' tactics differ depending on the type of issue (Bacheller 1977). Evans argues, for example, that when Congress is reviewing distributive legislation, such as special tax laws, the general public is not aware of the law's impact. Consequently, lobbyists prefer to use an inside strategy. The presumption is that a more public strategy can backfire (1991, 258–59). Moreover, a public strategy takes time to implement—more time than the 936 companies had during TEFRA.

42. The rift among the pharmaceutical companies was apparent when the Pharmaceutical Manufacturers Association could not reach a consensus with its members on what policy to pursue with members of Congress.

43. In fact, Famadas explained that every time he argued that pharmaceuticals' tax-free profits in Puerto Rico were not excessive, he "felt like Jack Ruby's lawyer arguing that his client was not in the parking lot when Harvey Oswald was killed."

44. Local 936 deposit rates paid by commercial banks were significantly below current market rates.

45. The number of corporate PACs increased from 433 in 1976 to 1,557 by 1982 (Plotke 1992, 191).

46. One of this book's premises is, however, that to get a true picture of business political behavior, a researcher must collect qualitative data based on interviews with corporate officials. The conventional wisdom is that businesses do not like to talk about the methods they use to try to influence the policy process. I found, however, that most business lobbyists are willing to provide researchers with the information necessary to acquire a more complete understanding of their political activities.

47. During the 1981–82 election cycle, less than half of the Fortune 1,000 had PACs (Masters and Kein 1985, 1168). G. K. Wilson (1990) makes this point about DuPont, an otherwise politically active company that did not establish a PAC for many years.

48. R. L. Hall and Wayman 1990; Wright 1990.

49. For PAC contributions, see appendix A.

50. According to Wright, at minimum, access means "an advantage in making appointments and getting phone calls returned" (1990, 418).

51. G. K. Wilson 1990, 284.

52. See Wright 1990; Evans 1991; Bauer, Pool, and Dexter 1972, chap. 28; Berry 1977, chap. 8; Denzau and Munger 1986.

53. Bureau of National Affairs 1982, G-5. Though negotiations had broken off in late 1981, Puerto Rican officials and U.S. firms had received the impression that Treasury would work with them for a regulatory solution and had forwarded this message to the companies. After Finance's proposal became public, some officials realized that Treasury was telling them one thing but lobbying for another in Congress.

54. Ibid, G-4.

55. R. Smith 1984, 47.

56. Carr 1984, 12.

57. According to this lobbyist, "Democrats, not Republicans, were especially notable for this attitude."

58. Former Senator Bill Bradley (D-N.J.) also had a Puerto Rican constituency and many 936 companies with operations in his state, but in 1982 he was not perceived as a strong supporter of 936.

59. *Congressional Record,* 97th Cong., 2d sess., 1982, 17227–35

60. Ibid., 17235.

61. Ibid.

62. In spite of the administration's position, Treasury staffers would not commit themselves to securing passage of their compromise with Puerto Rican officials. In a letter to the governor of Puerto Rico, John Chapoton, assistant secretary for tax policy, explained that although Treasury would prefer to see the compromise enacted,

> [w]e recognize, however, the responsibility of the Senate Finance Committee to meet the revenue target mandated in the First Concurrent Budget Resolution for fiscal year 1983. Consequently, we can support amending the Senate Bill to incorporate this proposal only if it is acceptable to the Committee in meeting their revenue targets. (Chapoton to Barceló, 23 July 1982, Washington, D.C.)

63. Yoffie 1987, 46.

64. Olson 1968.

65. See Neustadt 1960; Salisbury 1979; G. K. Wilson 1982.

66. Consistent with a weakening party identification was an increase in the importance of incumbency in determining congressional outcomes (Erikson 1972; Mayhew 1974b). This trend implied that members of Congress had become more independent from party leadership than they had been in the 1960s and early 1970s. See also Sundquist 1981; Rieselbach 1986.

67. By constitutional requirement, all bills for raising revenue must originate in the House. To bypass this requirement, Dole brought his committee's bill to the Senate floor as an amendment to a minor tax bill (H.R. 4961).

68. Rudder 1983, 207.

69. According to one Puerto Rican official, when he went to see Rangel, the congressman was very straightforward, saying, "What can you do for me?" What supporters of 936 did was give the congressman a fund-raiser in Puerto Rico. According to a Puerto Rican official, that fund-raiser, held after the Dole amendment passed the Senate but before it was discussed in conference, raised $141,000 for Rangel. The fund-raiser was attended mostly by company officials from the island affiliates. In 1980 Rangel had spent $90,344 for his reelection campaign; in 1982 the congressman spent $200,000.

70. It was clear that Brockway was more in tune with the Treasury staff's view of Section 936. H. Smith explained Brockway's attitude toward the tax code:

> Brockway . . . had studied tax law under Stanley Surrey—a former assistant secretary of the Treasury whose name is synonymous with knocking loopholes out of the tax code. While Brockway is politically neutral, he is not without an ideology: the ideology of reform. His professional bent is to eliminate tax credits, incentives, preferences, shelters, and loopholes and to use the tax code to collect revenues "on a level playing field"—the same for all—not to use the tax code as a instrument of social and economic engineering or to favor certain interest groups or to promote various policy goals. Indeed, the "nonpolitical" ethic of Joint Tax makes it an inevitable adversary to many special interests. (H. Smith 1988, 275)

In addition to Brockway, some of the Treasury staff members had also continued to advocate the replacement of Section 936 with a wage credit.

71. White and Wildavsky 1991, 254.

72. U.S. Treasury Department 1983, 121.

Chapter 5

1. White and Wildavsky 1991, chaps. 12–19.

2. "House Approves Major Rewrite of Tax Code" 1985, 480.

3. White and Wildavsky 1991, 475.

4. Ibid, 423.

5. Truman 1971.

6. Olson (1968, 146) argues that political goals alone do not suffice to induce individuals to join and support interest-group activity. Rather, he argues that "selective incentives" (i.e., material benefits) attract members to join an organization.

According to Yoffie (1987, 46), larger firms are more likely to organize for political action because "they can spread the costs of political action over a large volume of business," whereas "small firms would have to devote a larger percentage of their total revenues to participate in political activity" (see also Moe 1980, 193–94). This chapter argues that larger firms are also more likely to organize for collective action because they are both willing and able to bear the costs of organizing.

7. Heinz et al. 1993, 15.

8. Schlozman and Tierney 1986, 150.

9. See chap. 3.

10. Robert Nathan Associates 1985.

11. Common Cause, a public-interest lobby, criticized this aspect of PRUSA's lobbying strategy during the tax-reform process; see Kaplan 1986.

12. As early as 1982, Senator Bill Bradley (D-N.J.) and Representative Richard A. Gephardt (D-Mo.) had jointly proposed revising the tax system to eliminate most tax breaks and to reduce individual and corporate rates. When campaigning for the 1984 presidential elections began, Bradley tried to persuade the Democratic candidate, Walter Mondale, to take on the issue of tax reform as a campaign theme. Mondale chose to focus on the deficit and instead proposed raising taxes.

13. Birnbaum and Murray 1987, 47; see also Conlan, Wrightson, and Beam 1991, chap. 7.

14. "Treasury I," (U.S. Treasury Department, Washington, D.C., 1984, Duplicated).

15. The island government was so confident in this strategy that when Representative Robert García (D-N.Y.) offered to have the House Banking, Finance, and Urban Affairs Committee hold hearings on the issue, Puerto Rico rejected the offer (Turner 1985b; see also Lachica 1985).

16. Treaster 1985; Auerbach 1985.

17. Cintrón 1985. Under Puerto Rican law, the island's commercial banks were required to place 10 percent of the total amount of 936 funds on deposit (approximately $7 billion) in the government's development bank.

18. "All about Tax Breaks" 1986.

19. Berry 1997, 55–59; Shipper and Jennings 1984.

20. Skelly 1985b.

21. Cintrón 1985.

22. White and Wildavsky 1991, 501.

23. Birnbaum and Murray 1987, 66.

24. Ibid., 75.

25. Treasury believed that cost sharing enabled 936 companies to attribute most of the profit on a product with a very valuable intangible (e.g., a patent) to the Puerto Rican subsidiary and thus treated this gain tax-free. Treasury believed that profit split provided companies with an arbitrary return on marketing intangibles that might bear no relation to any economic activity carried out in Puerto Rico, which could also be overly generous.

26. "Treasury II," (U.S. Treasury Department, Washington, D.C., 1984, Duplicated).

27. McDonough 1989, 4–5.

28. Angulo 1986, 60; Gonzáles 1985.

29. White and Wildavsky 1991, 479

30. Birnbaum and Murray 1987, 103.

31. See, e.g., Skelly 1985a.

32. Bauer, Pool, and Dexter 1972, 403; Mayhew 1974a, 95.

33. R. L. Hall and Wayman 1990, 797–820.

34. House Committee on Ways and Means, *Comprehensive Tax Reform: Hearings before the Committee on Ways & Means,* 99th Cong., 1st sess., 1985, 5167–68.

35. Ibid., 4999–5014.

36. Ibid., 5005–6.

37. Ibid., 5107.

38. Ibid., 5094.

39. Ibid., 5157, 5168. Generic-drug manufacturers and pharmaceutical companies are generally at odds because generics start making money when the PMA members' patents expire.

40. Lowe 1985.

41. Turner 1985a; Castro Vélez 1985.

42. The Ways and Means Committee Report contained a section that required Puerto Rico's government to make good on its promise to encourage twin-plant investments in the Caribbean through the use of 936 funds. Puerto Rican officials were stunned. They had suggested the 936-CBI investment project on the condition that Section 936 was left intact. According to them, that had not been the case, since some changes were made to the tax law. However, according to some of the 936 company lobbyists interviewed for this study, the only reason why that requirement was made part of the report was because Copaken was scared that his idea would get lost and wanted to justify the kind of compensation he was charging the Puerto Rican government. So he worked behind closed doors to try to make sure that although the 936-CBI proposal had not been the reason why the House Ways and Means Committee had preserved Section 936, there was some mention of the proposal in the report (House Committee on Ways and Means, *Tax Reform Act of 1985,* 99th Cong., 1st sess., 1985, Report 99-426, 379–85; see also McDonough 1989).

43. White and Wildavsky 1991, 483.

44. Quoted in ibid.

45. Changes made to Section 936 are detailed in House Committee on Ways and Means, *Tax Reform Act of 1985,* 379–85.

46. White and Wildavsky 1991, 484.

47. Fessler 1986, 840; Birnbaum and Murray 1987, 209–13.

48. White and Wildavsky 1991, 501; Birnbaum and Murray 1987; Conlan, Wrightson, and Beam 1991.

49. Martin 1991, chap. 7.

50. White and Wildavsky 1991, 501.

51. Birnbaum and Murray 1987, 287–88, quotation on 287. See also Vogel 1989, 279–82; Martin 1991, 170–74.

52. Some pharmaceutical company lobbyists interviewed in the summer of 1992 challenged Treasury's interpretation of the superroyalty and had yet to pay a penny based on it.

53. "All about Tax Breaks" 1986, 20.

54. Birnbaum and Murray 1987.

Chapter 6

1. Johnson and Broder 1996, 90.

2. For example, according to the U.S. government in 1990, seventeen of the twenty-one most-prescribed drugs in the United States were manufactured in Puerto Rico (see Ward 1993).

3. Senate Special Committee on Aging, *The Drug Manufacturing Industry: A Prescription for Profits,* 102d Cong., 1st. sess., 1991, Print 102-50, p. 11.

4. *Congressional Record,* 102d Cong., 2d sess., 1992, 3183. See also U.S. Government Accounting Office 1992; 1994.

5. *Congressional Record,* 102d Cong., 2d sess., 1992, 3182–90.

6. Ibid., 3195.

7. Ibid., 3328–29.

8. Ibid., 3230.

9. Bradley 1996, 40.

10. Some of the largest pharmaceutical companies headquartered in New Jersey with operations in Puerto Rico included Johnson and Johnson, SmithKline Beecham, Merck, Bristol-Myers Squibb, American Home Products, Warner-Lambert, American Cyanamid, and Becton Dickinson. At the time, the pharmaceutical industry employed 50,000 workers in New Jersey (see Richmond 1993).

11. The issue also received considerable publicity outside Washington. Some opponents of the amendment were criticized. One Arizona newspaper, for example, published an article highly critical of Senator John McCain (R-Ariz.), implying that the senator's vote had been for sale because six days after he voted against the amendment, pharmaceutical companies held a fund-raiser for him (Barker 1992).

12. U.S. Government Accounting Office 1992.

13. U.S. Treasury Department 1978.

14. *Federal News Service,* 24 September 1992.

15. Puerto Rican elections are held on the same day as U.S. presidential elections. For a discussion of the meaning of *commonwealth* and an explanation of the Puerto Rican office of resident commissioner, see chap. 3, n. 10.

16. Barceló had always felt this way about Section 936. In 1982, however, he was the governor, and according to one of his aides at the time, he "did not want Section 936 to be repealed under his watch."

17. Midwest Center for Labor Research 1991.

18. Rohter 1993b.

19. Galib Bras, 1991.

20. Clinton and Gore 1992.

21. Victor 1992, 2714.

22. Hager and Cloud 1993a, 120; Hager 1992, 3634–36.

23. Birnbaum and Murray 1987, 88.

24. Rhoades and Langer 1997, chap. 8.

25. Salisbury 1990; Heinz et al. 1993.

26. Hager 1993a, 362.

27. Ward 1993.

28. The budget process begins when Congress votes on a budget resolution that contains a general blueprint or reconciliation instructions for the year's budget. In turn, reconciliation instructions contain dollar targets and suggestions on how to meet them. The committees can disregard the suggestions but must comply with the dollar targets. In 1993 the budget resolution was particularly important because for the first time since 1990 the president's proposal contained far-reaching deficit-reduction recommendations (Hager 1993b, 446). By March both the House and Senate had voted to endorse Clinton's budget plan embodied in the budget resolution. The different committees now had to meet the targets.

The committees' proposals are embodied in a budget-reconciliation bill. First the House and then the Senate vote on versions of the bill. The reconciliation bill is then sent to the conference committee, where the differences between the House and Senate versions are resolved. Finally, the conference agreement is sent to the House and Senate for approval.

29. House Committee on Ways and Means, *President Clinton's Proposals for Public Investment and Deficit Reduction: Hearing before the Committee on Ways & Means,* 103d Cong., 1st sess., 1993, 1311.

Another indication that Clinton's attack on pharmaceuticals was working was an NBC News/*Wall Street Journal* poll that found that only 18 percent of Americans had a favorable impression of the industry (Ostrowski 1993, 18).

30. House Committee on Ways and Means, *President Clinton's Proposals,* 480–85, 1249–66.

31. Ibid., 172–73, 1355–73.

32. Ibid., 172–73, 1267–1302, 1349–54, 1505.

33. Memorandum from Peter Holmes to PRUSA Tax and Washington Representatives, 2 April 1993.

34. Rohter 1993a.

35. Senate Committee on Finance, *Administration's Tax Proposal: Hearing before the Committee on Finance,* 103d Cong., 1st sess., 1993, 9–12.

36. Woodward 1994, 198–99; Krauss 1993.

37. U.S. Government Accounting Office 1993.

38. See De George and Magnusson 1993, 52.

39. Novak 1993c.

40. Hager and Cloud 1993b.

41. Harney 1993.

42. Board members included Abbott Laboratories, American Cyanamid, American Home Products, Banco Santander, Baxter Healthcare, Bristol-Myers Squibb, Chase Manhattan Bank, Citibank, Coca-Cola, E. I. DuPont de Nemours, Eli Lilly, General Electric, Johnson and Johnson, Medtronic, Merck, PepsiCo, Pfizer, RJR Nabisco, Schering-Plough, Upjohn, Warner-Lambert, and Westinghouse.

43. Friedman 1993.

44. "Tax Proposal," 1993.

45. Cunningham 1993, 1452.

46. Woodward 1994, 342; Krauss 1993.

47. Gigot 1993.

48. Friedman and Hemlock 1993.

49. Cloud 1993a, 1636; 1993b, 1799; Novak 1993b.

50. Novak 1993a, 1763; see also Weisskopf 1993.

51. Rogers and Wartzman 1993.

52. For a discussion of the new version of Section 936, see Adams and Riedy 1993.

53. Cloud 1993c, 2133. Interestingly, the bill gave capital-intensive companies a relief from the AMT enacted as part of the Tax Reform Act of 1986. The new provision was expected to cost $4.3 billion.

54. Hager and Cloud 1993c; Pulliam 1993.

55. Martin 1991, 198–99.

Chapter 7

1. March and Olsen 1984.
2. For a good review of the domestic-policy literature, see Pierson 1993. For a review of the more extensive foreign-policy literature, see Levy 1994. It should be carefully noted that learning by firms differs from the conception of policy feedback by interest groups. Policy feedback entails interest groups responding to public policies that create incentives or provide resources that may affect the groups' political behavior (Pierson 1993). As such, policy feedbacks produce a response to external factors (i.e., government policies, policy-making structures, and so forth), whereas experiential learning is reflected in the internal biases of firms. Experiential learning by firms is, however, compatible with the concept of policy learning, which entails policymakers learning from the effects of prior policy decisions and devising a new agenda, taking into account past successes and failures. Some good examples of this approach include Deeg 1995; P. Hall 1993; Heclo 1974; Neustadt and May 1986.
3. Vogel 1983, 1989; Martin 1994, 1995; G. K. Wilson 1990.
4. Feldman and March 1981; Heinz et al. 1993, 359–60, 389.
5. Berry 1997; Schlozman and Tierney 1986.
6. Lindblom 1977; Vogel 1983, 1989; Grier, Munger, and Roberts 1994.
7. Vogel 1989, 12.
8. Heinz et al. 1993, 59.
9. March 1981, 215.
10. Plotke 1992, 175–98.
11. Bauer, Pool, and Dexter 1972; Martin 1995.
12. Scott 1992, 110.
13. Salisbury 1990.
14. Gale and Buchholz 1987.
15. Collins 1981; Cyert and March 1963; DiMaggio and Powell 1983; Martin 1994, 1995; Miner and Haunschild 1995; Useem 1984; Vogel 1989; Plotke 1992.
16. Yoffie 1987, 44.
17. Vogel 1989, 37.
18. Ibid., chaps. 3, 4.
19. Ibid., 76.
20. Plotke 1992; Yoffie 1987, 44.
21. Masters and Kein 1985; see also Sabato 1984, 164.
22. Cyert and March 1963; DiMaggio and Powell 1983; Martin 1994, 1995; Miner and Haunschild 1995; Useem 1984.
23. March 1962; Thompson 1982.
24. Heinz et al. 1993, chap. 11.
25. Ibid., 90–94; Lusterman 1988, 2–3.
26. Heinz et al. 1993, 189.
27. Ibid., 249, 251.
28. Berry 1997, 205
29. According to Yoffie (1989, 46–47), firms will be followers if they can afford it and if they perceive that some collective benefit can be secured by political action.
30. Heinz et al. 1993, 90–94; Berry 1997, 205; J. Q. Wilson 1995, 328–29.

31. Quirk 1980, 1981.

32. Quoted in Ostrowski 1993, 18.

33. See also Waldolz 1993.

34. G. K. Wilson 1996, 225–30. For more on the divisions among pharmaceutical companies, see Stone 1993.

35. Vogel 1989; Martin 1991.

36. For a good review of the limits of presidential power, see Kernell 1993.

37. Mizruchi 1992, 34.

38. Examples include Neustadtl and Clawson 1986, 1988; Mizruchi 1989, 401–24.

Epilogue

1. Rubin 1996b.

2. Rubin 1996a.

3. Wines 1995; Chandler 1995.

4. Swoboda 1994.

5. Hershey 1995; Shapiro 1995.

6. Rubin 1996c.

Bibliography

Adams, Mathew T., and James A. Riedy. 1993. Possessions Corporations Face Two New Limitations. *Journal of International Taxation* 4: 445–49.

All about Tax Breaks. 1986. *Economist,* 16 August, 20.

Angulo, Marie Elena. 1986. American Foreign Policy towards Puerto Rico: A Record of Cultural, Political, Military and Economic Imperialism. Bachelor's thesis, Princeton University.

Auerbach, Stuart. 1985. Caribbean Program's Reviews Mixed. *Washington Post,* 30 April, D2.

Bacheller, John M. 1977. Lobbyists and the Legislative Process: The Impact of Environmental Constraints. *American Political Science Review* 71:252–63.

Baer, Werner. 1959. Puerto Rico: An Evaluation of a Successful Development Program. *Quarterly Journal of Economics* 73:645–71.

Balz, Daniel J. 1974a. Tax Report/Split Committee Is Unlikely to Produce Passable Bill. *National Journal,* 5 October, 1500–1502.

———. 1974b.Tax Report/Ways and Means Seeks to Maintain Power and Prestige. *National Journal,* 22 June, 913–20.

———. 1975. Slow Progress on Tax Reform Issues. *National Journal,* 30 August, 1237.

———. 1976. Tax Report/Congress Looks at Death and Taxes but Outlook Is Far from Certain. *National Journal,* 13 March, 328–30.

Barker, Jeff. 1992. McCain Upsets the Elderly over Ties to Drug Firms. *Phoenix Arizona Republic,* 28 March, A1.

Bauer, Raymond A., Ithiel de Sola Pool, and Lewis Anthony Dexter. 1972. *American Business and Public Policy.* Chicago: Aldine-Atherton.

Baumgartner, Frank, and Bryan D. Jones. 1993. *Agendas and Instability in American Politics.* Chicago: University of Chicago Press.

Berry, Jeffrey. 1997. *Lobbying for the People.* Princeton: Princeton University Press.

———. 1997. *The Interest Group Society.* Glenview, Ill.: Little, Brown.

Birnbaum, Jeffrey H., and Alan S. Murray. 1987. *Showdown at Gucci Gulch: Lawmakers, Lobbyists, and the Unlikely Triumph of Tax Reform.* New York: Vintage.

Bradley, Bill. 1996. *Time Present, Time Past.* New York: Knopf.

Browne, William. 1990. Organized Interests and Their Issue Niches: A Search for Pluralism in a Policy Domain. *Journal of Politics* 52:477–509.

Bureau of National Affairs. 1982. *Taxation and Accounting.* Report 134. Washington, D.C.: Bureau of National Affairs.

Business International Corporation. 1980. *Puerto Rico: Critical Choices for the 1980s.* New York: Business International Corporation.

Canellas, Jorge M. 1985. Eli Lilly tax court decision confirms 936 valid. *San Juan (Puerto Rico) Star,* 28 July, 8.

Carr, Raymond. 1984. *Puerto Rico: A Colonial Experiment.* New York: Random House.

Casellas, Salvador. N.d. Memorandum: A History of Section 936 of the U.S. Internal Revenue Code.

Castro Vélez, Alfredo. 1985. Inminente la Reforma a la 936. *El Mundo* (San Juan), 27 August, 33.

Caves, Richard E. 1996. *Multinational Enterprise and Economic Analysis.* Cambridge: Cambridge University Press.

Chandler, Clay. 1995. Bid to End Puerto Rican Tax Break Shows Tax Reform's Political Peril. *Washington Post,* 16 September, COI.

Cintrón, Isabel. 1985. Pondrán los Fondos 936 a Trabajar. *El Mundo* (San Juan), 4 January, 1.

Clark, Truman R. 1975. *Puerto Rico and the United States, 1917–1933.* Pittsburgh: University of Pittsburgh Press.

Clark, Timothy B. 1981a. The GOP Is Looking over Its Shoulder at the Specter of High Interest Rates. *National Journal,* 7 November, 1972–77.

———. 1981b. Reagan's Balanced Budget—One Step Closer, One Step Further Away. *National Journal,* 26 September, 1712–16.

———. 1982a. Business May Be Victim of Congressional Drive to Increase Taxes. *National Journal,* 27 February, 355, 389.

———. 1982b. Reagan's Budget: Economic, Political Gambles. *National Journal,* 13 February, 268–85.

———. 1982c. Tax Lobbyists Scrambling in the Dark to Fight Taxes That Hit Their Clients. *National Journal,* 22 May, 896–901.

———. 1982d. Tax-Raising Proposals Off and Running, but Few Generate Strong Support. *National Journal,* 3 April, 576–80.

Clinton, William J., and Al Gore. 1992. *Putting People First: How We Can All Change America.* New York: Times Books.

Closing in on Puerto Rico's Tax Haven. 1978. *Business Week,* 22 May, 154, 156.

Cloud, David S. 1993a. Conferees Must Wrestle with Major Differences. *Congressional Quarterly Weekly,* 26 June, 1636–38.

———. 1993b. It's Democrats vs. Democrats as Conference Nears. *Congressional Quarterly Weekly,* 10 July, 1799–1801.

———. 1993c. New Levies on Gas and the Rich Would Yield $240 Billion. *Congressional Quarterly Weekly,* 7 August, 2132–35.

Collins, Robert M. 1981. *The Business Response to Keynes, 1929–1964.* New York: Columbia University Press.

Congressional Actions. 1974. *National Journal,* 21 December, 1924–25.

Conlan, Timothy J., Margaret T. Wrightson, and David Beam. 1991. *Taxing Choices.* Washington, D.C.: CQ Press.

Culhane, Charles. 1972. Labor and Industry Gear for Major Battle over Bill to Curb Imports. *National Journal,* 15 January, 108–19.

Cunningham, Kitty. 1993. Caucus Rebuffs Clinton. *Congressional Quarterly Weekly,* 12 June, 1452.

Cyert, Richard M., and James M. March. 1963. *A Behavioral Theory of the Firm.* Englewood Cliffs, N.J.: Prentice-Hall.

Deeg, Richard. 1995. Institutional Transfer, Social Learning, and Economic Policy in Eastern Germany. *West European Politics* 18:38–63.

De George, Gail, and Paul Magnusson. 1993. A Hurricane Heads for Puerto Rico. *Business Week,* 14 June, 52.

Denzau, Arthur, and Michael C. Munger. 1986. Legislators and Interest Groups: How Unorganized Interests Get Represented. *American Political Science Review* 80:89–106.

DiMaggio, Paul, and Walter W. Powell. 1983. The Iron Cage Revisited: Institutional Isomorphism and Collective Rationality in Organizational Fields. *American Sociological Review* 48:147–60.

Dodd, Lawrence. 1986. A Theory of Congressional Cycles. In *Congress and Policy Change,* edited by Gerald Wright, Leroy Rieslback, and Lawrence C. Dodd, 3–44. New York: Agathon Press.

Doernberg, Richard L. 1989. *International Taxation in a Nutshell.* St. Paul, Minn.: West.

Erikson, Robert. 1972. Malapportionment, Gerrymandering, and Party Fortunes in Congressional Elections. *American Political Science Review* 66:1234–45.

Evans, Diana M. 1991. Lobbying the Committee: Interest Groups and the House Public Works and Transportation Committee. In *Interest Group Politics,* 3d ed., edited by Allan J. Cigler and Burdett A. Loomis, 257–76. Washington, D.C.: CQ Press.

Feldman, Martha S., and James G. March. 1981. Information in Organizations as Signal and Symbol. *Administrative Science Quarterly* 26:171–86.

Fenno, Richard F., Jr. 1973. *Congressmen in Committees.* Boston: Little, Brown.

Fessler, Pamela. 1986. Finance Panel Suspends Markup of Tax Bill. *Congressional Quarterly Weekly Report,* 19 April, 840–42.

FOMENTO. N.d. *Leading Companies Manufacturing in Puerto Rico.* San Juan, P.R.: Economic Development Administration.

Friedman, Robert. 1993. Moynihan May Save the Day for 936. *San Juan (Puerto Rico) Star,* 27 May, 3.

Friedman, Robert, and Doreen Hemlock. 1993. Clinton Favors Senate Version of 936. *San Juan (Puerto Rico) Star,* 23 July, 19.

Gais, Thomas, Mark Peterson, and Jack Walker. 1995. Interest Groups, Iron Triangles, and Representative Institutions in American National Government. *British Journal of Political Science* 14:161–85.

Galbraith, J. K., and Carolyn Shaw Solo. 1953. Puerto Rican Lessons in Economic Development. *Annals of the American Academy of Political and Social Science* 274:55–59.

Gale, Jeffrey, and Rogene A. Buchholz. 1987. The Political Pursuit of Competitive Advantage: What Business Can Gain from Government. In *Business Strategy and Public Policy,* edited by Alfred A. Marcus, Allen M. Kaufman, and David R. Beam, 31–60. New York: Quorum.

Galib Bras, Salomé. 1991. Posiciones Irreconciliables en la Pugna de las 936. *El Nuevo Día* (San Juan), 28 October, 14.

Gigot, Paul A. 1993. Senate Dems, Boren Play Tax and Pretend. *Wall Street Journal,* 18 June, Section A, p. 12.

Gilpin, Robert. 1975. *U.S. Power and the Multinational Corporation: The Political Economy of Foreign Direct Investment.* New York: Basic.

Gonzáles, Victor. 1985. Reagan Dispuesto a Alterar Enmienda a 936. *El Vocero* (San Juan), 23 May, 43.

Gover, James E. 1993. Review of the Competitive Status of the United States Electronics Industry. In *Technological Competitiveness: Contemporary and Historical Perspectives on the Electrical, Electronics, and Computer Industries,* edited by William Aspray, 57–74. New York: Institute of Electrical and Electronics Engineers Press.

Government Development Bank of Puerto Rico. 1982. The 1982 Amendment to IRC Section 936: Complete Text and Commentary. *Puerto Rico Business Review.*

Grier, Kevin B., Michael C. Munger, and Brian E. Roberts. 1994. The Determinants of Industry Political Activity, 1978–1986. *American Political Science Review* 88:911–926.

Griggs, Robert S. 1971. Current Tax Climate Favors Dealing with Affiliates in Puerto Rico. *Journal of Taxation* 35:376–78.

Hager, George. 1992. Clinton, Congress, the Deficit on a Collision Course. *Congressional Quarterly Weekly,* 14 November, 3634–36.

———. 1993a. Package of Tax Increases Reverses GOP Approach. *Congressional Quarterly Weekly,* 20 February, 360–64.

———. 1993b. Steps in the Budget Process. *Congressional Quarterly Weekly,* 27 February, 446.

Hager, George, and David S. Cloud. 1993a. Clinton Team's Similar Lines Focus on Deficit Reduction. *Congressional Quarterly Weekly,* 16 January, 120–23.

———. 1993b. Democrats Pull Off Squeaker in Approving Clinton Plan. *Congressional Quarterly Weekly,* 29 May, 1340–45.

———. 1993c. Democrats Tie Their Fate to Clinton's Budget Bill. *Congressional Quarterly Weekly,* 7 August, 2122–29.

Hall, Peter. 1993. Policy Paradigms, Social Learning, and the State: The Case of Economic Policy Making in Britain. *Comparative Politics* 25:275–96.

Hall, Richard L., and Frank W. Wayman. 1990. Buying Time: Moneyed Interests and the Mobilization of Bias in Congressional Committees. *American Political Science Review* 84:797–820.

Hamilton, Martha M. 1984. Drug Companies Lobby to Revise Compromise Bill. *Washington Post,* 29 July, G1.

Hansen, John M. 1991. *Gaining Access: Congress and the Farm Lobby, 1919–1981.* Chicago: University of Chicago Press.

Harney, John. 1993. The Fight over Puerto Rico's Fed Tax Break: Fear of Lost Jobs, Exodus to NYC. *New York Post,* 14 June, 6.

Heclo, Hugh. 1974. *Modern Social Policies in Britain and France.* New Haven: Yale University Press.

———. 1978. Issue Networks and the Executive Establishment. In *The New American Political System,* edited by Anthony King, 87–124. Washington D.C.: American Enterprise Institute.

Heinz, John P., Edward O. Laumann, Robert L. Nelson, and Robert H. Salisbury. 1993.

The Hollow Core: Private Interests in National Policy Making. Cambridge: Harvard University Press.

Hernández Colón, Rafael. 1974. Section 931 and 332 of the U.S. Internal Revenue Code and the Economy of Puerto Rico. 31 May, 1–16. Commonwealth of Puerto Rico. Duplicated.

Hershey, Robert D., Jr. 1995. A Hard Look at Corporate "Welfare." *New York Times,* 7 March, Section D, page 1.

Holbrook, Robert S. 1977. *A Study of the Characteristics, Behavior, and Implications of "Possessions Corporations" in Puerto Rico.* Special report prepared at the request of the Treasury Department. U.S. Treasury Department, Washington D.C. Duplicated.

House Approves Major Rewrite of Tax Code. 1985. *Congressional Quarterly Almanac* 41:480–98.

James, Barrie G. 1977. *The Future of the Multinational Pharmaceutical Industry to 1990.* London: Associated Business Programmes.

Johnson, Haynes, and David S. Broder. 1996. *The System.* Boston: Little, Brown.

Kaplan, Sheila. 1986. Join Congress, See the World. *Common Cause Magazine* (September/October) 12:17–23.

Kernell, Samuel. 1993. *Going Public: New Strategies of Presidential Leadership.* Washington, D.C.: CQ Press.

King, Gary, Robert O. Keohane, and Sidney Verba. 1994. *Designing Social Inquiry.* Princeton: Princeton University Press.

Krasner, Stephen. 1978. United States Commercial and Monetary Policy: Unraveling the Paradox of External Strength and Internal Weakness. In *Between Power and Plenty: Foreign Economic Policies of Advanced Industrial States,* edited by Peter J. Katzenstein, 51–88. Madison: University of Wisconsin Press.

Krauss, Clifford. 1993. Threat of Statehood in Puerto Rico Leads to a Restored Tax Break. *New York Times,* 23 July, Sec. 1, p. 26.

Lachica, Eduardo. 1985. Puerto Ricans Fear Tax Overhaul Would Force Island's Retreat to "Rum and Textile Economy." *Wall Street Journal,* 13 February, Sec. 1, p. 64.

Lenhart, Harry, Jr. 1971. Economic Report/Labor Fears Loss of Jobs in U.S. as Firms Expand Their Overseas Facilities. *National Journal,* 17 July, 1485–93.

Levinthal, Daniel A., and James G. March. 1993. The Myopia of Learning. *Strategic Management Journal* 14:95–102.

Levitt, Barbara, and James G. March. 1988 Organizational Learning. *Annual Review of Sociology* 14:319–40.

Levy, Jack S. 1994. Learning and Foreign Policy: Sweeping a Conceptual Minefield. *International Organization* 48:279–312.

Lewis, Gordon K. 1955. Puerto Rico: A Case Study of Change. *Journal of Politics* 17:614–50.

———. 1963. *Puerto Rico: Freedom and Power in the Caribbean.* New York: Monthly Review Press.

Lindblom, Charles. 1977. *Politics and Markets.* New York: Basic.

Lowe, Karen. 1985. Hay "Consenso" Congressional en Apoyo de las 936. *El Mundo* (San Juan), 31 July, 6.

Lowi, Theodore. 1964. American Business, Public Policy, Case-Studies, and Political Theory. *World Politics* 16:677–715.

Lusterman, Seymour. 1988. *Managing Federal Government Relations.* New York: Conference Board.

Mahon, John F., and James E. Post. 1987. The Evolution of Political Strategies during the 1980 Superfund Debate. In *Business Strategy and Public Policy,* edited by Alfred A. Marcus, Allen M. Kaufman, and David R. Beam, 61–78. New York: Quorum.

Manley, John F. 1970. *The Politics of Finance: The House Ways and Means Committee* Boston: Little, Brown.

March, James G. 1962. The Business Firm as a Political Coalition. *Journal of Politics* 24:662–78.

———. 1981. Decisions in Organizations and Theories of Choice. In *Perspectives on Organization Design and Behavior,* edited by Andrew H. Van de Ven and Willam F. Joyce, 205–44. New York: John Wiley.

March, James G., and Johan P. Olsen. 1976. *Ambiguity and Choice in Organizations.* Bergen: Universitetsforlaget.

———. 1984. The New Institutionalism: Organizational Factors in Political Life. *American Political Science Review* 78:734–49.

March, James G., and Herbert A. Simon. 1958. *Organizations.* New York: John Wiley.

Martin, Cathie Jo. 1991. *Shifting the Burden.* Chicago: University of Chicago Press.

———. 1994. Business and the New Economic Activism: The Growth of Corporate Lobbies in the Sixties. *Polity* 27:19–43.

———. 1995. Nature or Nurture? Sources of Firm Preference for National Health Reform. *American Political Science Review* 89:898–913.

Masters, Marick F., and Gerald D. Kein. 1985. Determinants of PAC Participation among Large Corporations. *Journal of Politics* 47:1158–73.

Mayhew, David R. 1974a. *Congress: The Electoral Connection.* New Haven: Yale University Press.

———. 1974b. Congressional Elections: The Case of Vanishing Marginals. *Polity* 6:195–317.

McDonough, James. 1989. *A Special Report: The 1985 Negotiations to Save Section 936.* Washington, D.C.: Granada.

Midwest Center for Labor Research. 1991. *Impact of Internal Revenue Code Section 936 on Manufacturing Jobs in the U.S.* Chicago: Midwest Center for Labor Research.

Mihaly, Zoltan M. 1963. Tax Advantages of Doing Business in Puerto Rico. *Stanford Law Review* 16:75–106.

Miner, Anne S., and Pamela R. Haunschild. 1995. Population Level Learning. *Research in Organizational Behavior* 17:115–66.

Mizruchi, Mark S. 1989. Similarity of Political Behavior. *American Journal of Sociology* 95:401–24.

———. 1992. *The Structure of Corporate Political Action.* Cambridge: Harvard University Press.

Moe, Terry M. 1980. *The Organization of Interests.* Chicago: University of Chicago Press.

Morales Carrión, Arturo. 1983. *Puerto Rico: A Political and Cultural History.* New York: Norton.

Mucciaroni, Gary. 1995. *Reversal of Fortunes.* Washington, D.C.: Brookings Institution.

Novak, Viveca. 1993a. From the K Street Corridor. *National Journal,* 10 July, 1763.

———. 1993b. It's Almost Time to Deal. *National Journal,* 26 June, 1654–55.

———. 1993c. Yo! We Need a Senator to Carry Some Water! *National Journal,* 29 May, 1298.

Neustadt, Richard E. 1960. *Presidential Power.* New York: John Wiley.

Neustadt, Richard E., and Ernest May. 1986. *Thinking in Time.* New York: Free Press.

Neustadtl, Alan, and Dan Clawson. 1986. The Logic of Business Unity: Corporate Contributions in the 1980 Election. *American Sociological Review* 51:797–811.

———. 1988. Corporate Political Groupings: Does Ideology Unify Business Political Behavior? *American Sociological Review* 53:172–90.

Olson, Mancur. 1968. *The Logic of Collective Action.* Cambridge: Harvard University Press.

Ostrowski, Helen. 1993. Drug Makers Prescribe Cure for Ailing Reputation. *Public Relations Journal* 49 (10): 18–23.

Packenham, Robert A. 1973. *Liberal America and the Third World: Political Development Ideas in Foreign Aid and Social Science.* Princeton: Princeton University Press.

Pantojas-García, Emilio. 1990. *Development Strategies as Ideology: Puerto Rico's Export-Led Industrialization Experience.* Boulder: Lynne Rienner.

Pastor, Robert A. 1980. *Congress and the Politics of U.S. Foreign Economic Policy.* Berkeley: University of California Press.

Perloff, Harvey. 1953. Transforming the Economy. *Annals of the American Academy of Political and Social Science* 274: 44–54.

Pierson, Paul. 1993. When Effect Becomes Cause: Policy Feedback and Political Change. *World Politics* 45:595–628.

Plotke, David. 1992. The Mobilization of Business. In *The Politics of Interest: Interest Groups Transformed,* edited by Mark Petracca, 175–98. Boulder, Colo.: Westview.

Polsby, Nelson. 1968. The Institutionalization of the House of Representatives. *American Political Science Review* 62:144–68.

Puerto Rico Government Position on Section 936. 1986. *Puerto Rico Business Review,* April, 3.

Pulliam, Susan. 1993. This Time, Drug Stocks Take a Hit over Loss of Much Coveted Puerto Rican Tax Break. *Wall Street Journal,* 10 August, 2.

Quintero Rivera, Angel G. 1974. Background to the Emergence of Imperialist Capitalism in Puerto Rico. In *Puerto Rico and Puerto Ricans: Studies in History and Society,* edited by Adalberto López and James Petras, 87–117. New York: John Wiley.

Quirk, Paul J. 1980. Food and Drug Administration. In *The Politics of Regulation,* edited by James Q. Wilson, 191–235. New York: Basic.

———. 1981. *Industry Influence in Federal Regulatory Agencies.* Princeton: Princeton University Press.

Regan, Donald T. 1988. *For the Record: From Wall Street to Washington.* San Diego: Harcourt Brace Jovanovich.

Restructuring of Puerto Rico Tax Aids Debated. 1981. *Tax Notes,* 2 November, 1054–55.

Rhoades, Rufus von Thülen, and Marshall J. Langer. 1997. *Rhoades and Langer U.S. International Taxation and Treaties.* Vol. 1. New York: Matthew Bender.

Rich, Spencer. 1984. Senate Votes to Make More Generic Drugs Available to Public. *Washington Post,* 13 September, A2.

Richmond, Kelly. 1993. Voting for Their Future: Statehood Side Effects Drug Companies Fear Loss of Tax Exemption. *Hackensack N.J. Record,* 8 November, A1.

Rieselbach, Leroy N. 1986. *Congressional Reform.* Washington, D.C.: CQ Press.

Ripley, Randall B., and Grace A. Franklin. 1987. *Congress, the Bureaucracy and Public Policy.* Chicago: University of Chicago Press.

Robbins, Sidney M., and Robert B. Stobaugh. 1973. *Money in the Multinational Enterprise.* New York: Basic.

Robert Nathan Associates. 1985. *The Employment, Economic, and Fiscal Impacts of Replacing 936 with a Wage Credit in Puerto Rico.* Washington, D.C.: Robert Nathan Associates.

Rogers, David, and Rick Wartzman. 1993. Companies' Fight to Protect Credit for Operations in Puerto Rico Illustrates the Stakes in Deficit Bill. *Wall Street Journal,* 16 July, Sec. A, p. 10.

Rohter, Larry. 1993a. Puerto Rico Fighting to Keep Its Tax Breaks for Business. *New York Times,* 10 May, Sec. A, p. 1.

———. 1993b. Trade Pact Threatens Puerto Rico's Economic Rise. *New York Times,* 3 January, Sec. 1, p. 1.

Rubin, Alissa J. 1996a. Bipartisan Tax Cut Plan May Break Stalemate. *Congressional Quarterly Weekly,* 18 May, 1375–77.

———. 1996b. Congress Clears Wage Increase with Tax Break for Business. *Congressional Quarterly Weekly,* 3 August, 2175–77.

———. 1996c. Tax Bill Would Have Big Impact on U.S. Business Overseas. *Congressional Quarterly Weekly,* 6 July, 1913–15.

Rudder, Catherine E. 1983. Tax Policy: Structure and Choice. In *Making Economic Policy in Congress,* edited by Allen Schick, 196–220. Washington, D.C.: American Enterprise Institute.

Rudick, Harry J., and George S. Allan. 1952. Tax Aspects of Operations under the Puerto Rican Exemption Program. *Tax Law Review* 7:403–37.

Sabato, Larry. 1984. *PAC Power: Inside the World of Political Action Committees.* New York: Norton.

Salisbury, Robert H. 1979. Why No Corporatism in America? In *Trends towards Corporatist Intermediation,* edited by Philippe Schmitter and Gerhard Lehmbruch, 213–30 . Beverly Hills, Calif.: Sage.

———. 1984. Interest Representation: The Dominance of Institutions. *American Political Science Review* 78:44–63.

———. 1990. The Paradox of Interest Groups in Washington—More Groups, Less Clout. In *The New American Political System,* edited by Anthony King, 203–30. Washington, D.C.: American Enterprise Institute.

Salvador Casellas: A Look at 936 Legislation and Its History. 1977. *Caribbean Business,* 16 June, 16. 10.

Sanders, Elizabeth. 1988. The Presidency and the Bureaucratic State. In *The Presidency and the Political System,* edited by Michael Nelson, Pp. 379–409. Washington, D.C.: CQ Press.

Schlesinger, Arthur M., Jr. 1965. *A Thousand Days: John F. Kennedy in the White House.* New York: Fawcett World Library.

Schlozman, Kay, and John T. Tierney. 1986. *Organized Interests and American Democracy.* New York: Harper and Row.

Schoene, Robert P. 1983. Casellas Recalls Birth, Dramatic Details of Tax Provision's History. *Caribbean Business,* 16 February, 546.

Scholes, Myron S., and Mark A. Wolfson. 1992. *Taxes and Business Strategy: A Planning Approach.* Englewood Cliffs, N.J.: Prentice-Hall.

Scott, W. Richard. 1992. *Organizations: Rational, Natural, and Open Systems.* Englewood Cliffs, N.J.: Prentice-Hall.

Shapiro, Robert. 1995. "End Corporate Welfare." *Washington Post,* 1 December, A27.

Shipper, Frank, and Marianne M. Jennings. 1984. *Business Strategy for the Political Arena.* Westport, Conn.: Quorum.

Sierra, Ralph J. 1973. Tax Advantages Available to U.S. Companies Doing Business in Puerto Rico. *Journal of Taxation* 38:310–14.

Skelly, John T. 1985a. 936 Misión Cameral a San Juan. *El Nuevo Día* (San Juan), 29 March, 5.

———. 1985b. Nueva Estrategia Para Salvar las 936. *El Nuevo Día* (San Juan), 22 February, 12.

Smith, Hendrick. 1988. *The Power Game.* New York: Ballantine.

Smith, Richard. 1984. Advocacy, Interpretation, and Influence in the U.S. Congress. *American Political Science Review* 78:44–63.

Steinmo, Sven. 1993. *Taxation and Democracy.* New Haven: Yale University Press.

Stone, Peter H. 1993. Drug Makers Splintered, Stymied by Health Reform? *Orlando Sentinel,* 12 December, G1.

Strahan, Randall. 1990. *New Ways and Means: Reform and Change in a Congressional Committee.* Chapel Hill: University of North Carolina Press.

Sundquist, James. 1981. *The Decline and Resurgence of Congress.* Washington, D.C.: Brookings Institution.

Swoboda, Frank. 1994. Reich: Cut "Corporate Welfare" Welfare Too. *Washington Post,* 22 November, C1.

Tax Increases Meet Deficit Reduction Target. 1982. *Congressional Quarterly Almanac* 38:29–39.

Tax Proposal for Puerto Rico. 1993. *New York Times,* 15 February, Sec. D, p. 7.

Tax Reform: No Final Action in 1974. 1974. *Congressional Quarterly Almanac* 30:181–93.

Taylor, Milton. 1954. Industrial Tax Exemption in Puerto Rico. *National Tax Journal,* December, 359–71.

Thompson, Graham. 1982. The Firm as a "Dispersed" Social Agency. *Economy and Society* 11:233–50.

Thurston, Charles. 1988. Branded Offshore Manufacturing Finds a Home in Ireland and Singapore. *Chemical Market Reporter* 253.

Tierney, John T. 1992. Organized Interests and the Nation's Capitol.In *The Politics of Interest: Interest Groups Transformed,* edited by Mark Petracca, 201–20. Boulder, Colo.: Westview.

Treaster, Joseph B. 1985. The Caribbean Restless for Recovery. *New York Times,* 17 February, Sec. 4, p. 2.

Truman, David. 1971. *The Governmental Process.* New York: Knopf.

Turner, Harry. 1985a. Fuster Convinced Wage Credit Plan Is Dead. *San Juan (Puerto Rico) Star,* 3 August, 2.

———. 1985b. Tax Plan Delay Allows Time to Build 936 Defense. *San Juan (Puerto Rico) Star* 23 January, 3.

U.S. Commerce Department. 1979. *Economic Study of Puerto Rico.* 2 vols. Washington, D.C.: Government Printing Office.

U.S. Government Accounting Office. 1992. *Pharmaceutical Industry: Tax Benefits of Operating in Puerto Rico.* Washington, D.C.: Government Accounting Office.

———. 1993. *Tax Policy: Puerto Rico and the Section 936 Tax Credit.* Washington, D.C.: Government Accounting Office.

———. 1994. *Prescription Drugs: Companies Typically Charge More in the United States than in the United Kingdom.* Washington, D.C.: Government Accounting Office.

U.S. Treasury Department. 1978. *The Operation and Effect of the Possessions Corporation System of Taxation: First Annual Report.* Washington, D.C.: Government Printing Office.

———. 1979. *The Operation and Effect of the Possessions Corporation System of Taxation: Second Annual Report.* Washington, D.C.: Government Printing Office.

———. 1980. *The Operation and Effect of the Possessions Corporation System of Taxation: Third Annual Report.* Washington, D.C.: Government Printing Office.

———. 1983. *The Operation and Effect of the Possessions Corporation System of Taxation: Fourth Annual Report.* Washington, D.C.: Government Printing Office.

——— 1985. *The Operation and Effect of the Possessions Corporation System of Taxation: Fifth Annual Report.* Washington, D.C.: Government Printing Office.

———. 1989. *The Operation and Effect of the Possessions Corporation System of Taxation: Sixth Annual Report.* Washington, D.C.: Government Printing Office.

Useem, Michael. 1984. *The Inner Circle.* New York: Oxford University Press.

Victor, Kirk. 1992. A Capital Idea. *National Journal,* 28 November, 2714–18.

Vogel, David. 1983. The Power of Business in America: A Re-Appraisal. *British Journal of Political Science* 13:19–43.

———. 1989. *Fluctuating Fortunes.* New York: Basic.

Waldolz, Michael. 1993. Drug Firms Plan Blitz to Counter Clinton Moves. *Wall Street Journal,* 25 March, Sec. B, p. 1.

Walker, Jack. 1991. *Mobilizing Interest Groups in America: Patrons, Professions, and Social Movements.* Ann Arbor: University of Michigan Press.

Walsh, James P., and Gerardo Rivera Ungson. 1991. Organizational Memory. *Academy of Management Review* 16:57–71.

Ward, Leah Beth. 1993. The Offshore Threat to Pharmaceuticals. *New York Times,* 14 March, Sec. 3, p. 5.

Washington Update. 1976. *National Journal,* 8 August, 1157.

Weisskopf, Michael. 1993. Congress Divided on Puerto Rico Tax Break: Plan to Cut Incentive Credit for Island-Based U.S. Drug Companies Draws Heavy Lobbying. *Washington Post,* 27 July, A8.

White, Joseph, and Aaron Wildavsky. 1991. *The Deficit and the Public Interest.* Berkeley: University of California Press.

Wilson, G. Peter. 1993. The Role of Taxes in Location and Sourcing Decisions. In *Studies in International Taxation,* edited by Alberto Giovannini, R. Glenn Hubbard, and Joel Slemrod, 195–234. Chicago: University of Chicago Press.

Wilson, Graham K. 1981. *Interest Groups in the United States.* Oxford: Oxford University Press.

———. 1982. Why Is There No Corporatism in the United States? In *Patterns of Corporatist Policy-Making,* edited by Gerhard Lehmbruch and Phillippe C. Schmitter, 219–36. Beverly Hills, Calif.: Sage.

———. 1990. Corporate Political Strategies. *British Journal of Political Science* 20:281–87.

———. 1992. American Interest Groups in Comparative Perspective. In *The Politics of Interests,* edited by Mark P. Petracca, 80–95. Boulder, Colo.: Westview.

———. 1996. The Clinton Administration and Interest Groups. In *The Clinton Presidency: First Appraisals,* edited by Colin Campbell and Bert A. Rockman, 212–33. Chatham, N.J.: Chatham House.

Wilson, James Q. 1995. *Political Organizations.* Princeton: Princeton University Press.

Wines, Michael. 1995. Now G.O.P. Head of Tax Panel Seeks End to Some Loopholes. *New York Times,* 15 September, Sec. A, p. 28.

Woodward, Bob. 1994. *The Agenda: Inside the Clinton White House.* New York: Pocket.

Wright, John R. 1990. Contributions, Lobbying, and Committee Voting in the U.S. House of Representatives. *American Political Science Review* 84:417–38.

Yoffie, David B. 1987. Corporate Strategies for Political Action: A Rational Model. In *Business Strategy and Public Policy,* edited by Alfred A. Marcus, Allen M. Kaufman, and David R. Beam, 43–60. New York: Quorum.

Index

AARP. *See* American Association of Retired Persons
Abbott Laboratories, 33, 56, 123, 127, 145, 153n. 54, 169n. 42
Accounting rules, 65, 104, 161n. 17, 166n. 25
Acme Boot Company, 122
AFL-CIO, 41–42, 111. *See also* Labor unions
AHP. *See* American Home Products
Alcoa, 156n. 49
Allergan, 115, 125, 127
Alternative Minimum Tax (ATM), 117
American Association of Retired Persons (AARP), 111
American Bankers Association, 7
American Business and Public Policy, 135
American Cyanamid, 81, 153n. 54, 169n. 42
American Home Products, 88, 114–15, 121, 145, 153n. 54, 169n. 42
American Hospital Supply, 101
American Samoa, 152n. 52
Anthony, Beryl F., 121
Aqueduct and Sewer Authority, 24
Archer, Bill, 146
ATM. *See* Alternative Minimum Tax

Baker, James, 68, 96, 97, 105, 117
Ballantine, Greg, 60–61, 81
Banco Santander, 169n. 42
Bangladesh, 104
Barceló. *See* Romero Barceló, Carlos
Bauer, Raymond A., 1, 135, 151n. 6
Baxter Healthcare, 169n. 42

Baxter International, 15, 79, 88, 90, 117, 125, 127, 145, 153n. 54
Benítez, Jaime, 44–46
Bentsen, Lloyd, 76–77, 113, 116, 122
Birnbaum, Jeffrey H., 93, 107
Boggs, Tommy, 80
Boyd, Charles E., 25
Bradley, Bill, 111–12, 125, 126, 164n. 58, 166n. 12
Branch operations, 20
Bristol Myers Squibb (formerly Bristol Myers), 33, 112, 121, 123, 153n. 54, 169n. 42
British Thermal Units (BTUs), 127
Brockway, David H., 70, 81, 85, 104, 106–8, 165n. 70
Budget Act of 1990, 13
Budget Committee, U.S. Senate, 67
Budget deficit, 12, 16, 55–56, 66–71, 85–86, 120–23; Clinton and, 115; Reconciliation bill, 126, 168n. 28; redefinition of, 12, 66–67; resolution, 121, 168n. 28
Burke, James A., 46, 157n. 3
Bush, George, 75, 99
Business: conflict within, 63–66, 78–79, 123–25, 145; investment strike by, 44, 52–53, 63, 65, 133, 161n. 16; political activity of, 1–3, 131–34; political outcomes for, 142–43; structuralist, interest-group and fragmented approaches to the study of, 6–7, 52–53, 55, 78; tax-free profits of, 3, 30–38, 56–59, 97, 117–18. *See also* Interests, of business; Political strategies

185

Economic Development Administration
(FOMENTO), Puerto Rico, 25, 26, 44, 62
Economic Recovery Act of 1981
(ERTA), 56, 66–78, 160n. 2
E. I. DuPont de Nemours, 169n. 42
Electronics industry, 36–38, 63–66, 145
Eli Lilly, 3, 33, 35, 73, 75, 117, 153n. 54, 169n. 42
Emergency Committee for American Trade, 122
Energy and Natural Resources Committee, U.S. Senate, 74–75
ERTA. *See* Economic Recovery Act of 1981
Eurodollar market, 30–31, 49
Experiential learning. *See* Learning
Experimental response. *See* Political strategies

Fair Labor Standards Act, 28
Famadas, Nelson, 59, 63, 72, 73, 163n. 43
Federal Coal Mine Health and Safety Act of 1969, 137
Federation of German Industries, 7
Feldman, Martha S., 10
Fifty-fifty profit split. *See* Accounting rules
Finance Committee, U.S. Senate, 18, 22, 51–52, 67–73, 75–78, 93–107, 112, 123–27; Democratic caucus of, 69; Republican caucus of, 69; staff interviewed from the, 18. *See also* Bentsen, Lloyd; Dole, Robert; Long, Russell; Moynihan, Daniel Patrick; Packwood, Robert
Flammable Fabrics Act of 1967, 137
FOMENTO. *See* Economic Development Administration (FOMENTO), Puerto Rico
Food and Drug Administration (FDA), 63, 140
Foraker Act of 1900, 153n. 4
Ford, Gerald, 52
Foreign Direct Investment (FDI), 19–22

Foreign tax credit, 19–22, 30–32
Fortune 500 corporations, 15, 78, 122, 138
Free-rider problem, 6, 7, 78, 79, 140
Frenzel, Bill, 100, 105
"Friend of Bill," 121

Gang of Seventeen, 68, 69
GAO. *See* General Accounting Office
García, Robert, 166n. 15
G. D. Searle, 3, 33, 35, 59, 112, 127, 160n. 3
Genentech, 136–37, 153n. 54
General Accounting Office, 112–13, 124
General Electric, 15, 37, 50, 79, 88, 96, 124, 127, 139, 145, 153n. 54, 169n. 42
Generic Pharmaceutical Industry Association (GPIA), 103
Gephardt, Richard, 91, 105, 166n. 12
Gibbons, Sam, 81
Glasmann, Jay W., 157n. 5
Gore, Albert, 127
Government Development Bank, Puerto Rico, 24, 94, 107
Government structures, 13–14; centralized, 48–49; decentralized, 71–80. *See also* Ways and Means Committee, U.S. House of Representatives
GPIA. *See* Generic Pharmaceutical Industry Association
Great Britain, 21
Grenada, 95
Groom and Nordberg (law firm), 88, 89
Guam, 30–31, 152n. 52
Guarini, Frank, 102
Guinier, Lani, 125
Gutiérrez, Luis V., 126–27

Haddad, William F., 103
Hartke, Vance, 157n. 3
Hall, Richard L., 101
Hawley-Smoot Tariff, 154n. 13
Health care costs and reform, 109–13, 115–16, 123, 141–42
Hearings. *See* Ways and Means Committee, U.S. House of Representatives